The New Grolier

STUDENT
ENCYCLOPEDIA

VOLUME 15

Nevada–Palm

 Grolier Educational Corporation
SHERMAN TURNPIKE, DANBURY, CONNECTICUT 06816
Also published under the title Young Students Learning Library.

PHOTO CREDITS

ASCAP page 1835(bottom right); AMERICAN LIBRARY ASSOCIATION page 1746(top left); BBC HULTON PICTURE LIBRARY page 1763(bottom left); 1821(top right); 1836(top left); BAHAMAS TOURIST OFFICE page 1785(bottom left); BRITISH COLUMBIA TOURIST BOARD page 1786(bottom left); BRITISH MUSEUM page 1787(top right); CANADIAN GOVERNMENT TRAVEL BUREAU page 1796(top left); COLLINS page 1801(above center); DAVE COLLINS page 1781(top right); COLORSPORT page 1831(bottom right and top left); 1830(bottom center); ROBERT COTTON page 1760(bottom left); ARMANDO CURCIO EDITORE SPA page 1743(top right); 1744(top left); 1772(top left); 1775(top left); 1777(bottom left & right); 1778(bottom left); 1826(bottom left); 1828(bottom left); 1830(top left); 1832(top left); 1846(top left & top right); 1847(bottom right); 1848(top left & center left); 1855(bottom right); 1858(top left); 1860(top left); 1861(bottom left); 1862(bottom left & bottom right); 1863(both pics); ZOE DOMINIC page 1835(top left); FITZWILLIAM MUSEUM, COMBRIDGE page 1860(bottom left); GEOLOGICAL MUSEUM page 1793(bottom right); STANLEY GIBBONS page 1779(top right); GIRAUDON page 1847(bottom left); SONIA HALLIDAY page 1773(bottom right); 1844(bottom right); 1850(both pics); HARCOURT, BRACE, JOVANOVICH, INC page 1848(bottom left); R. HARVEY page 1750(top left); BRIAN HAWKES page 1852(top right); HEINEMANN page 1801(below center); RUSSELL F. HOGELAND page 1817(top right); MICHAEL HOLFORD page 1773(center right); 1807(top right); IMITOR page 1865(bottom right); KITT PEAK OBSERVATORY page 1813(bottom right); KEN LARSEN page 1792(bottom left); LIBRARY OF CONGRESS page 1812(bottom left); MANDER & MITCHENSON page 1775(center right); MANSELL COLLECTION page 1760(top left); 1772(center left); 1795(center right); 1802(top); 1834(top left); METHUEN page 1801(bottom right); JIM MILES page 1776(bottom left); MARY E. A. MITCHELL page 1784(top right); P. MORRIS page 1849(top right); NATIONAL GALLERY, LONDON page 1861(top right); NATIONAL PARK SERVICE page 1859(top right); NEW HAMPSHIRE DEPT. OF RESOURCES & ECONOMIC DEVELOPMENT page 1752(top left); NEW JERSEY DEPT. OF LABOR & INDUSTRY page 1754(bottom left); NEW YORK DEPT. OF COMMERCE page 1765(top right); 1770(bottom left); NEW ZEALAND HIGH COMMISSION page 1768(bottom left); PETER NEWARK page 1769(bottom right); OKLAHOMA CONVENTION page 1828(top left); OKLAHOMA TOURISM PHOTO BY MIKE SHELTON page 1827(bottom right); OREGON STATE HIGHWAY PHOTO page 1842(top left); PENGUIN BOOKS page 1801(top right); PHOTRI page 1751(bottom right); 1808(top left); 1809(top right); G.R. ROBERTS page 1768(top right); SHELL page 1794(bottom right); R.I. LEWIS SMITH page 1794(top left); SMITHSONIAN INSTITUTE, FREER GALLERY OF ART, WASHINGTON, D.C. page 1845(bottom right); SPECTRUN COLOUR LIBRARY page 1824(top left); U.P.I page 1851(bottom right); USDA PHOTO page 1842(bottom left); UNITED KINGDOM ATOMIC ENERGY AUTHORITY page 1804(top right); 1805(top right & bottom left); VICKERS page 1820 (top left); VICTORIA & ALBERT MUSEUM page 1846(bottom left); 1847(top right); WEST VIRGINIA GOVERNMENT OFFICE page 1853(top left); WESTERMAN FOTO page 1835(top right); S. WHITAKER page 1763(top right); YERKES OBSERVATORY page 1814(top left); ZEFA page 1742; 1744(bottom left); 1747(bottom left); 1748(top left); 1749(both pics); 1752(bottom left); 1754(top left); 1756(top left); 1757(bottom right); 1758(top left); 1762(top left); 1765(bottom right); 1766(top left); 1767(bottom); 1771(bottom right); 1774(bottom left); 1781(bottom); 1790(top left); 1791(bottom right); 1797(bottom right); 1798(top left); 1800(bottom right); 1823(bottom right); 1834(bottom left); 1839(bottom right); 1841(top right); 1844(top left); 1849(bottom left); 1855(top right); 1857(top left); 1864(top left).

CONTENTS

NEVADA Some of the world's biggest explosions have been set off underground in Nevada. The U.S. Government tests new kinds of atomic bombs there. They are exploded far down under the surface of the Earth. A major testing place is at Yucca Flat, which is about 65 miles (105 km) northwest of Las Vegas.

The Land and Climate Nevada is a western state. Only California lies between it and the Pacific Ocean. North of it are Oregon and Idaho. Utah and Arizona lie to the east of it. California also borders it on the south. Nearly all of Nevada is in the Great Basin, which is a vast desert highland walled in by mountains. The western rim of the Great Basin is formed by the Cascade Mountains and the Sierra Nevada Mountains. The eastern rim is part of the Rocky Mountains. The state gets its name from the Sierra Nevada. This Spanish name means "Snowy Range." The mountain range lies mostly in California, but a branch of it enters Nevada near Reno.

Numerous streams run down Nevada's mountains. Some flow into lakes, but most of them end in places called *sinks*. There the water either sinks into the ground or dries up.

Even the state's longest river, the Humboldt River, flows into a sink. It travels about 300 miles (480 km) across northern Nevada, only to disappear in the Humboldt Sink. This sink is sometimes called a lake, but it is filled with water only part of the year.

In 1985, records reported that Nevada's population had increased about 90 percent since 1970. About half of the state's people live in urban areas, such as Reno and Las Vegas.

No other state is quite so dry as Nevada. Rain falls chiefly on the slopes of the mountains, where forests of pine, spruce, and hemlock trees grow. The rest of Nevada gets very little rain, and only hardy desert

plants, such as sagebrush and cactus, grow wild there. It is easy to see why most of Nevada is unused. Its valleys have too little rain for agriculture, and its mountains are too steep and rocky for crops.

History Small bands of Paiute, Shoshone, and Washoe Indians once wandered the Great Basin. Lack of rain kept them from raising crops. Grass was scarce, so there were few large animals to hunt. The Indians gathered seeds and dug roots for food. They trapped rats and lizards.

White trappers from Canada explored the Humboldt River in the early 1800's. At that time, Nevada was part of Northern Mexico, but the Mexicans took no interest in the barren land. After the Mexican War (1846–1848), what had been northern Mexico was taken by the United States. Soon afterward, the first settlers came to Nevada. Many of them were members of a religious group called the Church of Jesus Christ of Latter-Day Saints. The Mormons, as other people called members of this group, built a trading post in the Carson River Valley in 1851. But most of them moved on to Utah.

Silver was discovered in Carson County in 1859. A man named Henry Comstock staked out a claim. He sold it for $11,000, but the lode, or mass of silver ore, continued to be called the Comstock Lode. It was one of the richest bodies of ore ever found. Virginia City grew up near the mines and became one of the wildest cities in the Wild West. Many people came there hoping to "strike it rich." Those who

▲ *Vast areas of the state of Nevada are sandy, barren desert.*

Nevada is often called the Silver State because of the large amount of silver once mined there.

Bones and other remains discovered near Las Vegas, Nevada, indicate that some of the earliest American Indians lived there more than 20,000 years ago.

◀ *New Guinea natives elaborately decorated with body paint—possibly the earliest form of art. One carries a ritual drum. See* NEW GUINEA.

▲ *Virginia City is a ghost town near Reno, Nevada, which has been preserved as a tourist attraction.*

did not mine the silver tried to get money from those who did. Much silver changed hands in gambling. Gold and other minerals were later found elsewhere in the state. Most mining is now done in the northwestern and southwestern parts of the state.

On October 31, 1864, Nevada became the 36th state of the Union.

Nevadans at Work Copper is the most important mineral mined in Nevada today. There is a huge open-pit copper mine near Ely. Iron ore, tungsten, lead, zinc, barite, and mercury are mined in parts of the state. Central Nevada has deposits of oil. Some manufacturing, mainly food-processing and the production of lumber products, is carried on in Nevada. Livestock-raising is the chief form of farming. Hay for feeding the animals is the principal crop.

But mining, manufacturing, and agriculture are unimportant in comparison with another Nevada industry—tourism. This state of about 940,000 people has more than 25 million visitors a year! Most of these people go to Las Vegas and Reno. Tourists spend more than $2 billion each year in Nevada. Much of the money pays for hotel accommoda-

tions and entertainment, but at least half of it is spent in gambling. Nevada allows kinds of gambling that are unlawful in most states, so people who like to gamble flock there. Nevada also has laws that save time for people who want to marry—or get divorces. These laws bring outsiders to the state. While they are in Nevada, they spend money.

Many Nevadans are unhappy about the picture that other U.S. citizens have of their state. They do not want the nation to think of Nevada as simply Reno and Las Vegas. The state has much that is beautiful and interesting. It shares Death Valley and Lake Tahoe with California, and the great Hoover Dam and Lake Mead with Arizona. Tourists can go through the Lehman Caves near the Utah border or visit some of the ghost towns built during the early mining days. Visitors can also attend rodeos and go trout-fishing, hunting, and skiing. Above all, visitors should see the desert at dawn and at sunset. The desert at these times takes on rich colors that change with the light.

ALSO READ: DEATH VALLEY, DESERT, SIERRA NEVADA.

▼ *Las Vegas, in southeastern Nevada, is probably the gambling capital of the world.*

NEWBERY MEDAL Of all the children's books published in the United States each year, one is very special. It is the book whose author wins the Newbery Medal for the "most distinguished contribution to American literature for children." Members of the American Library Association judge the books and present the award at an annual dinner.

The Newbery Medal is named in honor of an English writer and publisher, John Newbery (1713–1767). It was established in the United States by Frederic G. Melcher, a publisher, in 1922. The first winner was Hendrik van Loon for *The Story of Mankind*, a book about the history of the

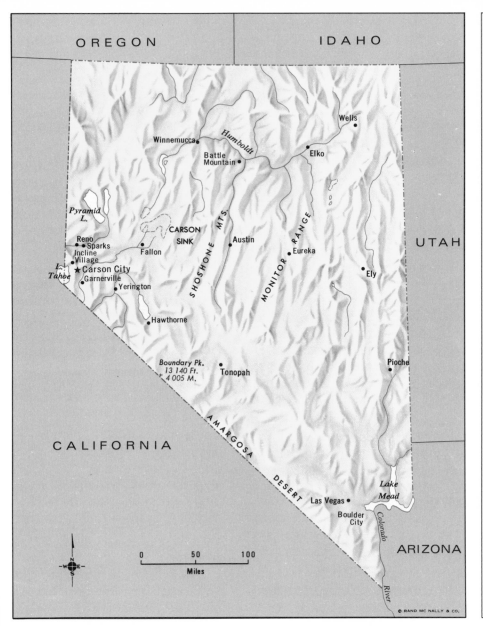

NEVADA

Capital
Carson City (34,000 people)

Area
110,540 square miles
(286,297 sq. km)
Rank: 7th

Population
1,058,000
Rank: 43rd

Statehood
October 31, 1864
(36th state admitted)

Principal river
Humboldt River

Highest point
Boundary Peak
13,140 feet (4,005 m)

Largest city
Las Vegas (211,000 people)

Motto
"All For Our Country"

Song
"Home Means Nevada"

Famous people
Patrick A. McCarran, Wovoka
(a Paiute Indian prophet)
Paul Laxalt, Pat Nixon

STATE EMBLEMS

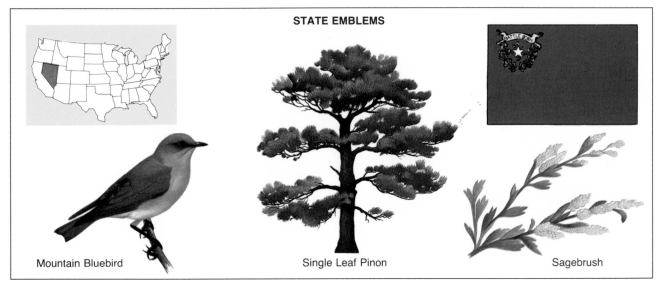

Mountain Bluebird

Single Leaf Pinon

Sagebrush

▲ *The front and back faces of the Newbery Medal, awarded each year to the author of the best children's book of the previous year.*

In 1922, Andrew Bonar Law of New Brunswick became the only person born outside the British Isles to become prime minister of Great Britain.

world. Among the most popular Newbery winners is Hugh Lofting's humorous *Voyages of Dr. Dolittle*, which won the award in 1923. Esther Forbes's *Johnny Tremaine*, about a boy helping the American colonies win their independence, won the award in 1944. Katherine Paterson, who won the Newbery Medal in 1978 for *Bridge to Terabithia*, won it again in 1981 for *Jacob I Have Loved*, a story of sibling rivalry.

ALSO READ: CALDECOTT AWARD, CHILDREN'S LITERATURE.

NEW BRUNSWICK New Brunswick is one of the four maritime provinces of Canada that border on the Atlantic Ocean. It is slightly smaller in size than its western neighbor, the state of Maine in the United States. New Brunswick is bounded on the north by the Gaspé Peninsula of Quebec, on the east by the Gulf of St. Lawrence and the Northumberland Strait, on the southeast by Nova Scotia, and on the south by the Bay of Fundy.

The Bay of Fundy, which has the highest tides in the world, provides spectacular sights at high tide. The St. John's River system empties into the bay through a rock gorge. At high tide, the bay waters race upstream through the gorge, creating the Reversing Falls. Also at high tide, a *tidal bore*, or wall of water, rushes up the Petitcodiac River near the city of Moncton. The possibility of using the power in the 40- to 50-foot (12- to 15-m) tides of the Bay of Fundy for industry has been under study for many years.

New Brunswick is a hilly area with many rivers and lakes, and broad, fertile river valleys. The hills are richly forested with red spruce, white birch, balsam, and Canadian maple. Campers in the Fundy National Park can see moose, black bear, deer, and other wildlife.

Occupations Fishing is an important occupation in this province bordered by the sea. About half the people in New Brunswick work in manufacturing, primarily of wood pulp and paper. Construction work, forestry, and farming are other occupations. Potatoes and apples are grown, and livestock is raised.

Bituminous (soft) coal is the most important mineral mined. Deposits of lead, zinc, silver, and copper sulfite have been discovered.

Saint John, the largest city and chief seaport, is one of the few ice-free ports in Canada. The University of New Brunswick in Fredericton, the capital, dates from 1800, and is the oldest university in Canada.

History Giovanni da Verrazano, an Italian who sailed for the French, touched the southern coast of New Brunswick in 1512. Jacques Cartier of France explored the northern coast in 1534. In 1604, Samuel de Champlain established a French settlement in New Brunswick, the first colony in what was later to be called Canada. The French settlement of Acadia included New Brunswick, Nova Scotia, Prince Edward Island, and parts of present-day Quebec and Maine.

After the British defeated the French in Queen Anne's War (1702–1713), Acadia was given to Britain. Later, Acadians caused trouble for Britain because they sympathized with France in the French and Indian War. In 1755, during the war, the British *deported* (sent out of the country) Acadians who refused to take an oath of allegiance to the British king. About 6,000 men, women, and children were sent to the American colonies. Some of them returned after the Treaty of Paris in 1763. Others went south to Louisiana, a former French colony. Descendants of the Acadians still live in Louisiana, where they are called Cajuns. Longfellow tells the Acadians' tragic story in his long poem, *Evangeline*.

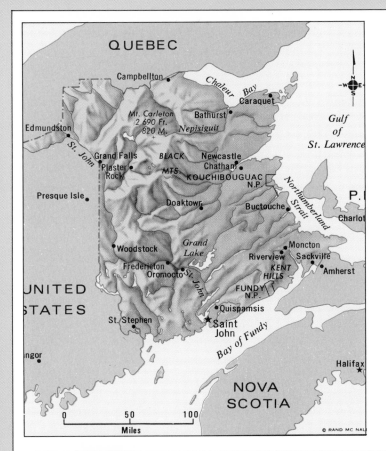

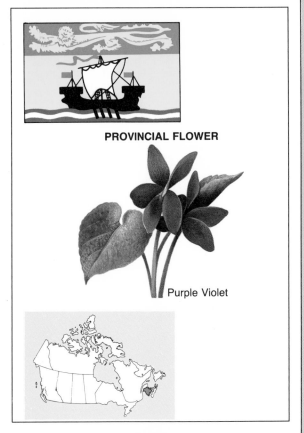

PROVINCIAL FLOWER

Purple Violet

NEW BRUNSWICK

Capital
Fredericton (47,500 people)

Area
27,834 square miles (72,090 sq. km)

Population
711,000

Entry into Confederation
July 1, 1867

Principal river
St. John River

Highest point
Mount Carleton 2,690 feet (820 m)

Largest city
Saint John (110,000 people)

Famous people
Richard B. Bennett, Bliss Carman, Andrew Bonar Law, Sir Charles Roberts

▲ *The strange formations of Hopewell Rocks are caused by the strong tides of the Bay of Fundy wearing away the rocks.*

▲ *Attractive weatherboard houses line this leafy avenue in Fredericton, capital of New Brunswick.*

The first transatlantic radio signal was received by Marconi in 1901 at Signal Hill, St. John's, Newfoundland.

By 1760, the British had conquered all the French colonies in Canada. During the American Revolution, many Tories, refugees from the United States, who were called United Empire Loyalists in Canada, settled in New Brunswick. Their descendants and others of British origin form almost 60 percent of today's population. Descendants of the original French settlers, called Acadians, form nearly 40 percent. Both French and English are official languages of New Brunswick.

In 1867, New Brunswick joined three other colonies to form the four original provinces of a new country called Canada.

ALSO READ: CANADA.

NEW ENGLAND see UNITED STATES OF AMERICA.

NEWFOUNDLAND-LABRA-DOR Newfoundland-Labrador is one of the four maritime provinces on the east coast of Canada. The other three maritime provinces are New Brunswick, Nova Scotia, and Prince Edward Island. Sometimes the four provinces are called the "Atlantic Provinces." The province includes the island of Newfoundland and the area on Canada's coast north and east of Quebec called Labrador. The whole province is about the size of the states of New York and Pennsylvania and the New England area combined, but its population is only slightly more than a half million people.

Newfoundland-Labrador is a rugged land of rocky hills, crystal lakes, and fast-flowing streams. The spectacular 245-foot (75 m) high Churchill Falls on the Churchill River in Labrador is the site of one of the largest hydroelectric-power plants in the world. Newfoundland's rocky coast has many fine natural harbors. Only a few hardy trees can withstand the

severe winters in the northern region of Labrador. But rich forests cover much of Newfoundland island, which is farther south.

Newfoundland-Labrador boasts one of Canada's best universities. This is the Memorial University of Newfoundland at St. John's, the capital city.

History Scandinavian Vikings (seafaring adventurers) probably discovered the island of Newfoundland about A.D. 1000. When the Vikings landed in North America, they founded a settlement they called Vinland (Wineland) the Good. But the settlement was later abandoned and forgotten until it was rediscovered at present-day L'Anse-au-Meadow in 1963.

Newfoundland was visited in 1497 by the explorer, John Cabot, who claimed it for England. The first English fishing colonies in North America were set up on the island shortly after this date. But the first official settlement was not until 1610.

In 1855, the British allowed the Newfoundland colony to govern itself. The colony by this time included the Labrador coast. But Newfoundland-Labrador's economy collapsed during the great economic depression of the 1930's, and the British again took control of the government. In 1949, a majority of Newfoundland-Labrador citizens voted to join Canada as the tenth Canadian province.

The People Most families in Newfoundland-Labrador came originally from the British Isles. Many Newfoundlanders ("Newflies") are of Irish origin and speak with an Irish lilt.

Fishing is one of the main occupations in Newfoundland-Labrador. The waters around the province are rich in cod, flounder, herring, and other fish. Most of Newfoundland-Labrador's wealth comes, however, from the great iron-ore mines in Labrador. Oil has recently been discovered offshore from St. John's. Lumbering is a major industry in the

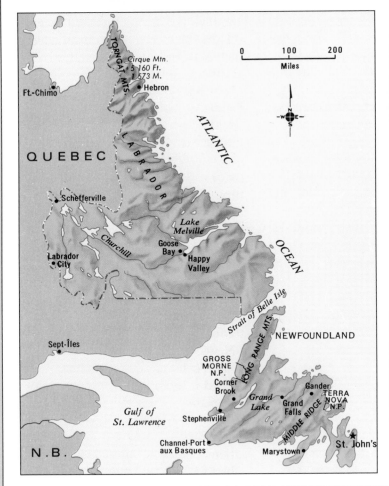

▲ Eskimo children dressed for the arctic-type weather in Labrador, build an igloo in which to play.

▲ L'Anse-au-Meadow, where Viking seafarers landed in A.D. 1000 and established the first settlement.

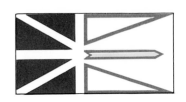

PROVINCIAL FLOWER

Pitcher Plant

NEWFOUNDLAND —LABRADOR

Capital and largest city
Saint John's (164,000 people)

Area
143,510 square miles (371,690 sq. km)

Population
570,000

Entry into Confederation
March 31, 1949

Principal river
Churchill River

Highest point
Cirque Mountain
5,150 feet (1,573 m)

Famous people
Robert Bartlett, Sir Wilfrid Grenfell, Maurice D. Prendergast

▲ *Although Western culture is making an impact on New Guinea, many of the people still live the way that their forefathers did.*

▲ *New Guinea is located north of Cape York Peninsula, Australia.*

province's forests. Much of the timber is processed into pulp and paper at mills in the province.

Most of the people of this province live around the coasts. Some of the smaller fishing villages can be reached only by sea. Life in these villages has changed little in two centuries. The villages have such charming names as Rattling Brook, Heart's Delight, Joe Batt's Arm, Leading Tickles, and Come by Chance.

"Newflies" enjoy their traditional way of life and would not change it. They call their homeland "Canada's happy province."

ALSO READ: CABOT, JOHN AND SEBASTIAN; CANADA; VIKINGS.

NEW GUINEA The largest and second largest islands on Earth are at opposite ends of the world. Greenland, the largest, is in the North Atlantic Ocean. New Guinea, the second largest, is in the southwest Pacific Ocean. New Guinea is part of the large group of islands, named Melanesia, that lie north and northeast of the continent of Australia. (See the map with the article on AUSTRALIA.)

New Guinea has an area more than twice that of California. The island is about 1,500 miles (2,400 km) long and about 430 miles (690 km) wide at the center. Much of the interior is covered by high, rugged mountains.

In the highlands of the mountain ranges, temperatures are less hot and humid than in the swampy lowlands of the coastal areas. The average temperature is 80° F (27° C). Tropical rain forests cover much of the island's highlands. The lowlands are largely swampy and grassy. New Guinea's jungles are filled with fascinating wildlife. There are crocodiles and snakes, such as pythons and death adders. There are tree kangaroos, various rodents, and colorful birds, such as the bird of paradise. More plentiful

are malaria-carrying mosquitoes, and leeches (bloodsucking worms that live mainly in water).

Most of the four million or so people of New Guinea are Melanesians—the native inhabitants of the island. There are also some Malaysians and Polynesians (people from other parts of the South Pacific), and some Europeans, Australians, and Chinese—most of them live along the coast.

Life moves at a slow pace on New Guinea except in the cities where trade increases activity. Most people—especially inland—meet their own needs by farming, fishing, hunting, and gathering food that grows wild. Many of the island's tribes practiced head-hunting and cannibalism not so long ago, and a few still do. There is still little evidence of Western civilization in the interior. Some tribes still use stone tools. Often the tribes wage small-scale wars against each other.

Early Spanish and Portuguese navigators saw New Guinea's shores. In 1606, the Spanish explorer, Luis de Torres, sailed between New Guinea and Australia through the strait now called the Torres Strait. The Dutch took over the western half of the island in 1793. Germany and Great Britain set up protectorates in the eastern half in 1884. Later, the eastern half came under Australian control.

During World War II, the Japanese captured parts of New Guinea to use as a base to try to conquer Australia. Australian and U.S. troops fought and defeated the Japanese in the jungles.

New Guinea is now divided into two parts. The western half of the island, Irian Jaya, has been under Indonesian control since 1963. Its capital is Jayapura. To the east of Irian Jaya lies the independent nation of Papua New Guinea. Australia used to govern this area, formerly called the Territory of Papua (in the south) and the United Nations Trust Territory of New Guinea (in the north). Papua New Guinea is now a member of the British Commonweatlh.

ALSO READ: INDONESIA, MELANESIA, PACIFIC ISLANDS, PAPUA NEW GUINEA.

NEW HAMPSHIRE One of New England's most famous sculptures is in the state of New Hampshire. This sculpture is strictly nature's work—a rock formation called the "Old Man of the Mountain." It became famous because of Nathaniel Hawthorne's short story, "The Great Stone Face," written in 1849.

To see this stone face, you have to go to the White Mountains of New Hampshire, to a deep, narrow valley named Franconia Notch. There, beside Profile Lake, you will find a marker on a large rock. Look up. Against the sky you will see the rock-formed features of the Old Man.

The face made the great New Hampshire-born statesman Daniel Webster (1782–1852) think of signs that craftworkers of his day hung over their doors. "Shoemakers hang a gigantic shoe," he said, "jewelers a monster watch . . . but up in the Franconia Mountains God Almighty has hung out a sign to show that in New England He makes men."

The Land New Hampshire is the middle state of northern New England. Vermont lies to the west across the Connecticut River. Maine lies to the east. Canada is north and Massachusetts is south of New Hampshire.

The mountains of northern New Hampshire are wooded. But some peaks rise above the timberline. Their tops are too high and cold for trees. Mount Washington in the White Mountains has the highest peak in the northeastern United States. Its top is cold even in midsummer. You can reach the top by a cog railroad that is more than 100 years old. Only cog-wheels can climb the steep slope here.

A winding motor road takes the climb more gradually.

South of the White Mountains is a belt of lakes that stretches from Maine in the east to the Connecticut Valley in the west. New Hampshire shares the northern part of the valley with Vermont. Dairy cattle graze the meadows of the valley, which has New Hampshire's best farmland. Other good farmland is in the southern part of the state, where the Merrimack River flows. The river provides waterpower for manufacturing in such cities as Concord and Manchester that lie beside it.

New Hampshire has only 18 miles (29 km) of coast, but there are some fine beaches on it. Portsmouth is the state's only seaport. Its harbor is near the mouth of the Piscataqua River. This city is more than 350 years old and has been a shipbuilding center since the days of wooden ships. Today, steel submarines are built and repaired there.

History When the first Europeans came, they found two main Indian groups living in what is now New Hampshire. These Indians were the Pennacook and the Abnaki (also called Abenaki). The word "abnaki" means "eastern land."

The highest wind speed ever recorded on the Earth's surface was measured at 231 mph (372 km/h) on Mount Washington, New Hampshire, on April 12, 1934.

New Hampshire was the only one of the original 13 states in which no fighting occurred during the Revolutionary War. In January 1776, New Hampshire became the first colony to form a government that was totally independent of Great Britain.

▼ *There are many popular summer camps in New Hampshire. Sometimes the camps are made up of log cabins way out in the country, surrounded by forests, lakes, and rivers—ideal for all kinds of outdoor activities, including canoeing.*

▲ *The best farms in New Hampshire are in the Connecticut River valley.*

▼ *Mount Jackson rises above the vast forest lands of the White Mountain National Forest in New Hampshire.*

Early explorers visited the coast of New Hampshire. Captain Martin Pring of England sailed up the Piscataqua River in 1603. Two years later, the French colonial leader Samuel de Champlain arrived. Captain John Smith drew the Piscataqua River on a map in 1614.

The history of New Hampshire begins with four towns. Dover was settled by British colonists in 1623. Portsmouth was then founded, followed by Exeter and Hampton. These towns were separate and had their own governments.

In 1679, King Charles II of Britain made New Hampshire a separate province. But the governors he sent over from Britain proved to be tyrants. As a result, in 1698, New Hampshire insisted on being under the governor of Massachusetts. For more than 40 years, the two colonies had the same governors. Otherwise, their governments were separate.

Wars with the Indians and with the French caused trouble until 1763, when the French were defeated. But there was soon war with the mother country, Britain. In a way, the American Revolution began in New Hampshire. On December 14, 1774, a band of New Hampshirites took a small British fort without firing a shot. They carried off the fort's cannon and gunpowder. In January 1776, New Hampshire declared itself independent of Britain.

After the American Revolution, the state grew swiftly. Its first cotton mill was built at New Ipswich in 1803. The machinery was powered by the Souhegan River. The state's first shoe factory was started at Weare in 1823. Manufacturing leather goods is still a leading business in New Hampshire.

New Hampshirites at Work The state's largest business is manufacturing. There are many small plants and large industrial factories located in southern New Hampshire. Electrical and nonelectrical machinery, paper and wood products, and leather goods (especially shoes) are the chief manufactured items. Some textiles are made in the state.

The second largest business is tourism. Beaches, mountains, and woodland lakes draw visitors in summer, when the weather is warm and pleasant. Snowy slopes bring them in winter. Skiing is an important sport in New Hampshire. Berlin, in the White Mountains, has one of the tallest ski-jump towers in the United States.

Many people come to New Hampshire when autumn has colored the leaves. Forests in the southern part of the state are a magnificent sight then. (The northern forests consist mostly of evergreen.)

Agriculture is the state's third largest business, although it is far behind the other two in terms of dollars earned. Many dairy and poultry farms are in the state's southern half. Apples, corn, and potatoes are grown. Despite New Hampshire's nickname as the "Granite State," the quarrying (mining) of granite is only a minor business. New Hampshire has a number of other nicknames. It is called the "White Mountain State," the "Mother of Rivers," and the "Switzerland of America."

ALSO READ: GRANITE; HAWTHORNE, NATHANIEL; WEBSTER, DANIEL.

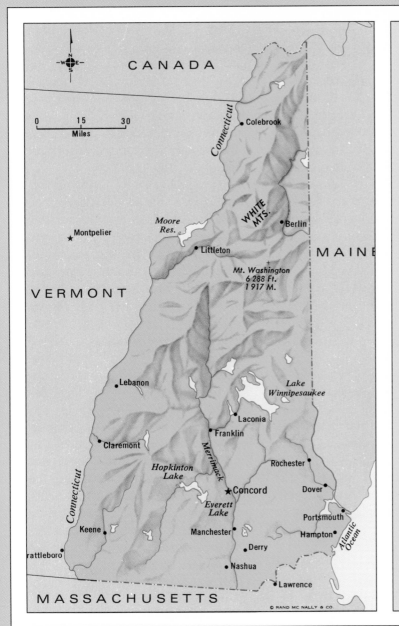

NEW HAMPSHIRE

Capital
Concord (34,500 people)

Area
9,304 square miles
(24,097 sq. km)
Rank: 44th

Population
1,110,000
Rank: 42nd

Statehood
June 21, 1788
(Ninth of the original 13 states to ratify the Constitution)

Principal rivers
Connecticut River
Merrimack River

Highest point
Mount Washington
6,288 feet (1,917 m)

Largest city
Manchester (101,000 people)

Motto
"Live Free or Die"

Songs
"Old New Hampshire"

Famous people
Josiah Bartlett, Mary Baker Eddy, President Franklin Pierce, Alan B. Shepard Jr., Daniel Webster

STATE EMBLEMS

Purple Finch   White Birch   Purple Lilac

▲ *Cape May at the tip of southern New Jersey has miles of ocean beaches that vacationers can enjoy in the summer months.*

▼ *Fishermen enjoy a day's sport in one of the many seaside resorts in southern New Jersey.*

NEW JERSEY Of every ten people who live in the state of New Jersey, nine live in cities and towns. New Jersey has been called a state of cities. The six largest New Jersey cities, in order of size, are Newark, Jersey City, Paterson, Elizabeth, Trenton (the capital), and Camden.

The Land and Climate New Jersey is a Middle Atlantic State, bounded on the east by the Atlantic Ocean and on the northeast by the Hudson River, which separates New Jersey from New York. To the southwest, across the Delaware River, are the states of Delaware and Pennsylvania.

New Jersey lies across three long geographical regions of the East Coast. Farthest inland is the Appalachian, which is covered with wooded mountains and lakes. The state's highest point is in the Kittatinny Mountains in the Appalachian region.

The Piedmont region is a highland between the mountains and the coastal plain. Near the mountains it consists of rounded hills, but becomes rolling plains farther east. The eastern, lower Piedmont has several rocky ridges. The most famous of these is the Palisades, which rises sharply along the Hudson River opposite New York state. Newark, Jersey City, Paterson, and Elizabeth are in the lower Piedmont. Camden and Trenton are on the line where the Piedmont meets the coastal plain.

The Atlantic Coastal Plain covers the entire southern half of the state. Here the land rolls very gently, and slow-moving rivers wind across the plain. Smooth beaches line much of the coast, where there are also some salt marshes. Ducks like the shallow swamp water, and long-legged birds wade among the reeds.

New Jersey has a mild climate. Breezes from the mountains and the Atlantic Ocean keep summers from being too hot. During the winter, the southern part of the state is warmed by winds from the Delaware Bay and the ocean. The mountains in the north are much colder.

History The first known inhabitants of what is now New Jersey were the Lenni-Lenape Indians. The Lenni-Lenape, called the Delaware by the English, were peaceable and usually friendly toward the Europeans who came to their land. The first European to arrive was an Italian, Giovanni da Verrazano, who was exploring for France in 1524. A British sea captain, Henry Hudson, arrived in 1609, while exploring for the Dutch. The Dutch claimed New Jersey as part of their colony of New Netherland and established settlements there between 1614 and 1621.

The British claimed the territory too, basing their claim on the explorations of Sebastian Cabot in 1509. They captured the land from the Dutch in 1664, during the Anglo-Dutch wars. Charles II of Britain granted the land between the Hudson and Delaware rivers to two British subjects. One of them, Sir George Carteret, had previously been the governor of the island of Jersey in the English Channel. He named the land "New Jersey."

In 1702, the owners of New Jersey gave up their right of self-government to the British king. There was much quarreling between the colonists and the governors sent from Britain. New Jersey joined the other colonies that

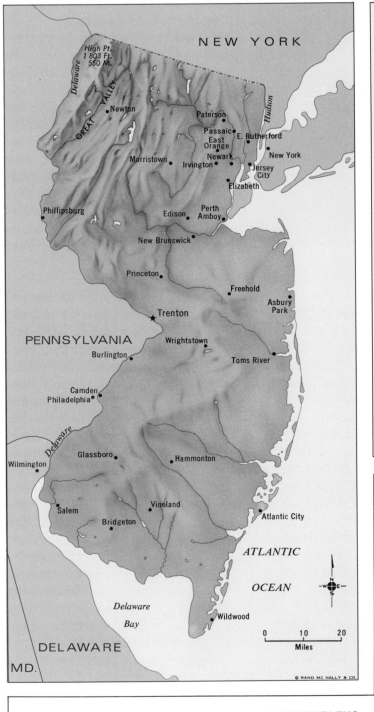

High Pt.
1,803 Ft.
550 M.

NEW YORK

Delaware

GREAT VALLEY

Newton

Paterson

Passaic
East
Orange

E. Rutherford

Morristown

Irvington

Newark

New York

Hudson

Jersey
City

Elizabeth

Phillipsburg

Edison

Perth
Amboy

New Brunswick

Princeton

Freehold

Asbury
Park

★ Trenton

PENNSYLVANIA

Wrightstown

Burlington

Toms River

Camden
Philadelphia

Delaware

Wilmington

Glassboro

Hammonton

Salem

Vineland

Bridgeton

Atlantic City

ATLANTIC

OCEAN

N W E S

*Delaware
Bay*

Wildwood

0   10   20
Miles

DELAWARE

MD.

© RAND MC NALLY & CO.

NEW JERSEY

Capital
Trenton (92,000 people)

Area
7,836 square miles
(20,295 sq. km)
Rank: 46th

Population
7,728,000
Rank: 9th

Statehood
December 18, 1787
(Third of the original 13 states to ratify the
Constitution)

Principal river
Delaware River

Highest point
Kittatinny Mountains
1,803 feet (550 m)

Largest city
Newark (314,000 people)

Motto
"Liberty and Prosperity"

Song
None

Famous people
Count Basie, James Fenimore Cooper,
Thomas Edison, Albert Einstein, Molly Pitcher,
Paul Robeson, Frank Sinatra, Bruce
Springsteen

Red Oak

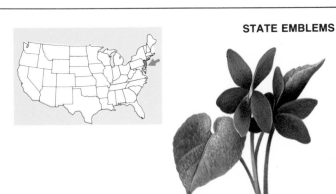

STATE EMBLEMS

Purple Violet

Eastern Gold Finch

▲ *Princeton, about 50 miles (80 km) southwest of New York City. This small town is home to the famous ivy-league college, Princeton University. The town also served briefly as the nation's capital in 1783 during the American Revolution.*

New Jersey has more people per square mile than any other state— 965 (373 per square km). As a comparison, Alaska has only 1 person per square mile.

rose up against the British in 1775. On July 2, 1776, New Jersey adopted its first constitution, and in December 1787 it ratified the U.S. Constitution. New Jersey was the site of many important battles during the American Revolution, including the battles of Trenton and Monmouth. George Washington's headquarters were located for a time in Morristown.

Once the war was over, New Jerseyites settled down to farming and industry. They were soon manufacturing products with newly invented power-driven machinery. In 1791, Alexander Hamilton started the United States's first planned factory town, Paterson. The falls of the Passaic River provided power for the machines spinning cotton yarn. After that, more factories were built in New Jersey.

In 1870, a wooden platform about 6½ miles (10.5 km) long was built along New Jersey's coast. This is the Boardwalk, featured in the game "Monopoly."

New Jersey at Work New Jersey leads the nation in the making of chemical products and pharmaceuticals. Other important industrial activities are food-processing, petroleum-refining, and the manufacture of machinery, transportation equipment, metal products, textiles, and glass products.

Business executives saw that a good

transportation system could help industry. New Jersey has more highways and railroad lines per square mile than any other state. Tunnels, bridges, harbors, and canals all serve to bring in and take out manufactured products and raw materials. The excellent transportation system has also helped the tourist trade. Tourism accounts for more than $11 billion of New Jersey's economy each year. Most of the visitors go to beach resorts, such as Asbury Park, Atlantic City, and Cape May. In 1978, legalized casino gambling began in Atlantic City.

New Jersey's agriculture industry is also important. Millions of chickens and thousands of dairy cows are raised in New Jersey. Vegetables and fruits are grown on modernized farms in "The Garden State." The agricultural products are processed (canned, frozen, and packaged) in the state's factories.

The population has grown faster than the number of jobs. Unemployment and poverty make life very difficult for thousands of people.

Destructive riots occurred in several New Jersey cities in the late 1960's. Black and white people demonstrated against the poor living conditions and high unemployment. The worst riot took place in Newark, where 26 persons were killed and almost $15 million in property damage was done in July 1967.

Today, urban renewal projects are underway in many of the state's cities. New industrial, commercial, residential, and recreational areas are being established. Old buildings are being repaired. New Jersey is working to solve its social and economic problems. In 1970, Newark elected Kenneth A. Gibson, the first black mayor of a New Jersey city. He was reelected in 1974 and 1978.

ALSO READ: AMERICAN REVOLUTION; CITY; HAMILTON, ALEXANDER; VERRANZO, GIOVANNI DA.

NEW MEXICO If you were traveling through the southwestern desert region of New Mexico, you might spot, walking ahead of you, a large brown bird. It is the roadrunner, the state bird of New Mexico. The roadrunner likes people—if they are moving. It enjoys a race. People on foot cannot hope to get ahead of it. Motorists can beat it, of course, but they often slow down to watch the bird. The roadrunner then sees its chance. It spreads its wings and takes long, gliding leaps. When it passes the car, the race is over. The bird disappears behind a rock or into a clump of bushes.

Roadrunners are only one of the unusual sights to see in New Mexico. The state's nickname—the "Land of Enchantment"—suggests the wonders found in this rugged land. Some of its other nicknames give the same impression: it is known also as the "Land of Delight Makers," the "Land of Heart's Desire," and the "Sunshine State." Other nicknames for New Mexico include the "Spanish State," referring to its history, and the "Land of Opportunity"—a nickname it shares with Arkansas.

The Land and Climate New Mexico is a southwestern state. It lies between Arizona on the west and Texas on the east. Mexico is its southern neighbor, and Colorado its northern one. The Great Plains cover the eastern third of New Mexico. The long Pecos River flows through this area. The river was thought of as a boundary in the early days of ranching. Cowboys used to say "West of the Pecos" when they referred to the wild, lawless land beyond the Great Plains. The area west of the river is covered with scattered mountain ranges and high valleys. The Sangre de Cristo ("Blood of Christ") Range extends southward from Colorado. It is part of the Rocky Mountains. The Sacramento Mountains to the south link the Rockies and Mexico.

West of these ranges is the valley of the Rio Grande. This river rises in Colorado and flows south through New Mexico. Water from the Rio Grande irrigates land not only in New Mexico but in Texas and Mexico as well. The Elephant Butte Reservoir, located on the river near the town of Truth or Consequences, forms the state's largest lake. The Rio Grande valley is an important part of the state. New Mexico's largest city, Albuquerque, and its capital, Santa Fe, are located in the valley. Not far from the capital is Los Alamos, a center for atomic research. South of Santa Fe, the Rio Grande valley becomes what is called "basin-and-range country." Mountain ranges enclose broad plains, making them basins. Southwestern New Mexico, too, is basin-and-range country.

Northwestern New Mexico is part of the Colorado Plateau. This area is broken up by sharp cliffs and deep canyons. Strangely colored rocks give it a beauty all its own.

History The remarkable Pueblo Indians have lived in New Mexico for thousands of years. *Pueblo* is Spanish for "town." Unlike other Indians in our country, these people lived in towns of well-constructed houses. The houses were built of stone or *adobe* (sun-dried brick). The Pueblo Indians belonged to several tribes. The Zuni and Hopi were two of the most important tribes. They had pueblos in the basin of the Rio

The Carlsbad Caverns National Park in New Mexico has the world's largest known system of caverns. They are still not fully explored. The area is one of stunning natural beauty.

▼ *Much of New Mexico is desert with mesas (flat-topped hills) and sparse vegetation of cactus and sagebrush where it is not just rocky desert.*

▲ *A complex of adobe dwellings of the ancient Taos Pueblo Indians. Such buildings were the first U.S. "apartments"—communal homes already in use when the first white settlers arrived.*

Grande. The Pueblo Indians were skillful farmers. They raised corn, beans, and squash for food, and cotton for cloth.

They often had to fight off enemies. Navaho and Apache Indians from the Great Plains attacked the Pueblo Indians.

Francisco Coronado, a Spanish explorer, visited the region during the 1540's. He was searching for the legendary Cibola (seven cities supposedly built of gold) and was disappointed to find only the pueblos. Spanish colonists built their first settlement in the valley of the Chama River near the Rio Grande in 1598. Twelve years later, they founded Santa Fe a little to the southeast. Its full name was La Villa Real de la Santa Fe de San Francisco, "The Royal City of the Holy Faith of Saint Francis." This name was too long for everyday use, and it was soon shortened to Santa Fe. The Spaniards made the Indians pay taxes. Since the Indians had no money, they paid in corn, cloth, or labor. They were forced to become Christians and were forbidden to perform their old religious ceremonies. In 1680, the Indians rebelled and drove the Spaniards to the south. For a dozen years, the Indians were free. Then the Spanish regained control.

Mexico won independence from Spain in 1821. The territory that is now New Mexico was part of Mexico at that time. But by the end of the Mexican War in 1848, the United States had conquered almost all of New Mexico. A strip along the southern boundary was bought from Mexico in 1853, in a 10 million dollar deal called the Gadsden Purchase.

U.S. settlers who came to live in the new territory fought the Navaho and Apache. The U.S. Army finally defeated these Indians and forced them to live on reservations. Many cattle and sheep ranchers came to New Mexico. They needed grass and water for their animals. During the

1870's, these two groups began to fight over the land. Gradually, the fighting ended. Irrigation brought farmers. The territory became a state in 1912.

During World War II, U.S. scientists developed atomic bombs. The first one was tested near Alamogordo, New Mexico, on July 16, 1945. There and then the human race entered the Atomic Age.

New Mexicans at Work New Mexico's biggest industry is mining. Oil, natural gas, and copper are the three most valuable minerals found in the state. New Mexico mines more uranium, an element used to produce atomic energy, than any other state. It also leads the country in the production of potash, a substance used in fertilizers.

Manufacturing is important in New Mexico. Chemicals, machinery, food products, and lumber products are manufactured. Agriculture is a large business, too. Raising cattle and sheep is the main type of farming.

The U.S. Government employs many people in New Mexico. Scientists and others do research at Los Alamos. New weapons are tested at several bases in the state. Many people work on equipment for space exploration.

The "Land of Enchantment" naturally attracts tourists. Many people come to see the ruins of pueblos and the "cliff dwellings" of ancient Indians. Acoma, a pueblo built on a flat-topped rock 357 feet (109 m) high, is a favorite attraction. Indians still live there. Acoma has an adobe church built in the 1600's. The beautiful and enormous Carlsbad Caverns are another popular tourist attraction. The largest cave is more than a half mile (800 m) long and sometimes as much as 650 feet (200 m) wide.

ALSO READ: APACHE INDIANS; CIBOLA, SEVEN CITIES OF; CLIFF DWELLERS; CORONADO, FRANCISCO; NAVAHO INDIANS; PUEBLO INDIANS; RIO GRANDE.

COLORADO

OK.

Aztec · *Navajo Res.* · Raton
Shiprock · Farmington
Wheeler Pk.
13,161 Ft.
4,011 M.
COLORADO
Espanola
Gallup ·
Los Alamos · Las
★ Vegas
Santa Fe
Grants ·
Zuni · Alameda · Tucumcari ·
Albuquerque ·
PLATEAU
Rio Grande
ROCKY MOUNTAINS
GREAT PLAINS
Pecos
Socorro · Clovis ·
Portales ·
Elephant Butte Res.
Roswell ·
Ruidoso · Lovington ·
Alamogordo · Hobbs ·
Artesia ·
Silver City ·
Carlsbad · *Pecos*
Deming · Las Cruces · CARLSBAD CAVERNS N.P.
El Paso · TEXAS
Ciudad Juarez ·
0   50   100
Miles

ARIZONA

MEXICO

© RAND MC NALLY & CO.

NEW MEXICO

Capital
Santa Fe (51,800 people)

Area
121,666 square miles
(315,113 sq. km)
Rank: 5th

Population
1,514,000
Rank: 37th

Statehood
January 6, 1912
(47th state admitted)

Principal rivers
Rio Grande
Pecos River

Highest point
Wheeler Peak
13,160 feet (4,011 m)

Largest city
Albuquerque (380,000
people)

Motto
Crescit Eundo ("It Grows as
it Goes")

Song
"O, Fair New Mexico"

Famous people
Billy the Kid, Geronimo,
Conrad Hilton

STATE EMBLEMS

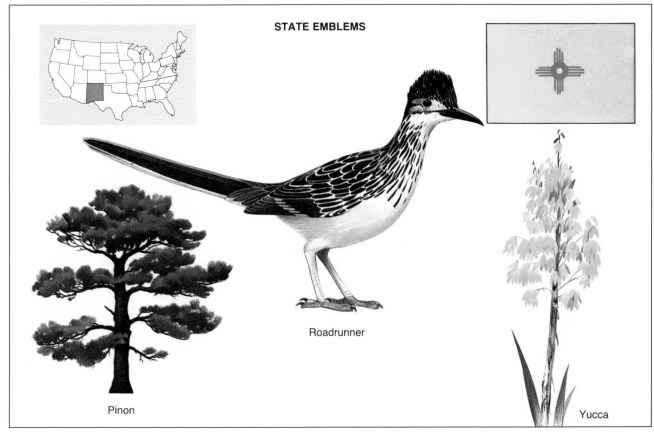

Pinon

Roadrunner

Yucca

▲ The Scottish Dove *was a weekly newspaper, small in size. The edition shown here is for the week beginning November 3, 1643. It brings news of the English Civil War.*

▼ *A modern, open-plan newspaper room. Here journalists and editors process news stories and features on electronic keyboards with visual display units (VDU's).*

NEWSPAPER A daily newspaper brings you the written word about news happenings all over the world. Wherever a big event is taking place, a news reporter is very likely there, reporting details of the story. A newspaper's job is to get that news to its readers as accurately and as quickly as possible.

Newspapers are printed to give fast information, if that is all a reader wants. Just a glance at the front page can give a newspaper reader a quick indication of the important events occurring around the world. Each story is written in such a fashion that the reader can get the essential facts quickly. The first paragraph of the story usually contains most of the key facts. Newspaper writers call these facts the *five w's*: the who, what, where, when, and why of a story.

There is much more in a newspaper besides straight news reports. *Editorials* have the newspaper editor's or owner's opinions about different subjects. *Columns* are articles written regularly about special topics—such as politics or gardening—by writers who are familiar with these topics. *Feature stories* entertain or inform readers with information that may not be current news. A common type of feature story is the travel article, which tells readers about faraway places.

Cartoons and comic strips provide entertainment.

Newspapers are often divided into sections according to subject matter. For example, banking and stock-market news are often found in the financial section of a metropolitan daily paper. Other sections may be devoted to entertainment, real estate, food, sports, and travel news.

The price you pay for a newspaper usually covers only a fraction of the cost of its production. Newspapers make most of their money from advertisements. The two main kinds of advertisements are called *display* advertisements and *classified* advertisements. Display ads usually take up several columns of space and contain pictures as well as facts. Businesses use display ads to promote their products. Classified ads are lists of items, set in small type. They are set under headings, such as "Help Wanted" or "For Sale," in a particular section of the paper.

Although most major U.S. newspapers are published every day, some are published weekly. Many of them appear on Thursday or Friday because much of the advertising depends on weekend specials. Weekly newspapers are usually smaller than a local daily, but millions of people read them to know who in their town, suburb, or community within a city is getting married, has a new job, or is doing something else locally newsworthy. More than 7,000 weekly newspapers are published in the United States.

But the most important type of newspaper is the metropolitan daily. It is published in a large city and prints international and national as well as state and local news. A metropolitan daily may sell more than a million copies each day because it carries information that is interesting not only to the people who live in the city where it is published, but also to people all over the state. It may even reach people in other states or other countries.

History of Newspapers The first newspaper in the world of which there is a record was the bulletin *Acta Diurna* ("Actions of the Day") that Julius Caesar had posted in the public places of Rome about 2,000 years ago.

Less than 100 years after Johannes Gutenberg developed the printing press in 1447, the first newspapers were printed in Europe. They appeared in several German cities. The first full-size daily newspaper was published in Leipzig in 1660. Five years later the first full-size English-language newspaper, the Oxford *Gazette*, appeared in Britain. That publication invented the word "newspaper" in 1670.

The first North American newspaper was published in 1690 in Boston. It was called *Publick Occurrences*. It lasted for only one issue because the colonial governor protested that the printer, Benjamin Harris, had no license. Another newspaper, the Boston *News-Letter*, was started 14 years later. It lasted until 1776.

Many important American colonists wrote for or published early American newspapers. Among them were Benjamin Franklin, Samuel Adams, Thomas Jefferson, Thomas Paine, and Richard Henry Lee. These early North Americans believed strongly that newspapers should have the right to publish the facts. They made sure that the U.S. Constitution's Bill of Rights guaranteed freedom of the press.

The first daily newspaper in the United States—the Pennsylvania Evening Post and Daily Advertiser— was published in 1793. Until the 1800's, only a few people could receive newspapers. But during the 1830's, new printing presses enabled publishers to produce newspapers faster and cheaper. More people were learning to read, and they wanted newspapers. Printers lowered the price of their papers to one penny. With the coming of the "penny press," more newspapers were sold, and widespread publishing of news

papers began in the United States. In 1841, Horace Greeley founded the *New York Tribune*—the first low-priced newspaper to include book reviews and other literary features. His editorials became famous and strongly influenced public opinion. Ten years later, Henry J. Raymond founded the *New York Times*. The *Times* presented the news in a thorough and largely impartial way. It grew to have the largest national and international staff of any newspaper in the United States. It is now one of the world's leading newspapers. The *Christian Science Monitor*, published in Boston, established a reputation of honesty and thoroughness.

By the late 1800's, newspapers had become very popular. Some attracted many readers by printing sensational news about crime and disaster, often distorting the truth. This was called "yellow journalism." The newspapers owned by William Randolph Hearst did much to get the United States into the Spanish-American War in 1898. The Hearst papers printed stories about the conditions in Cuba under Spanish rule. These stories were sometimes highly exaggerated.

Radio and television have brought strong competition to newspapers in recent years. Newspaper circulation has gone down in cities and up in the suburbs as people have left the cities. Several large city daily newspapers, such as the Washington *Star*, have ceased publication because of decreasing circulation and advertising. But some small city dailies have increased their circulation in recent years. Each day, people in the United States buy more than 62 million copies of daily newspapers.

How Newspapers Are Made A newspaper office usually has three kinds of workers. The editorial department is headed by the editor in chief, who makes all the big decisions about what goes into the newspaper. He or she supervises the news staff

▲ *A journalist keys in his story of the day on to a word processor. The story is filed on a floppy disc which can be called up anytime by the editor and prepared for the page layout and production states.*

Half the world's 10,000 daily newspapers are in the English language.

The world's largest-selling daily newspaper is *Komsomolskaya Pravda*, a daily paper for young people in the Soviet Union. Nearly 22 million copies are sold every day.

▲ *A newspaper press. The plates that print the newspaper are fitted onto two huge drums. Paper is fed into the press from a giant roll so that one turn of the drums prints an entire newspaper. Another machine cuts and folds the newspaper.*

▲ *Export editions of several U.S. newspapers are available around the world.*

and a board of editorial writers. The managing editor heads the news staff, which can consist of a city editor (in charge of gathering local news), a foreign editor (in charge of international news), and editors who handle the sports, food, financial, entertainment, and other special sections. Most section editors have their own staffs of reporters and photographers.

The business staff is headed by a business manager. His or her job is to supervise the workers who sell ads, manage the office, distribute the papers, and carry out all the details needed to make the business end of the newspaper work. The production staff includes the photoengravers, layout artists, typesetters, and press workers who turn the typewritten copy into a printed newspaper.

Imagine there has been a fire. The city editor of a newspaper gets a report of a large fire in progress at a big downtown hotel. A reporter goes quickly to the scene of the fire. The press card on the car's windshield gets him or her a parking spot not far from the fire engines. The reporter talks to the fire chief, the hotel manager, and to people the fire fighters have rescued. He or she makes some notes, goes to the nearest telephone, and calls the newspaper. An editor there decides how much space this news should get and switches the reporter

to a rewrite person. The reporter tells the rewriter what happened at the scene, and the rewrite person quickly writes the basic story. The story is then given to a copy editor, who checks it for clearness and accuracy and writes a headline. The managing editor reviews the final story and sends it to the composing room to be set into type and printed. A proofreader checks the printed copy for mistakes and takes it to the layout artist, who shows the printer where the story should appear on the printed page. The printer and his or her staff set up the pages according to the layout artist's instructions and print the paper. The papers are counted, bundled, and packed into trucks that deliver them to homes and newsstands. When you receive your newspaper, you read all about the fire.

Many modern newspapers use computers so that, instead of a reporter writing a story and then a printer setting it into type, the words the reporter types are set directly into type by the computer. This saves a great deal of money because the system is quicker and because the proprietor has to employ fewer printers. But, although the system is cheaper, there are some disadvantages—for example, newspapers today contain many more printing errors than newspapers used to. However, it seems certain that the newspapers of the future will all be produced in this way.

ALSO READ: ADVERTISING; CARTOONING; COMICS; COMMUNICATION; FRANKLIN, BENJAMIN; JOURNALISM; PRINTING; PUBLISHING; TYPESETTING.

NEWTON, SIR ISAAC (1642–1727) The falling of an apple may have led the great British scientist, Isaac Newton, to make his most important discovery. A story tells that one day he saw an apple fall to the ground. He realized that a force must be making the apple fall downward instead of flying off into the air. Newton later explained how the same force—*gravity*—caused the moon to move around the Earth and the planets around the sun.

Isaac Newton was born in Woolsthorpe, England. As a boy, he was very interested in scientific experiments. He studied mathematics at Cambridge University and later taught mathematics there.

One of Newton's most important achievements was his discovery of the three laws of motion. These laws explain how motion occurs and the relationship between an object's movement and the forces that act on the object. Newton created a special type of mathematics to calculate (work out) the forces of gravity between objects. This mathematics, which later became known as *the calculus*, is widely used in science today—although we use the superior method devised independently by the German mathematician, Gottfried Leibniz.

Newton also made important discoveries about light and color. He found that so-called white light is actually made up of a *spectrum* of many colors. He first saw these colors by looking at light through a glass *prism* (three-sided block). His research was of great value in the science of *optics*, or the study of light. Newton invented a *reflecting telescope*, which shows a clear and powerful image by reflecting it from a curved mirror. Most large telescopes are now made in this way.

Newton had the ability to concentrate completely on whatever he was doing. He devoted his whole life to his work. He received many honors and was knighted in 1705. Scientific researchers today still rely on Newton's basic discoveries about the nature of the universe.

ALSO READ: COLOR, GRAVITY AND GRAVITATION, LIGHT, MATHEMATICS, MOTION, SPECTRUM, TELESCOPE.

▲ *A portrait of British scientist Sir Isaac Newton at the age of 46. He is widely regarded as the greatest scientist of all time.*

▼ *The first reflecting telescope, made by Isaac Newton in 1668.*

NEW YEAR'S DAY January 1, New Year's Day, is celebrated as a holiday in many parts of the world. In the past, New Year's Day came at different times of the year. March 25 was New Year's Day in Europe during the Middle Ages. January 1 became New Year's Day when the Gregorian calendar was adopted in 1582. The Chinese New Year's Day falls between January 20 and February 19. The Jewish New Year is celebrated during Rosh Hashanah, which usually occurs in September.

New Year's Eve, the night before the holiday, is usually celebrated with parties or church services. Many people make New Year's *resolutions*, promises to improve themselves in the coming year.

ALSO READ: CALENDAR, HOLIDAY.

NEW YORK The northernmost of the Middle Atlantic States, New York is bordered by five other states, two rivers, two lakes, an ocean, and an-

Newton made his three momentous scientific discoveries in a burst of inspiration from 1665 to 1667. He was not yet 26 years of age when he achieved this.

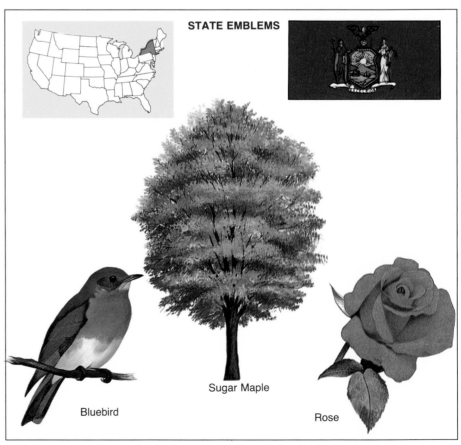

NEW YORK

Capital
Albany (111,000 people)

Area
49,576 square miles
(128,401 sq. km) Rank: 30th

Population
17,990,000
Rank: 2nd

Statehood
July 26, 1788 (11th state)

Principal rivers
Hudson River, Mohawk River

Highest point
Marcy 5,344 feet (1,629 m)

Largest city
New York City (7,440,000
people)

Motto
Excelsior ("Ever Upward")

Song
"I Love New York"

Famous people
Aaron Copland, George
Gershwin, Julia Ward Howe,
Herman Melville, John D.
Rockefeller, Theodore
Roosevelt, Franklin D.
Roosevelt

STATE EMBLEMS

Bluebird

Sugar Maple

Rose

other nation! On the north, New York is bordered by Lake Ontario, the St. Lawrence River, and Canada; on the east, by Vermont, Massachusetts, and Connecticut; on the west, by Pennsylvania, Lake Erie, and the Niagara River; and on the south, by Pennsylvania, New Jersey, and the Atlantic Ocean.

Nearly 18 million people live in New York State. Over 40 percent of them live in New York City, in the southeast corner of the state—the largest city in the United States. The state has three important islands—Staten Island, Manhattan Island, and Long Island. The first two are part of New York City, as is the western end of Long Island.

The Land and Climate Mainland New York is largely hilly or mountainous. This part of the state is rough and the soil is thin, providing poor farming land. But the excellent forests and lakes make northern New York good country for vacationing.

The state's highest mountains, the Adirondacks, are in the north. Most of the state south of the Adirondacks lies in the Appalachian Highland. This highland stretches northward from Alabama. The Catskill Mountains, in southeastern New York, are also covered with forests and lakes. Like the Adirondacks, they also provide good vacation country. But much of the land of the Catskills has been cleared for farming.

Because so much of New York is hilly or mountainous, its flatlands are very important. The plains along the Great Lakes and much of the Hudson River valley provide excellent farming land. The river valleys have also been useful for lowland transportation routes through the mountains.

The climate varies greatly in different parts of the state. The average annual rate of precipitation (rain and snow) of 40 inches (100 cm) is excellent for farming—where the land is suitable. The western highlands and

the Adirondacks have cold winters, hot summer days, and cool summer nights. In the southeast, breezes from the Atlantic Ocean make winters milder and keep summer days from being extremely hot. Summer heat in New York City, however, is often stifling. The asphalt of the city's streets and concrete of its tall buildings soak up the heat and hold it.

History In 1609, the French explorer, Samuel de Champlain, entered New York from what is now Canada. He sailed south along the water route that led to what is now Lake Champlain. In the same year, the British Henry Hudson, exploring for the Dutch, sailed north on the river that was later named for him.

In 1624, the Dutch founded a settlement, which they named Fort Orange, near the point where the Hudson River joins the Mohawk River. The location of the settlement made water routes to the north, south, and west easily available. The Dutch became fur traders, buying furs from the Indians. In 1625, the Dutch established another settlement, New Amsterdam, at the lower end of Manhattan Island. The colony was named New Netherland.

Great Britain also claimed this territory. In 1664, an English fleet captured New Netherland from the Dutch. King Charles II of Britain awarded the territory to his brother,

▲ *Fort Ticonderoga in New York State has been restored as a historic landmark of the American Revolution.*

▼ *New York is a state with vast forests, lakes and rivers, rolling hills and fertile valleys. Fish are abundant in such lakes as this one near the Adirondack Mountains.*

▲ *Autumn in New York state brings out golden reds and yellows in the vast deciduous forests such as in the Catskill hills in the southeast.*

New York City has some of the world's most impressive structures including the Chrysler Building and the Empire State Building and the World Trade Center (all in their time the tallest buildings in the world), the largest natural-history museum (the American Museum of Natural History), the largest railroad station (Grand Central Terminal), and the largest port (New York Harbor).

the Duke of York and Albany. New Amsterdam was renamed New York. Fort Orange was renamed Albany. This city is the present-day capital of the state.

By 1775, when the Revolution began, New York was one of the 13 British colonies. Many major battles of the war were fought in New York. In 1788, New York became the 11th state to ratify the Constitution.

During the 1800's, the state grew in population and wealth. The fine harbor of New York City helped the city become a center of world trade and finance. The Hudson and Mohawk rivers provide good inland water routes through the state.

The state quickly developed its natural transportation advantages. Ports, canals, highways, railroad tracks, and airports are located throughout the state. In addition to the port of New York, several ports on the Hudson River can be used by oceangoing ships, and Buffalo is one of the leading ports of the Great Lakes. The St. Lawrence Seaway enables oceangoing ships to use ports on the Great Lakes. The New York State Barge Canal, a system of 525 miles (845 km) of canals, provides inland water transportation. The 559-mile-long (900-km-long) Governor Thomas E. Dewey Thruway (the New York State Thruway), linking New York City with Buffalo and ex-

press highways in neighboring states, is the world's longest toll superhighway. There are about 220 airports within the state. La Guardia and John F. Kennedy International Airports are major terminals in New York.

New Yorkers at Work New York ranks as the foremost manufacturing state in the nation. This is mainly due to the leading position of New York City as a port and financial center. Manufacturing earns many millions of dollars for the state each year. The chief item manufactured in the state (and New York City) is clothing and related products. Other major industries are printing and publishing, food-processing, and the manufacture of machinery, chemicals, and glassware.

Although the income from agriculture seems small compared with manufacturing, New York has extensive agricultural industries. The state's leading crops are potatoes, corn, hay, onions, apples, and grapes. A large part of the grape crop is used to produce New York State wines. Livestock products are even more important than crops. The state has a good climate for breeding dairy cattle and growing the hay the cattle eat. The principal value of the dairy farming is that it produces the huge amounts of milk consumed in the state.

Thousands of visitors come to New York State each year. Many travel to work in New York City each day. Others are tourists who come to enjoy the countless attractions of the state. These attractions include the military academy at West Point, the Baseball Hall of Fame at Cooperstown, President Franklin D. Roosevelt's home at Hyde Park, the spectacular Niagara Falls, and the more than 300 state forests, 100 state parks, and 8,000 lakes and ponds. Visitors also come to see New York's many sports teams in action at its many stadiums.

ALSO READ: APPALACHIAN MOUNTAINS; CHAMPLAIN, SAMUEL DE; EMPIRE STATE BUILDING; FIVE NATIONS; GREAT LAKES; HARBORS AND PORTS; HUDSON, HENRY; INTERNATIONAL TRADE; IROQUOIS INDIANS; NEW YORK CITY; NIAGARA FALLS; STATUE OF LIBERTY; ST. LAWRENCE SEAWAY; STUYVESANT, PETER; VERRAZANO, GIOVANNI DA.

NEW YORK CITY The largest city in the United States, New York City, covers more than 320 square miles (830 sq. km) in the southeastern corner of New York State. Nearly seven and a half million people live in the five-borough city. The five boroughs, in order of population, are Brooklyn, Queens, Manhattan, the Bronx, and Staten Island (formerly Richmond). Only seven *states* in the United States (excluding New York State) have larger populations than New York City! If you include the people living in the neighboring counties and suburbs of New York State, New Jersey, and Connecticut, "Greater New York" has a population of more than 18 million people. Every day a million people travel into the city from these suburbs to work.

A Dutch settlement called New Amsterdam was founded on Manhattan Island in 1625. Peter Minuit, the governor of the settlement, bought the island from the Manhattan Indians for about $24 worth of beads, shells, and other small objects. The settlement grew into a busy fur-trading and commercial center. The British captured the settlement in 1664 and renamed it "New York" after the Duke of York. After the American Revolution, New York City served as the first capital of the United States until 1790. George Washington was inaugurated there as the country's first President.

New York City originally consisted of Manhattan Island. The surrounding communities were joined with Manhattan as the City of New York in 1898. The Bronx is the only borough on the mainland. Queens and Brooklyn are on part of Long Island, Manhattan is on Manhattan Island, and Staten Island is in New York Bay. The boroughs are connected by bridges and tunnels, which are used by thousands of cars, subway trains, and buses every day.

New York's industry and prosperity have attracted many immigrants. The original Dutch and British have been joined by thousands of others, including Italians, Russians, Germans, Irish, Jews, Africans, West Indians, and Puerto Ricans.

The early Dutch settlers built a wooden wall near the southern end of Manhattan Island for protection against Indian attacks. Today, the same area, called Wall Street, is the financial center of the nation. The New York and American stock exchanges and large international banks have their headquarters there. Finances in every nation of the world

▲ *New York City at night. The "Big Apple" is famous for its nightlife and international restaurants.*

▼ *Part of Manhattan Island, where skyscrapers dominate the skyline. Because space is limited in Manhattan, people have to build* up, *rather than spreading out to the sides.*

▲ *The official flag of New York City.*

It is a curious fact that New Zealand has no native land mammals. All the cattle, sheep, pigs, deer, rabbits, goats, opossums, weasels, and ferrets were brought to the country by European settlers.

are affected by decisions made on Wall Street.

New York City is also the shipping capital of the United States. The excellent natural harbor, with some 1,600 piers, is one of the busiest in the world.

Many tourists come to New York City each year from every state and country to see such famous places as the World Trade Center, the Empire State Building, Rockefeller Center, and the headquarters of the United Nations. They also visit such familiar landmarks as the Statue of Liberty, Central Park in the center of Manhattan, and Greenwich Village, the home of many artists and writers.

The bright lights of Times Square and New York's theater district are known throughout the world. Restaurants serving food of almost every nation can be found in the city. New York City's several museums include the Museum of Natural History and the large Metropolitan Museum of Art.

ALSO READ: EMPIRE STATE BUILDING, NEW YORK, STATUE OF LIBERTY.

NEW ZEALAND Few countries in the world offer scenery of greater contrast than New Zealand. This English-speaking island nation lies about 1,200 miles (1,930 km) southeast of Australia in the southern Pacific Ocean. New Zealand has snowy

▲ *Sheep are the mainstay of New Zealand's economy. New Zealand exports wool and lamb all over the world.*

mountains and warm sandy beaches; icy glaciers and boiling volcanic mud pots; calm lakes, deep fiords, and rushing rivers; and rich soil and mineral deposits. The big, modern cities of Auckland and Wellington (the capital) contrast sharply with rugged, sparsely populated areas of southern New Zealand. (See the map with the article on PACIFIC OCEAN.)

New Zealand consists of two main islands, the North Island and the South Island, and some smaller islands, the largest of which is Stewart Island. The islands combined have an area about the same as that of Colorado. North Island has the largest cities and the best farmland. South Island has the most dramatic scenery. But little Stewart Island has the most imaginative names—such as Halfmoon Bay, Murder Cove, and Hidden Island.

The original inhabitants of New Zealand were the Maoris, a Polynesian people who still make up about nine percent of the country's population of more than three million people. In 1840, the Maoris signed a treaty making New Zealand part of the British Empire. The country was settled largely by people from Great Britain. Today, New Zealand is an independent member of the British Commonwealth of Nations.

A governor-general represents the

▼ *The Maori are the native people of New Zealand. This Maori meeting hall is decorated with beautiful woodcarving.*

NEW ZEALAND

Capital City: Wellington (134,000 people).

Area: 103,736 square miles (268,676 sq. km).

Population: 3,300,000.

Government: Independent state within the Commonwealth of Nations.

Natural Resources: Natural gas, coal, iron ore, sand, hydropower, gold.

Export Products: Wool, lamb, mutton, beef, fruit, fish, cheese.

Unit of Money: New Zealand dollar.

Official Lanugage: English.

British monarch in New Zealand, but the political leader of the government is the prime minister, who heads the cabinet. There is a House of Representatives, whose 95 members serve for three-year terms, and a High Court of Appeal. New Zealand was the first country in the world to give women the vote.

Wellington and Auckland are New Zealand's chief ports. Along with Christchurch, they are also the leading manufacturing centers. The raising of cattle and sheep is a major business in New Zealand. Meat is the country's largest export, followed by wool, hides, and dairy products. Publishing is an increasingly important industry. Valuable timber comes from the forests. Iron ore, coal, and natural gas are being extracted.

In recent years, New Zealand has been at the forefront of a movement among Pacific island nations to halt nuclear weapons testing in the Pacific Ocean.

ALSO READ: AUSTRALIA, PACIFC OCEAN.

NEZ PERCÉ INDIANS These Indians of the Northwest were named by French fur trappers. *Nez* means "nose" in French; *percé* means "pierced." The French gave them the name because they pierced their noses for wearing ornaments. The Indians' name for their tribe is Nimipu, which means "The People."

The Nimipu lived in central Idaho, northeastern Oregon, and southeastern Washington. They fished, mainly for salmon, in the rivers. They also raised fine horses that they traded with other Indian tribes for things they needed. The Nimipu also hunted buffalo each year. During winter they lived on the riverbanks in houses built partly underground. They went to the mountains to camp during the hot days of the summer.

The Nimipu experience with the white settlers was a sad one. The Nimipu had always been friendly to white settlers. But they were forced to give up most of their land in treaties. About 1860, white prospectors found gold on the remaining Nimipu land. Miners moved in, violating a government treaty. Chief Joseph, leader of one group of the Nimipu, protested that the Indian land was being stolen by the whites. U.S. Army troops were ordered to remove Chief Joseph's band to a small reservation. Bloody battles were fought. In desperation, Chief Joseph led his people on a brilliant 1,000-mile (1,600-km) retreat to Canada in 1879. But the Indians were overtaken and forced to surrender. Today, a few thousand Nimipu live on reservations particularly in Idaho and also in Montana and Washington.

ALSO READ: INDIANS, AMERICAN; JOSEPH, CHIEF.

The *tuatara*, a "living fossil," is found on New Zealand's offshore islands. This dragonlike reptile has a scale-covered lump on its head that in prehistoric days was a third eye. The tuatara grows to a length of 2½ feet (76 cm).

▲ *Chief Joseph, brilliant leader of the Nimipu Indians, against U.S. Army troops in the 1870's.*

1769

▲ *A cross-section of the Niagara Falls between the United States and Canada. At the top is a hard rock called* dolomite. *Underneath are much softer rocks. These softer rocks wear away as the water lashes against them. Finally the rocks at the top cave in, and the falls move slowly upriver.*

▼ *The Niagara Falls are in two parts, one in Canada and the other in the United States. The American Falls* (foreground) *are higher than Canada's Horseshoe Falls* (rear), *but not as wide.*

NIAGARA FALLS   Two separate waterfalls thunder over a high cliff to make the world-famous water spectacular, Niagara Falls. There are nearly 100 waterfalls in the world that are higher than Niagara Falls. But not many other falls are so wide or have such a tremendous amount of water falling over them.

The 36-mile-long (58-km-long) Niagara River connects two of the Great Lakes, Lake Erie and Lake Ontario. About 18 miles (29 km) from Lake Erie, the river is divided by Goat Island, and then the two sections plunge over the edge of a high cliff—the falls. The Niagara River forms part of the unguarded border between the United States and Canada. The border passes directly through Horseshoe Falls, named for its shape. American Falls is on the U.S. side. American Falls is 167 feet (51 m) high and 1,000 feet (305 m) wide. Horseshoe Falls, by far more majestic, is 158 feet (48 m) high and 2,600 feet (792 m) wide. About 95 percent of the water from the Niagara River, that is, more than 100 million gallons (378.5 million liters) flows over Horseshoe Falls every minute.

Water from the melted glaciers of the last ice age began flowing over the cliffs of Niagara Falls many thousands of years ago. The upper rock of the cliff is hard limestone. But the rock underneath the falls is soft shale and sandstone. As the water plunges over the cliff it slowly *erodes* (wears away) the rock. As the underlying rock erodes, the upper ledge is unsupported. In this way, the position of the falls is gradually changed. The falls are about seven miles (11 km) farther north than they were when the water first flowed over them.

The rock under the American Falls erodes about 50 feet (15 m) every 100 years. The rock under Horseshoe Falls is eroding even more rapidly—about 300 feet (90 m) every 100 years. In several thousand more years, Niagara Falls, as we know it, will have disappeared!

There are several exciting ways for visitors to see the falls. You can go aboard a small steamboat named *The Maid of the Mist*, which takes you close to the foaming torrent of water at the base of the falls. You can put on a shiny yellow raincoat and follow a guide to the Hurricane Deck, where you can look up at the American Falls. You can even take a cable-car ride 150 feet (46m) above the spinning whirlpool downriver from the falls.

Niagara Falls is an example of international cooperation. A high bridge over the gorge links New York State with the Canadian province of Ontario. The Welland Canal, built by the Canadians, enables ships to bypass the falls. The two nations have also agreed to divide the tremendous electric power generated by several hydroelectric plants that are located on both sides of the falls.

ALSO READ: ELECTRIC POWER, EROSION, HYDROELECTRICITY, WATERFALL.

NICARAGUA   The Republic of Nicaragua in Central America has an unusual lake named Lake Nicaragua. Its fresh water contains many fish, such as swordfish and sharks, that normally live in salt water. No one

NICARAGUA

Capital City: Managua (750,000 people).
Area: 50,193 square miles (130,000 sq. km).
Population: 3,560,000.
Government: Republic.
Natural Resources: Gold, silver, copper, tungsten, lead, zinc.
Export Products: Cotton, coffee, bananas, seafood, meat, sugar, chemicals.
Unit of Money: Córdoba.
Official Language: Spanish.

knows exactly why these fish live there, but some scientists believe that the lake was once part of the Pacific Ocean. (See the map with the article on CENTRAL AMERICA.)

Nicaragua stretches across Central America from the Pacific Ocean to the Caribbean Sea. It is the largest country in Central America, but much of the land is unpopulated. Most of the people live on the western (Pacific) coast, where the land is flat and suitable for farming. The capital city, Managua, is in this region. Several active volcanoes lie along the coastal plain north of Managua. A line of high mountains runs down the center of Nicaragua. Farther east, on the Caribbean Sea, is the Mosquito Coast—named for the Mosquito Indians. This region is flat and heavily forested. The highlands are cool. The coasts are hot and humid, and the Mosquito coast has heavy rainfall.

Most Nicaraguans are of mixed Spanish and Indian ancestry. Spanish is spoken throughout the country. Farming is the most important occupation. Cotton, rice, fruit, and sugarcane are grown on large farms along the Pacific coast. Cotton is Nicaragua's leading agricultural product. Coffee plantations line the slopes of the central highlands. Nicaragua's mineral resources include gold, silver, and copper.

The Italian explorer, Christopher Columbus, landed in Nicaragua in 1502. Spanish *conquistadors* (conquerors) later conquered the local Indians, and Spain ruled the region for almost 300 years. In 1838, Nicaragua became an independent republic. From 1936, the Somoza family dominated politics in Nicaragua. Anastasio Somoza Debayle became president in 1967. He was often accused of ruling like a dictator. Sandinista guerrillas began a civil war to overthrow him. In 1979, he left the country and the rebels set up a new government supported by the Soviet Union and Cuba. In the 1980's, anti-Sandinista forces, called *contras*, invaded the northeast, with U.S. aid.

In 1990, de Chamorro was elected president. The *Sandanistas* and the contras agreed to a tentative ceasefire. But the demobilization of the contras led to renewed violence.

ALSO READ: CENTRAL AMERICA.

NICHOLAS, CZARS OF RUSSIA Nicholas was the name of two czars (emperors) of Russia.

Nicholas I (1796–1855) became czar on December 25, 1825. Two days later, several army officers revolted against the czar. They wanted a reform of the Russian government, which had become very corrupt. Nicholas put down the revolt. For the rest of his reign, Nicholas was a very severe ruler. He used the Russian army to govern the country. Russian secret police pried into the lives of the people. Nicholas became known as

▼ *A young Nicaraguan guides his cows pulling an old wooden cart along the Pacific shoreline.*

▲ *Czar Nicholas I of Russia.*

▲ *Czar Nicholas II and his family.*

the Iron Czar. But he also introduced a few measures to lessen the extreme poverty and hardships that the Russian peasants were suffering at that time. While Nicholas was czar, the Russians were defeated in the Crimean War by the armies of France, Britain, and Turkey. Some of Russia's most famous writers, such as Alexander Pushkin, Leo Tolstoy, and Ivan Turgenev, lived during Nicholas's reign.

Nicholas II (1868–1918) was the last czar of Russia. He became czar on November 1, 1894. When Nicholas came to the throne, the sufferings of the Russian peasants were growing worse. The government was too corrupt to do anything for the people, and rebellion was beginning to break out. Nicholas agreed to several reforms, but he was anxious not to weaken his own power. He depended very much on the advice of his wife, the Empress Alexandra. But the empress was an unsuitable counselor. She was deeply influenced by a crafty and villainous monk named Rasputin, who claimed he could cure her son's attacks of *hemophilia* (a bleeding disease). When World War I started, the Russians were unprepared. They lost several battles. Food became scarce, and the peasants began to starve. In 1917, a major revolution broke out. Nicholas was forced to give up his throne, and a new government was formed. The czar and his family were sent to a town in Siberia. When the Bolshevik (Communist) Party eventually won control, Nicholas, Alexandra, and their family were shot to death.

ALSO READ: CRIMEAN WAR, RUSSIAN HISTORY, WORLD WAR I.

NICHOLAS, SAINT Most children know about the tradition of Santa Claus, the kindly old man who brings presents for children at Christmastime. Santa Claus is named after a Christian saint called Nicholas, who lived during the A.D. 300's. Saint Nicholas was archbishop of the seaport town of Myra in Asia Minor (now Turkey). Many legends surround his name. He is said to have performed miracles and many good deeds, especially for children and sailors. After his death, several countries, including Russia and Greece, chose him as their patron saint. People celebrated his feast day, December 6, with gift-giving. This celebration later became a part of Christmas. The tradition was brought to the United States very early by the Dutch colonists. The name "Santa Claus" comes from *Sinterklaas*, the Dutch for Saint Nicholas.

ALSO READ: CHRISTMAS.

NIGER Lying mostly in the Sahara Desert, Niger is a West African country that has no seacoast. Niger is bounded on the north by Algeria and Libya, on the east by Chad, on the south by Nigeria, Benin, and Burkina Faso, and on the southwest and west by Mali. Niamey is the capital. (See the map with the article on AFRICA.)

The southern Sahara Desert stretches across northern Niger, giving way to sub-Sahara savannas and steppes, open grassy plains where cattle, sheep and goats find pasture. The Niger River's water and the wet and dry seasons make some farming possible. Peanuts, cotton, and livestock are important exports. Uranium is mined and is an important mineral export.

Many African tribes of different origins live in Niger. Among them are the Hausa, Djerma-Songhai, Peul, and Toubou. Among the best-known peoples are the Tuareg, who cross the desert in camel caravans, trading goods of all kinds. Most people are Muslims, but some practice local religions and others are Christians.

Niger has a rich tradition. It was

NIGER

Capital City: Niamey (368,000 people).
Area: 489,191 square miles (1,267,000 sq. km).
Population: 7,620,000.
Government: Supreme Military Council.
Natural Resources: Coal, phosphates, iron ore, uranium.
Export Products: Uranium, livestock, cowpeas, onions, hides, skins.
Unit of Money: Franc of the African Financial Community.
Official Language: French.

once a part of the Songhai, Kanem, and Bornu empires. Its location between Arab Africa and Black Africa made it a crossroads for trade.

The Scottish explorer, Mungo Park, was the first European to open the territory to Westerners when he traveled up the Niger River in 1805.

Niger was entered by the French in the 1890's and became a French colony in 1922. In 1960, the country became independent. Its first president was ousted in a coup in 1974. A military government took over. In the 1970's and 1980's, severe droughts led to great losses of livestock and crops. Many people starved. Some country people have moved to the cities, looking for jobs, and the cities have become vastly overcrowded. Other people have moved to neighboring countries.

ALSO READ: AFRICA

NIGERIA The country of Nigeria has more people than any other country in Africa. Its territory extends inland from the Gulf of Guinea and is bordered by Cameroon to the east, Benin to the west, Niger to the north, and Chad to the northeast. (See the map with the article on AFRICA.)

There are swamps 10 to 60 miles (16–100 km) wide along the coast. Farther north are tropical rain forests 50 to 100 miles (80–160 km) wide. In the forests are palm trees from which oil is obtained, cacao trees whose beans yield cocoa, and mahogany trees, whose wood is used to make furniture. Nigeria extends deeply into the West African *savanna*—rolling, grassy country and open woodland. In northern and central Nigeria, cotton and peanut crops are raised on a plateau ranging from 1,000 to 4,000

▲ *A sculpture made by the Nok people, who lived about 900 B.C. in what is now Nigeria. They were the earliest people in Black Africa to make sculptures.*

◄ *A caravan of camels, laden with salt, at Bilma, in Niger.*

NIGERIA

Capital City: Lagos (1,251,000 people).
Area: 356,669 square miles (923,768 sq. km).
Population: 120,000,000.
Government: Federal republic, ruled by the Armed Forces Ruling Council.
Natural Resources: Oil, tin, coal, columbite, iron ore, lead, zinc, natural gas.
Export Products: Oil, cocoa, palm products, rubber.
Unit of Money: Naira.
Official Language: English.

feet (300–1,200 m) above sea level.

Nigerians belong to about 250 different tribes. The Ibo, Yoruba, Hausa, Fulani, Ijaw, Efik, Kanuri, Ibibio, and Tiv are the major groups.

In the early 1960's, Nigeria depended on the export of its agricultural products—specifically cocoa, peanuts and peanut oil, and palm oil. Since then, oil production and export has become very important to the country. Nigeria also produces tin and columbite.

Several great African kingdoms once existed in what is now Nigeria. They include the kingdoms of Burnu, Ife, Benin, and the Yoruba of Oyo.

The first European contact with the people of Nigeria was with the Portuguese in the 1470's. Contact with Europeans developed mainly because of the slave trade that flourished until Britain abolished it in 1807. The British occupied Lagos in 1861 and, by 1900, had established British rule. In 1960, Nigeria gained its independence. In 1967, the eastern region of the country declared itself the Republic of Biafra and seceded. A civil war ended with Biafra's surrender in January 1970. Since then, money from petroleum sales has helped Nigeria, but several coups have occurred. Successive governments have been overthrown.

ALSO READ: AFRICA, EQUATORIAL GUINEA.

▼ *Lagos, the capital of Nigeria, is also the country's most important port. It is one of the largest cities in Africa, having a population of over one million.*

NIGHTINGALE, FLORENCE
(1820–1910) As a result of the dedicated work of an Englishwoman, Florence Nightingale, nurses became important members of the medical profession.

Florence Nightingale was born in Florence, Italy, to a wealthy English family. She received the education that was considered proper for a wealthy young woman brought up in the 1800's. Her family was shocked when she expressed an interest in nursing. It was considered to be a lowly occupation, and most nurses

▲ *Florence Nightingale was the founder of modern nursing and campaigned for cleanliness in hospitals.*

were not even trained. Florence Nightingale traveled to various countries to study European hospital systems. She worked as a nurse in France and Germany. In 1853, she became superintendent of the Hospital for Invalid Gentlewomen in London.

When the Crimean War between Great Britain and Russia began in 1854, Florence Nightingale organized a group of 38 nurses and took them to the battlefront in Russia. There she found that nearly half the sick and wounded soldiers were dying because of primitive sanitation methods and poor nursing facilities. As a result of the nursing methods and strict sanitation she set up, the deathrate was greatly decreased.

Upon her return to Britain, she started the Nightingale School of Nursing at St. Thomas's Hospital in London. The opening of the school marked the beginning of professional education in nursing.

During several other wars, including the U.S. Civil War, Florence Nightingale was often consulted on questions concerning the organization and operation of battlefront hospitals. She received honors from many nations.

ALSO READ: CRIMEAN WAR, NURSING.

NIJINSKY, VASLAV (1890–1950)

Vaslav Nijinsky was one of the most brilliant and powerful ballet dancers who ever lived. He could move with amazing speed. And when he leaped, he seemed to "stand" in the air before coming down.

Nijinsky was born in Kiev, Russia. He was of the fifth generation in a family of well-known Polish dancers. When only nine years old, he was accepted by the Russian Imperial Ballet School. He was already dancing important parts before he graduated.

In 1909, Sergei Diaghilev, director of the Russian Ballet, took Nijinsky and other Russian dancers to perform in Paris, France. Audiences crammed the theaters to see Nijinsky perform. His dancing was like none they had ever seen. Diaghilev encouraged Nijinsky to *choreograph* (create dances) for the music of Claude Debussy and Igor Stravinsky. Nijinsky created the ballets *Afternoon of a Faun* and *The Rite of Spring*. Many people disliked these ballets.

While on tour in South America, Nijinsky married a young ballerina. In 1916, he danced at the Metropolitan Opera House in New York City. Nijinsky's last performance took place in 1917, when he was only 27 years old. Mental illness caused him to stop dancing. He was never able to perform again.

ALSO READ: BALLET; DANCE; PAVLOVA, ANNA.

▲ *Vaslav Nijinsky, the great Russian ballet dancer. His leaps were so high that many people claimed that he was able to fly!*

NILE RIVER The Nile is the longest river in the world. It flows about 4,145 miles (6,670 km) from central Africa to the Mediterranean Sea. Two rivers, the White Nile and the Blue Nile, meet in the Sudan and flow northward to the sea as one river. (See the map with the article on AFRICA.) Boats cannot travel the full length of the Nile because of dams, waterfalls, and rapids.

▲ *The Nile River which flows north from Lake Victoria, near the equator, and passes through Uganda, Ethiopia, Sudan, and Egypt. This map shows its winding course.*

▼ *Sunset on the Nile reveals the outline of this* felucca—*the common working boat of the river.*

The White Nile begins in the mountains of Burundi in small streams that flow into Lake Victoria. The river then flows over waterfalls and through canyons to Lake Kioga. From there, it rushes over Kabarega (formerly Murchison) Falls and goes into Lake Mobutu Sese Seko (formerly Albert). About 200 miles (320 km) farther on, the river flows through a swampy area called the Sudd, where many plants choke the river. The river flows through the Sahara desert in Sudan. At Khartoum, capital of Sudan, the White Nile meets the Blue Nile. Between the two rivers, just before they join, lies the fertile Gezira plain.

The Blue Nile starts at Lake Tana in the Ethiopian highlands, at a height of about 6,000 feet (1,830 m). The river rushes over many rapids on its trip of about 1,000 miles (1,600 km) to meet the White Nile.

A narrow strip of fertile land lies along the banks of the Nile as it flows northward. Once it approaches Egypt, the Nile broadens into a new, 300-mile-long (480-km-long) lake—Lake Nasser. This lake lies behind the Aswan Dam, built between 1960 and 1970. This dam is 375 feet (114 m) high and more than 2 miles (3 km) long. It provides enough water for 670,000 acres (271,100 hectares) that were once irrigated only when the river was in flood and for another million acres (4,000 sq. km) of farmland in Egypt.

As it flows through Egypt, the Nile passes many ancient Egyptian monuments. It passes the great temples and statues at Thebes, Luxor, and Karnak. The pyramids at Giza near Cairo can be seen from the river where *feluccas* (boats with large sails) and other more modern boats travel. The Nile glides though Cairo and goes on to the delta region bordering on the Mediterranean Sea. There, the river separates into many small streams that give water to the wide delta. The Damietta and Rosetta rivers are the main branches leading to the sea. Farmers in the delta build dikes. They irrigate their fields to produce crops of cotton, hay, and vegetables.

The ancient Egyptians considered the Nile River to be sacred because its water made life possible for them. They built temples and tombs along the riverbanks and held religious festivals to celebrate the yearly flooding of the land along the river that left rich fertile soil.

ALSO READ: ABU SIMBEL; AFRICA; CAIRO; EGYPT, ANCIENT.

NITROGEN Nitrogen is a gas that makes up four-fifths of our world's atmosphere. It is a chemical element. Nitrogen is vital in nature. Plants and animals cannot live without it.

Although there are vast amounts of nitrogen in the air, this nitrogen cannot be used directly by most living things. First, it must be combined with other elements to form *nitrates*. Bacteria that live in the soil or on the roots of plants called *legumes* change nitrogen into nitrates that plants can use for growth. The nitrogen becomes part of the plant tissues called *proteins*. Animals eat plants, and plant proteins become animal proteins. People get nitrogen from the plant and animal food they eat. When plants and animals die, the decayed

matter leaves nitrates in the soil. New plants then use the nitrates. When crops are harvested, some nitrogen is removed. Fertilizers put it back.

Nitrogen does not easily join with other chemical elements. It does not burn under normal conditions. It is slow to unite with other elements, but its compounds may break down explosively. Many explosives contain nitrogen. The nitrogen of the air can be combined with *hydrogen* through a process that subjects the mixture to great pressure. This combination forms a gas called *ammonia*. Ammonia gas combines with oxygen to form *nitric acid*. In the chemical industry, a large number of useful things are made by using ammonia and nitric acid. Aniline dyes for silk and wool cloth contain nitrogen. Nitrous oxide, a colorless gas, is prepared by heating ammonium nitrate. This gas is called "laughing gas" because it tends to cause hysterical laughter in people who inhale it. It is mixed with oxygen and used as an anesthetic.

Get a good-sized clump of clover. Dig up the roots and all. Wash the roots carefully. The tiny whitish bumps on the roots are where the nitrogen is being "fixed" by the bacteria that live there. This is natural fertilization going on.

ALSO READ: ELEMENT, HYDROGEN, OXYGEN, PLANT.

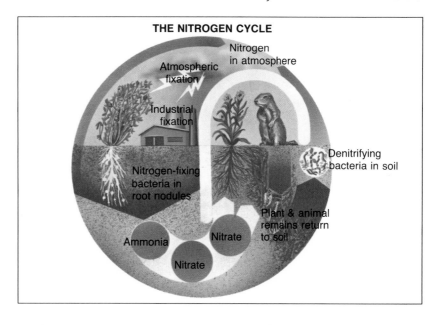

THE NITROGEN CYCLE

NIXON, RICHARD MILHOUS (born 1913) In 1960, the Republican Party of the United States chose the U.S. Vice-President, Richard Milhous Nixon, as the Republican candidate for President. Nixon lost the presidential election to John Fitzgerald Kennedy by only 119,450 votes. Two years later, Nixon was defeated in the election for Governor of California. Many U.S. citizens believed that his political career was over. He then joined a law firm in New York City. In 1968, the Republicans once more nominated Nixon for the Presidency. The election was again very close, but this time Nixon won, defeating the Democratic candi-

▲ *The nitrogen in the atmosphere can be used by living creatures because of the* nitrogen cycle. *Lightning in the air, bacteria in the soil, or people in factories turn the nitrogen first into* ammonia. Denitrifying bacteria *turn the ammonia into* nitrates, *which are used by plants as food. Animals eat the plants, and their wastes release more ammonia to the soil.*

▲ *President and Mrs. Nixon and Secretary of State William Rogers in Shanghai, with Chinese premier Chou En-Lai.*

RICHARD MILHOUS NIXON

THIRTY-SEVENTH PRESIDENT   JANUARY 20, 1969—AUGUST 9, 1974

Born: January 9, 1913, Yorba Linda, California
Parents: Francis Anthony and Hannah Milhous Nixon
Education: Whittier College and Duke University Law School
Religion: Society of Friends (Quaker)
Occupation: Lawyer
State Represented: California
Political Party: Republican
Married: 1940 to Thelma ("Pat") Ryan
Children: 2 daughters

During Richard Nixon's term of office the minimum voting age in all U.S. elections was lowered from 21 to 18.

▲ *Alfred Nobel, inventor of dynamite. He intended it to be used for peace, and was so horrified when he saw people use it for war that he left all his money for the Nobel Prizes.*

All five Nobel Prizes awarded in 1976 were won by U.S. citizens. No Peace Prize was given that year. Even so, this was the first time since the awards began that all winners were citizens of the same country.

1778

date, Hubert Humphrey, who was then U.S. Vice-President. Nixon's running mate, Spiro T. Agnew, became the Vice-President.

Nixon was born on a farm in Yorba Linda, California. His parents were Quakers. Nixon's boyhood was spent mostly in Whittier, a small town near Los Angeles, California. He helped in his father's gas station and general store. After he finished high school, he attended Whittier College, where he played on the college football team and was an outstanding member of the debating team. His record as a good student won him a full scholarship to the Law School of Duke University. At Duke, he was elected president of the student body and president of the university law association. After his graduation with honors in 1937, he returned to his hometown to practice law.

During World War II, Nixon served in the United States Navy and was promoted to the rank of lieutenant commander. After his release from active duty, he was elected to the United States House of Representatives in 1946 and, four years later, to the Senate.

During his term in the House of Representatives, Nixon served as a member of the Un-American Activities Committee. One of his duties was to investigate the charges made by a former Communist that Alger Hiss, a high-ranking U.S. State Department employee, had been a spy for the Soviet Union. Nixon became very well known for his controversial part in this investigation. In 1952, he was elected U.S. Vice-President. Nixon served in that office during the eight years that Dwight D. Eisenhower was President.

Nixon had pledged in his Presidential campaign to bring an end to the war in Vietnam. In 1969, he began a program for the gradual withdrawal of U.S. troops from Vietnam. But in 1970 he claimed that an invasion of the neighboring country of Cambodia

(now Kampuchea) was necessary to protect the withdrawing troops. In the United States, he favored stricter handling of lawbreakers and measures to reduce crime. He proposed a new system of welfare aid to the poor as well as new educational programs.

In 1971, he ordered a "wage-price freeze" designed to improve the nation's economy. He also announced that the dollar would be *devalued* (lowered in value) in order to increase trade with other countries. Nixon continued the U.S. space program begun under President John F. Kennedy. When the first U.S. astronauts landed on the moon, Nixon congratulated them by radio. Nixon visited China and Russia in 1972 and was reelected President that year. After securing a ceasefire in Vietnam, he withdrew all U.S. troops.

In 1973, the Nixon administration was hit by the Watergate scandal, caused by the burglary of the Democratic Party headquarters in the Watergate office complex in Washington, D.C., on June 17, 1972. Nixon publicly denied any wrongdoing, but tapes revealed that he had approved of and directed a cover-up of the burglary. Impeachment of Nixon seemed likely. On August 9, 1974, he resigned, becoming the first President ever to do so. Later, members of his administration were put in jail.

ALSO READ: FORD, GERALD RUDOLPH; IMPEACHMENT; VIETNAM WAR.

NOBEL PRIZE The Nobel Prize is probably the greatest award and honor a person can receive for his or her work. Each year, Nobel Prizes are awarded in the fields of chemistry, physics, physiology or medicine, economics, literature, and peace. Occasionally, prizes are not given or are awarded later. The winners are selected by groups of distinguished scholars from several European countries, including Sweden and Norway. The Peace Prize is presented in Oslo by the king or queen of Norway. The other prizes are presented in Stockholm by the king or queen of Sweden. The prizes consist of a medal, a certificate, and a cash award.

The prizes were established by Alfred Nobel, a Swedish chemist who invented dynamite, an explosive. Nobel had invented dynamite for peaceful purposes, but people soon discovered that dynamite could be a powerful weapon in war. This misuse of his invention saddened Nobel. The invention had brought him great wealth, and he decided to use his money to reward those who worked for peace and the good of mankind. Before he died in 1896, he willed that the yearly income from his fortune should be divided into the various annual awards.

The Nobel Peace Prize, perhaps the greatest prize of all, has been won many times by U.S. citizens. These U.S. winners include President Theodore Roosevelt (1906) for arranging a peace in the Russian-Japanese war, President Woodrow Wilson (1919) for founding the League of Nations, Ralph Bunche (1950) for arranging an armistice between the Arabs and Israelis, Linus Pauling (1962) for his efforts to end the testing of atomic bombs (he also won the 1954 Chemistry Prize), and Martin Luther King, Jr. (1964) for his peaceful campaigns to gain equal rights for blacks. Henry Kissinger shared the 1973 Nobel Peace Prize with Le Duc Tho of North Vietnam for arranging a truce in the Vietnam War. Winners of the Peace Prize from other countries include Lester Pearson of Canada (1957), Albert John Luthuli of South Africa (1960), Andrei Sakharov of Russia (1975), Menachem Begin of Israel and Anwar Sadat of Egypt (1978), Mother Teresa of Calcutta (1979), and the United Nations Peacekeeping Forces in 1988.

Several organizations have won the

Nobel Peace Prize including the International Red Cross (1917, 1944, and 1963), Amnesty International (1977), and the Office of U.N. High Commissioner for Refugees (1954 and 1981).

ALSO READ: BUNCHE, RALPH; KING, MARTIN LUTHER, JR.; LITERATURE; PEARSON, LESTER; ROOSEVELT, THEODORE; WILSON, WOODROW.

▲ *A collection of Swedish stamps commemorating some of the winners of the Nobel Prizes.*

NOBILITY In some countries, certain people are called by special names, or *titles*, such as "duke," "marquess," "earl," or "count." A person who has a title of this kind is called a noble. All the nobles together make up the nobility of a country.

Nobles are found only in countries that have, or once had, kings or emperors. These rulers gave titles and lands to their important followers. The different titles showed how important each noble was, and how much land he or she owned. Nobilities grew up in most European countries and in some Asian countries, such as Japan and India. The most important European titles are described in this article. They are listed in order of importance.

A *duke* (female: *duchess*) governed a large region of the kingdom. He was usually a military leader, with an army of his own.

A *marquess* (female: *marchioness*)

The Constitution of the United States forbids the giving of titles of any kind. The wording of the Constitution says: "No title of Nobility shall be granted by the United States. And no person holding any Office of Profit or Trust under them, shall, without the consent of Congress, accept of any present, Emolument, Office, or Title, of any kind whatever, from any King, Prince, or foreign state."

▼ *Louis XIV of France—the "Sun King"—looking at the plans for his great palace at Versailles.*

was usually given land at the border of the kingdom. His duty was to guard the border against enemies of the king. The French form of this title is *marquis*.

The title of *earl* (female: *countess*) is found only in Britain. An earl was the chief justice, or sheriff, of a small region of the kingdom. In some other countries, a *count* had the same rank, or importance, as an English earl.

A *viscount* (female: *viscountess*) was usually a deputy, or representative, of a count. In Britain, the title of viscount was sometimes granted as a special favor by the king.

The title of *baron* (female: *baroness*) was once used in England for all the important followers of the king. Other titles were later adopted for the higher ranks of nobility, and baron became one of the less important titles.

The title of *knight* was usually an honor given to a brave warrior by the king or by one of the higher nobility. Knights did not always own land. The wife of a knight is called a *lady*.

When a noble dies, the eldest son usually inherits (takes over) the title. If the noble has only daughters, the title sometimes passes to the eldest daughter. In this way, a title is passed down from generation to generation.

Many nobles still own their ancient family lands. But their titles no longer give them the same duties and powers that their ancestors had.

In many countries, the titles of prince and princess represent various ranks of nobility, but in Great Britain these titles are used only by members of the royal family.

New titles are granted today to men and women who have given service to their country, but in Britain these new titles are usually no longer passed on after the person has died.

ALSO READ: FEUDALISM, KINGS AND QUEENS, KNIGHTHOOD.

NOISE see SOUND.

NOMAD People who move from place to place with no fixed home are called nomads. Some nomads live in regions where the land is not rich enough for farming. They keep herds of cattle, sheep, or goats. Nomadic herders may move from one pasture to another as their animals eat up all the grass on the land. They may also move to different pastures in summer and winter. Other nomads are hunters who follow the herds of wild animals. Gypsies traveling the countryside as tinkers and horse traders are also nomads.

Nomadic herders in Mongolia drive herds of sheep across the vast *steppes*, or grasslands, of central Asia. They ride ponies and live in lightweight tents. Like most nomadic herders, they live off their animals—eating their meat and milk, and using their hides and wool for tents and clothing. The Bedouin herders of Arabia spend most of the year roaming through the desert with their herds of sheep and camels. But during the hottest season of the year, they pitch their tents near a village. They trade their camels with the villagers for grain and rifles.

Some of the Plains Indians of North America were nomadic hunters. On their horses, they followed the buffalo herds. They ate buffalo meat and used buffalo skins to make clothes and *tipis* (tents).

ALSO READ: ARABIA; ESKIMO; GYPSY; INDIANS, AMERICAN; MONGOLIA.

NORSEMEN see VIKINGS.

NORSE MYTH see MYTHOLOGY.

NORTH AMERICA Of the world's seven continents, North America is the third largest in size and fourth in population. Asia and Africa are larger in size, and Asia, Europe, and Africa have larger populations. Many natural wonders can be found in North America—from glaciers to deserts, from forests of giant redwood trees to smoking volcanoes. The Grand Canyon cuts through western lands. Between the United States and Canada, the Niagara River pours over two great falls. Modern cities offer skyscrapers and long bridges, while ancient cities reveal stone pyramids and temples.

The most northern part of North America is above the Arctic Circle, and the most southern part is in the tropical regions, where it is warm all year. All of North America lies north of the equator. The Atlantic and Pacific Oceans lie on the east and west.

The Arctic Ocean is to the north. North America lies a little west of South America, rather than directly north. The Isthmus of Panama connects the two continents. A canal cut through Panama provides a water route between the Atlantic and Pacific Oceans. At its widest part, North America is about 4,000 miles (6,440 km) wide, and 40 miles (64 km) wide at its most narrow section. From north to south it is about 4,500 miles (7,240 km) long.

Most scientists believe North and South America were once attached to Europe and Africa. There is a ridge of underwater mountains down the middle of the Atlantic Ocean. Scientists think the old landmass split along this ridge and the continents drifted apart to form the Atlantic. The 50-mile (80-km) wide Bering Strait separates Alaska in North America from Siberia in Soviet Asia.

Canada is the largest North American country in land area, with the United States second and Mexico third. These countries are independent nations. So are the larger islands in the Caribbean, such as Cuba, Trinidad, and Jamaica. Some of the smaller islands are still ruled at least

▲ *Few human beings live in hot deserts because there is very little food. But nomads have learned to move between oases (fertile spots) and survive the desert conditions.*

▼ *Denver is the capital of Colorado. It is the marketing and economic center of a large agricultural region in North America.*

▲ *The restored ship U.S.S. Constitution, famous for its part in the War of 1812, anchored in Boston Harbor.*

partly by European countries. Puerto Rico is joined with the United States in a commonwealth arrangement. All Puerto Ricans have U.S. citizenship. In the far north of the continent, Greenland, the largest island in the world, is a province of Denmark.

Geography North America has a long spine of mountain ranges running down its western side from Alaska to Panama. The ranges' highest peak is Mount McKinley in Alaska, 20,320 feet (6,194 m) high. Mount Logan, just across the border in Canada, and Mount Orizaba in Mexico are the highest in those two countries. Other high mountain peaks are Mount Whitney in California and Pikes Peak in Colorado.

Western ranges such as the Rocky Mountains were formed recently in the Earth's history and are rugged and sharp. Along the eastern part of the United States are the Appalachian Mountains, much older and smoother than the Rockies. The rounded mountains and hills of northern and eastern Canada are called the *Cana-*

dian or *Laurentian Shield*. The area, shaped like a giant knight's shield, surrounds shallow Hudson Bay.

The Appalachians and the Canadian Shield were covered by huge, creeping glaciers during the last ice age, much as Greenland is still covered today. As these glaciers retreated, they ground down the sharp peaks and deposited soil on the eastern mountains.

The Canadian Shield was the area most worn down by the glaciers of the last ice age. As a result, most of its minerals are close to the surface and easy to discover. Among the hills of the shield are some of the world's richest known deposits of gold, uranium, and other valuable metals.

On the west coast from southern Alaska to southern California are the coastal ranges of mountains. Between these mountains and such ranges as the Rockies farther east is the intermountain region. The western states of Nevada and Utah and the central plateau in Mexico are part of this area. The land here is high and dry, sometimes desert, because there is

NORTH AMERICA

Highest Point
Mount McKinley in Alaska, 20,320 feet (6,194 m).

Lowest Point
Death Valley in California, 282 feet (86 m) below sea level.

Longest River
Mississippi-Missouri, 3,860 miles (6,212 km).

Biggest Lake
Lake Superior, 31,800 square miles (82,362 sq. km).

Largest City
Mexico City (13,000,000 people).

Total Population
426,337,100

NORTH AMERICAN NATIONS

Country	Area in sq. miles	Area in sq. km	Population	Capital
Antigua and Barbuda	171	442	64,000	Saint Johns
Bahamas	5,380	13,935	247,500	Nassau
Barbados	166	431	258,500	Bridgetown
Belize	8,867	22,965	181,000	Belmopan
Canada	3,851,806	9,976,130	26,380,000	Ottawa
Costa Rica	19,575	50,700	2,980,000	San José
Cuba	44,218	114,524	10,470,000	Havana
Dominica	290	751	83,700	Roseau
Dominican Republic	18,816	48,734	7,300,000	Santo Domingo
El Salvador	8,124	21,041	5,325,000	San Salvador
Grenada	133	344	85,200	Saint George's
Guatemala	42,042	108,889	9,520,000	Guatemala City
Haiti	10,714	27,750	6,500,000	Port-au-Prince
Honduras	43,277	112,088	5,110,000	Tegucigalpa
Jamaica	4,244	10,991	2,525,000	Kingston
Mexico	761,605	1,972,547	89,080,000	Mexico City
Nicaragua	50,193	130,000	3,560,000	Managua
Panama	29,209	75,650	2,450,000	Panama City
St. Christopher and Nevis	101	262	40,200	Basseterre
St. Lucia	238	616	156,000	Castries
St. Vincent and the Grenadines	150	388	106,000	Kingstown
Trinidad and Tobago	1,981	5,130	1,285,000	Port of Spain
United States of America	3,615,122	9,363,123	252,630,000	Washington D.C.

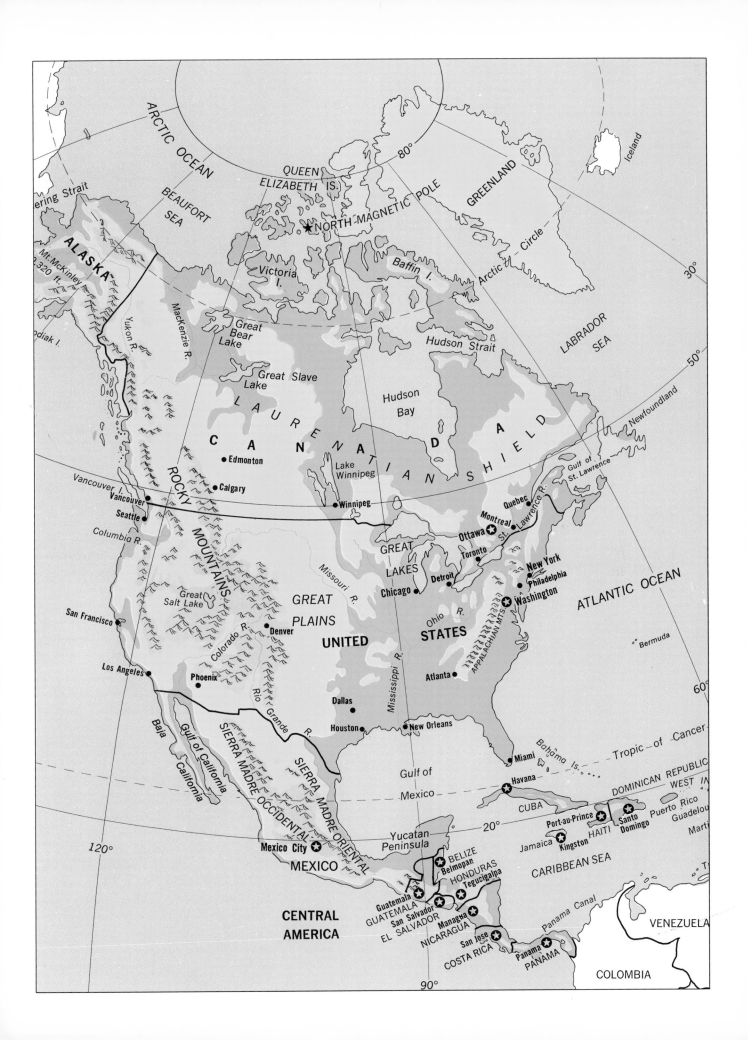

ARCTIC OCEAN

QUEEN
ELIZABETH IS.

GREENLAND

Iceland

80°

BEAUFORT
SEA

★ NORTH MAGNETIC POLE

ering Strait

ALASKA

Mt. McKinley
9,320 ft.

Baffin I.

Victoria
I.

30°

odiak I.

Yukon R.

Mackenzie R.

Great
Bear
Lake

Great Slave
Lake

Hudson Strait

LABRADOR
SEA

Arctic
Circle

50°

Hudson
Bay

L A U R E N T I A N   S H I E L D

C A N A D A

Newfoundland

Edmonton

Lake
Winnipeg

Gulf of
St. Lawrence

Vancouver I.

Calgary

Quebec

St. Lawrence R.

Vancouver

Winnipeg

Montreal

Ottawa ✪

St.

Seattle

ROCKY

GREAT

Toronto

New York

Columbia R.

MOUNTAINS

LAKES

Detroit

Philadelphia

Great
Salt Lake

Missouri R.

Chicago

Washington ✪

ATLANTIC OCEAN

San Francisco

GREAT

Ohio R.

APPALACHIAN MTS.

Denver

PLAINS

Colorado R.

UNITED

STATES

Bermuda

Los Angeles

Phoenix

Rio

Mississippi R.

Atlanta

Grande

Dallas

Baja

Gulf of California

R.

Houston

New Orleans

Tropic of Cancer

SIERRA MADRE OCCIDENTAL

SIERRA MADRE ORIENTAL

Gulf of

Miami

Bahama Is.

California

Mexico

Havana

DOMINICAN REPUBLIC

WEST IN

Yucatan
Peninsula

CUBA

Puerto Rico

Guadelou

120°

Mexico City ✪

20°

Port-au-Prince ✪

Santo
Domingo ✪

HAITI

Marti

MEXICO

BELIZE

Jamaica

Kingston

Belmopan ✪

HONDURAS

CARIBBEAN SEA

T

CENTRAL

Tegucigalpa ✪

Guatemala ✪

GUATEMALA

San Salvador ✪

Managua ✪

Panama Canal

AMERICA

EL SALVADOR

NICARAGUA

San Jose ✪

VENEZUELA

COSTA RICA

Panama ✪

PANAMA

COLOMBIA

90°

60°

The lowest point in North America is Death Valley, California, 282 feet (86 m) below sea level. Death Valley is also the hottest place on the continent. A temperature of 134° F (56° C) was registered there on July 10, 1913.

little rainfall. In the United States and Canada, the land changes east of the Rockies to the central plains and prairies. Wide rivers flow through the plains. The Mississippi River system is the largest in North America. The five Great Lakes in the plains region form the largest freshwater supply in the world.

Oil is found under the soft soils of the plains area between the mountain ranges from Texas and Louisiana through Alberta to the north Alaska coasts. The plains extend to the Appalachian range in the east. In many places a flat coastal area lies between the Appalachians and the Atlantic Ocean.

Climates The climates of the different regions of North America range from the polar to the tropical. In the far north, the ice and snow of Greenland and the northern Canadian islands never melt, and temperatures rarely reach 32° F (0° C).

Most of the northland in Canada

▲ *The Cathedral of Saint Prisca in the old Mexican city of Taxco is a fine example of the influence of the Spanish colonists on North American architecture.*

and Alaska has a subpolar climate. The short summers have temperatures that sometimes reach 50° F (10° C) and permit the growth of plant and animal life. This climate produces tundra, a vegetation of low shrubs, lichen, and moss. The ground is permanently frozen beneath the surface.

South of the subpolar climate, most of the interior of North America has a *continental* climate, fairly dry with extremes of temperature. Winters are cold and summers are hot. Because the wind and the weather in North America usually come from the west, the Atlantic coast of the continent also has a continental climate. But along the Pacific coast, warm, wet winds from the ocean make the climate mild, with much rain and few extremes of heat and cold.

To the east of the mountain ranges along the Pacific is a long region of dry climate stretching south into central Mexico. The Mexican coasts and the lands of Central America and the Caribbean have a warm, tropical climate. Heavy rains may fall during the wet seasons in the tropics, and almost

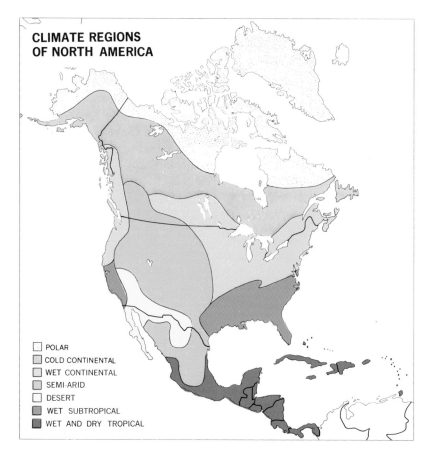

CLIMATE REGIONS OF NORTH AMERICA

☐ POLAR
☐ COLD CONTINENTAL
☐ WET CONTINENTAL
☐ SEMI-ARID
☐ DESERT
☐ WET SUBTROPICAL
☐ WET AND DRY TROPICAL

no rain falls during the dry seasons.

Plants and Animals In the short, hot summer of the northern regions, even the tundra has colorful blossoms. Orchids and other flowers bloom most of the year in the hot southern regions, where fruit trees bear many kinds of fruit. Canada has forests of spruce, fir, pine, and hemlock. Probably the thickest forests in the world are in Washington, Oregon, and northern California. Ponderosa pine, cedar, hemlock, Douglas fir, sugar pine, and the sequoia grow there.

Polar bears and huge Kodiak bears live in the cold areas of North America. Rabbits, squirrels, prairie dogs, skunks, beavers, chipmunks, and opossums are some of the smaller animals of the continent. Bright parrots, lively monkeys, and iguanas live in the steamy Central American jungles. Millions of bison once roamed the plains of North America, but now just a few thousand graze there. Northern forests are inhabited by moose, deer, elk, and varieties of foxes and wolves. The lynx, puma, and other wildcats are North American animals. Alligators and crocodiles swim in the rivers of the tropical regions.

Rattlesnakes and other snakes are found in North America. Many small birds, such as the robin, sparrow, and cardinal, nest in the trees. Wild ducks, geese, and other wildfowl and birds leave the cold north for the warmer south each winter.

People People from many other countries settled in North America. North Americans have American Indian, European, Asian, and African ancestors.

More than 250 million people in the United States, Canada, and some of the Caribbean islands speak English as their first language. More than 100 million people in Mexico, Cuba, the Dominican Republic, and the Central American republics mainly speak Spanish. More than six million Canadians, mainly in Quebec, speak French. French is also spoken in Haiti, the western third of the island of Hispaniola, and in other Caribbean islands, such as Guadeloupe and Martinique, controlled or first settled by the French.

Many of the Indian peoples of North America, perhaps 20 million, still speak their original Indian languages. Most of them live in Mexico and Central America. In the Arctic, about 50,000 Eskimo people use their own language.

In earlier days, most people in North America lived in the country or in small villages and settlements. But as industry developed and the population increased, great cities grew up. Probably nine persons out of ten will live in the various cities of North America by the year 2000. Fewer and fewer people are needed to operate modern farms, and most jobs are to be found in cities.

Great cities include Mexico City, New York City, Chicago, Los Angeles, Philadelphia, Montreal, and Toronto. The largest, Mexico City, has nearly nine million inhabitants—more than 16 million if the suburbs are included.

Indian tribes lived in most parts of North America before the European explorers arrived. The Aztecs and the Maya were two of the main Mexican tribes.

In North America there are more starlings than any other bird. It is estimated that there are more than 500 million of them. The world population of starlings may be as high as 2 billion.

Scientists believe that if the continents continue to move as they have been doing for millions of years, North and South America will separate completely. The Atlantic Ocean will grow wider as the Americas are pushed farther west.

▼ *Nassau, the capital of the Bahamas, which is one of the North American nations, is a major tourist center.*

▲ *Guatemalans work on a coffee plantation in the highlands. The* Volcano del Fuego *rises in the background. Guatemala and the other Central American states are part of the North American continent.*

▼ *The Coast Mountains of British Columbia form an impressive backdrop as this truck winds its way along an interstate highway.*

Europeans first reached North America when the Norwegian Viking, Eric the Red, discovered Greenland in the 900's. His son, Leif Ericson, was probably the first to reach the mainland. Remains of a Viking settlement nearly 1,000 years old have been found in Newfoundland.

After the voyage made in 1492 by Christopher Columbus, an Italian serving Spain, other explorers and settlers came to North America. The English, French, and Spanish controlled most of the settlements for many years.

When the Europeans discovered North America they were looking for Asia. Soon, however, they found North America had riches of its own. Perhaps its greatest resource was its size. It offered room for everyone who wished to find space to grow, discover, explore, and settle. The continent was a land of promise.

For further information on:
Arts, *see* ART HISTORY; INDIAN ART, AMERICAN.
Cities, *see* BOSTON, CHICAGO, DALLAS, DETROIT, DISTRICT OF COLUMBIA, LOS ANGELES, MEXICO CITY, MONTREAL, NEW YORK CITY, OTTAWA, PHILADELPHIA, SAN FRANCISCO, TORONTO.
History, *see* AMERICAN COLONIES; AMERICAN HISTORY; AMERICAN REVOLUTION; ANCIENT CIVILIZATIONS; BERING, VITUS; BLACK AMERICANS; CENTRAL AMERICA; CHAMPLAIN, SAMUEL DE; CIVIL WAR; CONFEDERATE STATES OF AMERICA; CONQUISTADOR; EXPLORATION; FOLSOM CULTURE; FRENCH AND INDIAN WAR; HISPANIC AMERICANS; HUDSON'S BAY COMPANY; INDIANS, AMERICAN; INDIAN WARS; LOUISIANA PURCHASE; MEXICAN WAR; MONROE DOCTRINE; NORTHWEST PASSAGE; NORTHWEST TERRITORIES; PANAMA CANAL; PILGRIM SETTLERS; SLAVERY; SPANISH-AMERICAN WAR.
Languages, *see* ENGLISH LANGUAGE, WRITTEN LANGUAGE.
Physical Features, *see* APPALACHIAN MOUNTAINS, ARCTIC, ATLANTIC OCEAN, CARIBBEAN SEA, CHESAPEAKE BAY, COLUMBIA RIVER, CONTINENTAL DIVIDE, DEATH VALLEY, EVERGLADES, GRAND CANYON, GREAT LAKES, GREAT PLAINS, GREAT SALT LAKE, GULF OF MEXICO, HUDSON BAY, MACKENZIE RIVER, MISSISSIPPI RIVER, MOHAVE DESERT, NIAGARA FALLS, PACIFIC OCEAN, PAINTED DESERT, RIO GRANDE, ROCKY MOUNTAINS, SIERRA NEVADA, ST. LAWRENCE SEAWAY, YOSEMITE VALLEY.
Travel, *see* EMPIRE STATE BUILDING, INDEPENDENCE HALL, MOUNT RUSHMORE, PETRIFIED FOREST, STATUE OF LIBERTY, STONE MOUNTAIN, WHITE HOUSE, YELLOWSTONE PARK.

NORTH ATLANTIC TREATY ORGANIZATION Peace did not come at the end of World War II. Forces of the Soviet Union that had driven the Germans out of Eastern European countries refused to leave. Instead, the Soviet Union took control of the governments of these countries. It seemed only a matter of time before the Soviet Union would also try to take over the countries of Western Europe. To prevent this, the North Atlantic Treaty Organization (NATO) was formed in 1949. The original NATO headquarters was in Paris, France.

NATO is a military alliance of 16 nations. Its purpose is to strengthen the nations of Western Europe so that no country would dare to attack. Member nations also work together on economic and political issues. NATO members are Belgium, Canada, Denmark, France, Germany, Great Britain, Greece, Iceland, Italy, Luxembourg, the Netherlands, Norway, Portugal, Spain, Turkey, and the United States, who is the dominant member because of its military capabilities. Member countries provide soldiers and supplies to NATO military forces. NATO members are represented on a governing council that decides military, political, and economic policies. NATO has two main military commands—SACEUR (Supreme Allied Command, Europe) and SACLANT (Supreme Allied Command, Atlantic). There is also a Canada-U.S. Regional Planning Group.

In the mid-1960's, some nations became unhappy with NATO. The French mistrusted certain NATO policies and withdrew their forces. The NATO headquarters had to be moved to Brussels in 1966.

The fall of Communism in the early 1990's meant that the original purpose of NATO no longer existed. It was still important economically and politically, and it offered associate membership to Eastern European countries. NATO has a military *rapid reaction force* for emergencies.

NORTH CAROLINA High sand dunes near the town of Kitty Hawk overlook Kill Devil Hill, North Carolina, where Wilbur and Orville Wright made the world's first successful flight of a power-driven airplane. The date was December 17, 1903.

The Land and Climate The Atlantic Coastal Plain covers the eastern third of North Carolina. Rivers wind across the plain on their way to the ocean. Much land between the river

mouths is swampy. The state's chief port, Wilmington, lies near the mouth of the Cape Fear River. The Dismal Swamp is in the coastal section. Lake Mattamuskeet is the largest natural lake in the state. Many wild ducks, geese, and other birds come here. The Sandhills in the inner coastal plains have sandy soil.

The Piedmont Plateau begins about 150 miles (240 km) inland. Here the land rises. The boundary between the Piedmont and the Atlantic Coastal Plain is known as the *fall line*. At points along this boundary, the rivers coming from the highlands drop down in waterfalls to the lower, sandy plain. The Piedmont is an area of low hills and forests, streams and lakes. About 20,000 square miles (51,800 sq. km) of central North Carolina are in the Piedmont. Most of the industry and people are in the Piedmont section.

The Appalachians are west of the Piedmont. These mountains stretch from Alabama and Georgia to New England. The North Carolina section is part of the Blue Ridge. The Blue Ridge includes the Black Mountains, the Great Smoky Mountains, and others. Many of North Carolina's rivers start in the Blue Ridge. Large dams

▲ *A painting of an Indian village by John White, a brilliant artist. During the late 1500's, he accompanied several English expeditions to what are now Virginia and North Carolina.*

When white men first arrived in north Carolina there were about 35,000 Indians, belonging to 30 different tribes in the region.

▲ *Lake Fontana lies in the mountainous western region of North Carolina.*

In 1795, the University of North Carolina became the first university in the United States to hold classes.

on rivers in the highlands have made reservoirs. The reservoirs, such as Fontana on the Little Tennessee River, are used for hydroelectric power and for boating and other recreation. Asheville, where the writer Thomas Wolfe lived, is the main mountain city.

Summers are hot in North Carolina. Winters are cold only in the mountains. Snow falls in the mountain regions, but seldom in the lowlands. Winter is mostly a time of blue skies and bright sunshine. Rain comes in all seasons but is heaviest in summer. Summer thunderstorms often bring hail and high winds.

History About 1526, the Spanish tried unsuccessfully to set up a colony near Cape Fear. In 1584, Sir Walter Raleigh, acting for Queen Elizabeth I of England, sent explorers who found the land around Albemarle Sound suitable for a colony. The fishing and hunting were good, and the Roanoke Indians seemed friendly. After Raleigh received the good news about the area, he sent out colonists (all men) in 1585. They built a settlement on Roanoke Island—the first English colony in the Americas. But the settlers suffered from disease and hunger and fought with the Indians. In 1586, they went home.

Under the leadership of John White, another group of colonists came with their families and settled on Roanoke Island in 1587. Virginia Dare, the first English child to be born in the New World, was born there on August 18, 1587. White returned to England for supplies and did not return to North America until 1590. The Roanoke colony was in ruins and deserted. No one knows what happened to the men, women, and children of the "Lost Colony."

The first North Carolina settlement that lasted was founded about 1653 by settlers from Virginia. It was built on the Chowan River, which flows into Albemarle Sound.

Ten years later, King Charles II of Britain decided to put a large colony south of Virginia. It was to cover all the land that is now North and South Carolina—and even beyond. The people to whom he gave the land named it *Carolina*. This name is from the Latin form of Charles. Later, the colony was divided into two separate parts, which were called North Carolina and South Carolina.

North Carolina had a large Indian population. The largest tribe, the Cherokee, lived in the mountains. Among the lowland tribes was a powerful one named the Tuscarora. The colonists clashed with the Indians. Two years of hard fighting were needed to defeat the Tuscarora.

The colonists quarreled constantly with the governors sent from Britain. In 1768, an uprising of Piedmont farmers took place. They said that their taxes were unfair and that the eastern plantation owners had too much power. They were called the Regulators. The governor called out troops to put down the uprising. The Regulators were defeated at the Battle of the Alamance on May 16, 1771.

In the Halifax Resolves of April 12, 1776, the North Carolina delegates to the Continental Congress were authorized to vote for independence. One of the last battles of the American Revolution, the Battle of Guilford Courthouse, was fought in the state on March 15, 1781. North Carolina became one of the 13 original states.

North Carolina stayed in the Union until President Lincoln called for troops in April 1861. Then the state seceded to join the other Southern states during the Civil War.

Shortly after the Civil War, white citizens used force to put black citizens under their control. Blacks were kept from voting and from the better paid occupations.

The University of North Carolina opened at Chapel Hill in the late 1700's. In the 1800's, cotton mills were started near the rivers because of

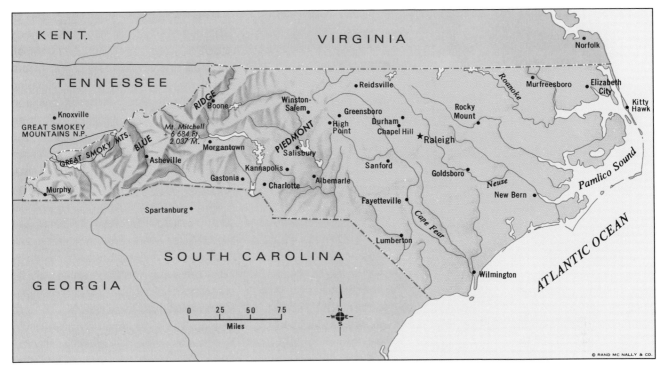

NORTH CAROLINA

Capital
Raleigh (172,000 people)

Area
52,712 square miles
(136,523 sq. km)
Rank: 28th

Population
6,530,000
Rank: 10th

Statehood
November 21, 1789
(12th of the original 13 states
to ratify the Constitution)

Principal rivers
Roanoke River
Neuse River
Cape Fear River

Highest point
Mount Mitchell
6,684 feet (2,037 m)

Largest city
Charlotte (383,000 people)

Motto
Esse quam Videri
("To be, rather than to
Seem")

Song
"The Old North State"

Famous people
Virginia Dare, Billy Graham,
President Andrew Johnson,
Dolly Madison, President
James Knox Polk

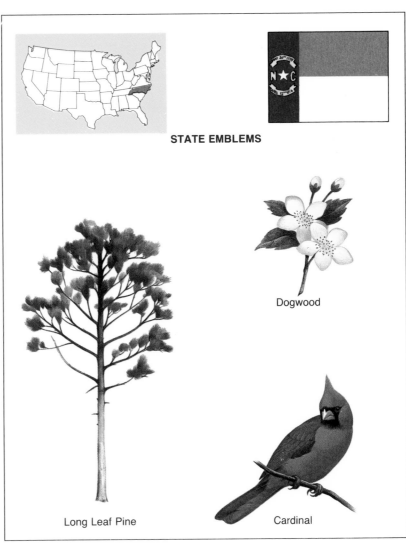

STATE EMBLEMS

Dogwood

Long Leaf Pine

Cardinal

▲ *Though not the capital of North Carolina, Charlotte is the largest city and a manufacturing and trading center in the south of the state.*

A nickname for North Dakota is the "Flickertail State." The name comes from the little flickertail ground squirrel that lives in the North Dakota prairies.

waterpower. Cotton and tobacco were the main crops that brought money to the farmers. By the 1920's, the manufacture of cotton cloth was a large industry.

The 1960's brought progress of another kind. Step by step, blacks moved toward gaining their full rights as citizens. The city of Chapel Hill showed that change was taking place. In 1969 the city, most of whose population is white, elected a black mayor, Howard Lee.

North Carolinians at Work The manufacture of textiles (cloth products) is the leading industry. Greensboro and Charlotte are industrial centers. The state has the largest denim mill in the world. The manufacture of tobacco products and furniture are other important industries. Winston-Salem and Durham, home of Duke University, are tobacco centers. Food-processing and electronics provide many jobs.

Agriculture is important to the state. North Carolina grows more tobacco than any other state. Cotton, peanuts, corn, and soybeans are also grown. Livestock products nearly match tobacco in value.

Visitors to North Carolina can learn history through the outdoor dramas staged each summer. "The Lost Colony" is presented on Roanoke Island. In the western part of the state, "Horn in the West" tells about

Daniel Boone and pioneer life. "Unto These Hills" is the story of the Cherokee Indians. Many people drive on the beautiful Blue Ridge Parkway through the mountains. Others drive to the long beaches along the Atlantic coast.

ALSO READ: APPALACHIAN MOUNTAINS; CHEROKEE INDIANS; RALEIGH, SIR WALTER; TOBACCO; WRIGHT BROTHERS.

NORTH DAKOTA Here's a riddle: "When are badlands good lands?" The answer is: "When they are in the Dakotas—North and South."

The Badlands of North Dakota lie in its southwest. They were named by pioneers who found them bad lands to travel through. Rainfall is light there, and water is scarce. Grass grows in many places, but much of the land is bare. The scenery is startling. For thousands of years the Little Missouri River and the weather have been carving rock and clay into unusual shapes. Steep, flat-topped hills called *mesas* are in the Badlands. So are *buttes*, which are like mesas except not as broad. Mesas and buttes are colored in bands of red, yellow, blue, and gray.

The Land and Climate The Badlands are near the Montana border in the Great Plains region of North Dakota. This region covers the whole western part of the state. Most of the Great Plains was once grassland. Large areas are still grazing country. North Dakota's part of the Missouri Basin is in the Great Plains region. The Garrison Dam holds back some of the water of the Missouri River. This water makes a winding lake about 200 miles (320 km) long.

The eastern boundary of the Great Plains region is formed by two rivers. The Rivière des Lacs ("River of Lakes") is in the north. It starts near

Canada. The James River is in the south.

East of the two river valleys, the land slopes downward. From there on, North Dakota is prairie land. It is part of the plains that lie west and south of the Great Lakes. The prairie region is a rolling plain with fertile soil. The *black belt* has especially good land. This belt is the part of the river valley that North Dakota shares with Minnesota. The river is the Red River of the North.

North Dakota has very little natural woodland. The Turtle Mountains are wooded and so are parts of the Red River valley and some of the smaller valleys. But in most of the state the woods were planted by people.

North Dakota lies at the center of North America. No ocean winds can warm it in winter or cool it in summer. Winters are long and cold. Strong winds from northern Canada often bring snowstorms. Summers are short and hot with very dry air. The eastern part of the state has more rain than the western part, but rainfall is not heavy. In both east and west, farmers manage to raise huge crops of wheat.

History Europeans came late to the center of the continent. New France, New England, and Virginia were more than 100 years old by the time white people explored North Dakota. The first Europeans in North Dakota were the French, who came about 1740. The French were looking for Indians who would sell furs. They met Indians of two kinds. Some Indians were settled farmers, and others were wandering hunters. Among the farming tribes were the Mandan and the Cheyenne. They lived in villages protected by walls. Their crops were corn, squash, pumpkins, and beans. The farmers hunted enough to get some meat.

The wandering hunters lived differently. They did not stay in one place long enough to harvest crops. These Indians went wherever they could find game. Bison provided them with meat and with skins for *tipis* (tents) and warm robes. Deer and elk were useful, also. Two hunting tribes were the Sioux (Dakota) and the Chippewa (Ojibwa). The Sioux, especially, were feared by the farming tribes.

The southwestern part of North Dakota, claimed by France, was sold to the United States in 1803 as part of the Louisiana Purchase. Two explorers, Meriwether Lewis and William Clark, were the first to raise the Stars and Stripes in North Dakota in 1804. Northern and eastern North Dakota were held by Britain. Britain turned them over to the United States in 1818 with part of Minnesota.

For a while, the only white people in North Dakota were fur traders and soldiers. The soldiers lived in lonely little forts built at places where Indians were likely to attack. After 1850, white settlers came to the region in larger numbers. Some of them took land that the government had set aside for the Indians. White hunters slaughtered bison that the tribes needed. During and after the Civil War, Sioux warriors fought the white people. But they were too few to hold back the whites for long. The Sioux, led by Sitting Bull, surrendered in 1881 to U.S. troops.

▲ *A North Dakotan, wearing an over-sized cowboy mask, enjoys a carnival.*

▼ *Wind has eroded the Badlands region of North Dakota, creating strange formations including cliffs, buttes, and canyons. Sometimes strong winds whip up the soil making dust storms.*

NORTH DAKOTA

Capital City
Bismarck (48,000 people)

Area
70,665 square miles
(183,022 sq. km)
Rank: 17th

Population
672,000
Rank: 46th

Statehood
November 2, 1889
(39th state admitted)

Principal river
Missouri River

Highest point
White Butte
3,506 feet (1,069 m)

Largest city
Fargo (64,500 people)

Motto
"Liberty and Union,
Now and Forever, One
and Inseparable"

Song
"North Dakota Hymn"

Famous people
John Burke, Louis
L'Amour, Peggy Lee,
Lawrence Welk

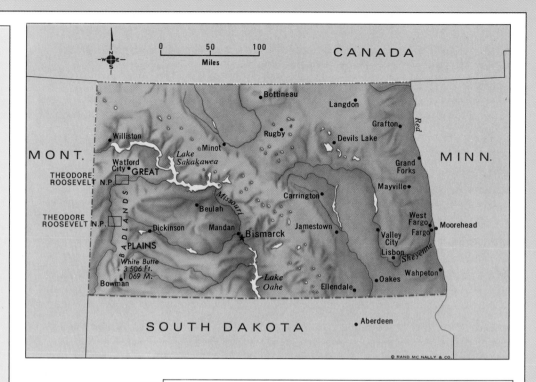

▼ *The Red River of the North, with its tributaries, flows north into Hudson Bay. It drains the eastern and northern parts of North Dakota.*

STATE EMBLEMS

Wild Prairie Rose

American Elm

Western Meadowlark

North and South Dakota were parts of the same territory. The settlers of both areas wanted them to be separate states. In 1889, Congress granted their wish. U.S. President Benjamin Harrison signed the papers on November 2 of that year. Which state became the 39th and which the 40th? No one can say for sure. President Harrison didn't want to put one Dakota ahead of the other. So he would not let anyone see which declaration of statehood he signed first. North Dakota is usually called the 39th state and South Dakota the 40th. But there is no way of telling which state was admitted to the Union before the other.

North Dakotans at Work By the time that North Dakota was made a state, wheat was being raised on large farms there. Agriculture has remained the state's largest business, and wheat is still the main crop. Only one state, Kansas, grows more wheat than North Dakota does. In North Dakota, wheat-fields stretch as far as the eye can see. Tall grain elevators rise from the plain. They are the buildings in which wheat is stored while waiting to be shipped.

Lack of rain in the 1920's and early 1930's brought drought and dust storms to North Dakota. Topsoil was blown away, ruining the farmland. Wheat prices went down and many people lost their farms. More than 70,000 persons left the state during that time. In the late 1930's, wheat prices rose. Farmers worked large farms by using modern machinery.

Crops earn more money for North Dakota than cattle do. Corn and oats grow in the southeastern part of the state. Food-processing is the leading industry. Vast amounts of petroleum, natural gas, and lignite lie under the lands of North Dakota. Oil was discovered in 1951 in the large Williston Basin near Tioga. This basin lies under the Dakotas, Montana, and parts of Canada. Many refineries have been built in the state to process the oil.

Theodore Roosevelt National Park, formerly a memorial park from 1947 to 1978, is located in western North Dakota. It contains the cattle ranches that Theodore Roosevelt operated in the 1880's, prairie-dog towns, and petrified forests.

ALSO READ: BISON, FUR, LEWIS AND CLARK EXPEDITION, LOUISIANA PURCHASE, PRAIRIE, SIOUX INDIANS, WESTWARD MOVEMENT.

NORTHERN IRELAND Northern Ireland, also called Ulster, consists of six counties in the northeastern corner of the island of Ireland, off the west coast of Great Britain. (See the map with the article on EUROPE.) Northern Ireland was separated politically from the rest of Ireland in 1921. In that year, the rest of Ireland (now the Republic of Ireland, or Eire) won independence from Great Britain. The residents of Northern Ireland's six counties (which were predominately Protestant) voted to remain part of Great Britain rather than become part of the predominantly Roman Catholic Republic of Ireland.

Belfast is the capital of Northern Ireland and its largest city. The Belfast shipyards are among the largest in the world. Londonderry (often called "Derry") is the second largest city.

The leading industries are the manufacture of textiles and clothing. Irish linen, considered the finest in the world, is produced mostly in Northern Ireland. Agriculture, especially dairy farming, is another important source of income. Crops and livestock are raised on small farms. Flax (used in making linen), oats, animal feeds, and potatoes thrive in the moist, moderate climate. Aircraft-manufacturing is a major industry.

Political problems in Northern Ireland date back to the early 1600's, when many English and Scottish

Armagh in Northern Ireland is a small town with two cathedrals and two archbishops, one Protestant and one Roman Catholic. The Roman Catholic archbishop of Armagh is Primate of all Ireland.

▲ *The Giant's Causeway, a spectacular rock formation on the coast of Northern Ireland. Thousands of pillars of a hard rock called basalt have been partly destroyed by the waves. The legend is that the giant Finn MacCool (Fingal) built the "causeway" (road through water) to cross from Ireland to Scotland.*

▲ *A howling sled dog of the Arctic. Notice the icebergs in the chilly waters of the Arctic Sea behind him. Near the North Pole, people rely on dogs for some transportation needs.*

The first ship to reach the North Pole was the U.S. atomic submarine *Nautilus*. It traveled under the ice-covered pole on August 3, 1958. The first surface ship to reach the pole was the Soviet nuclear ice-breaker *Arktika*. It broke its way through the ice to the top of the world on August 16, 1977.

Protestants settled there. The Protestants soon exceeded the Catholics in number, and a religious conflict developed. In the 1960's, protests by the Catholics against unfair treatment led to civil disorder. British troops were sent to restore order.

Today, Northern Ireland, as part of the United Kingdom, has representatives in the British House of Commons, but several of those representatives refuse to attend the House. The provisional wing of the Irish Republican Army (IRA) has vowed to achieve independence from British rule. Bombings, shootings, and other terrorist acts have led to great loss of life in Northern Ireland.

In 1985, the Republic of Ireland and Britain agreed to set up a joint commission to give the Republic an advisory role in the government of the north. But the northern Protestants opposed this plan.

ALSO READ: BRITISH ISLES, ENGLISH HISTORY, IRELAND, UNITED KINGDOM.

NORTH KOREA see KOREA.

NORTH POLE As the Earth moves around the sun, it also spins like a top. Most tops spin on a spike that runs through their center. The Earth has an imaginary line running through its center, around which it spins. The northern point of this line is called the North Pole. The southern point is the South Pole. The North Pole is geographically the northernmost point on the Earth. If you look at a globe, you will see that all the longitude lines (meridians) meet at the pole.

About 1,000 miles (1,600 km) away from the North Pole is the *North Magnetic Pole*. This is the northern point to which your compass needle points. It is located near Prince of Wales Island in Canada's Northwest Territories. The exact position of

both magnetic poles shifts slightly each year.

ALSO READ: AMUNDSEN, ROALD; ARCTIC; BYRD, RICHARD E.; COMPASS; EXPLORATION; MAGNET; PEARY, ROBERT.

NORTH SEA The North Sea lies between Great Britain and the northwestern part of the European continent. To the north, the sea opens straight into the Atlantic Ocean. To the southwest, the sea is linked to the Atlantic by the Strait of Dover and the English Channel. A narrow channel to the east links the North and Baltic Seas.

Ships' captains who sail the North Sea know the dangers of its sudden fogs, winter gales, and strong tides and currents. Nevertheless, this sea is one of the world's busiest shipping areas. Freighters and passenger ships steam to and from busy ports such as Rotterdam, in the Netherlands; Portsmouth, in England; Bremen and Hamburg, in West Germany; and Antwerp, in Belgium.

The North Sea is one of the richest fishing grounds in the world. Fisher-

▼ *A huge concrete oil rig being towed into position in the North Sea.*

men of several nations catch large quantities of cod on the Dogger Bank, a sandbank off the northeast coast of England.

Large amounts of oil and natural gas are under the North Sea. The North Sea is dotted with oil and gas rigs, and the oil is brought ashore by pipeline. The discovery of North Sea oil is important to the economies of Britain and Western Europe.

ALSO READ: ATLANTIC OCEAN, BALTIC SEA, ENGLISH CHANNEL, PETROLEUM.

NORTH STAR In the Northern Hemisphere, one star is used for telling direction more than any other star because it always stays in nearly the same place in the sky. It is the North Star, or *Polaris*, also called the *polestar*. Polaris is almost directly above the North Pole. The North Star is the star at the end of the handle of the constellation called the *Little Dipper*.

Other stars seem to move in the sky because of the turning of the Earth on its axis. Polaris stays in almost the same place, with the axis of the Earth pointed near it.

Ship captains have used the North Star as a guide for years. Although ships have radar and radio now, Polaris still helps tell direction.

You can find the North Star if you go out on a clear night. Look for the Big Dipper. Find the two stars farthest from the "handle." Follow the line of these two stars upward, and you will find the North Star.

ALSO READ: CONSTELLATION, STAR.

NORTHWEST PASSAGE The famous voyage to the Americas by Christopher Columbus in 1492 led other explorers to search for some way to sail past the American continents and reach Asia. The Portuguese explorer Ferdinand Magellan found a route around the southern tip of South America in 1520. But explorers continued to search for hundreds of years for a "Northwest Passage" around North America.

The English explorer, Sir Martin Frobisher, tried several times to find the Northwest Passage during the 1570's. He explored the eastern approaches to the Canadian Arctic. Another British explorer, Henry Hudson, reached as far as Hudson Bay in 1610. Hudson thought he had discovered the west coast of America and joyfully sailed south. When his journey was stopped at the south end of the bay, the Arctic winter had begun. When spring came, his starving crew mutinied and set him, his 10-year-old son, and several of his loyal followers adrift in a small boat. He and his companions perished.

Other explorers followed in Hudson's wake. They explored much of the region between northeast Canada and Greenland. In 1845, Sir John Franklin, the English explorer, and his crew were lost when their boat was crushed by the Arctic ice.

In 1906, after a three-year ordeal, the Norwegian explorer, Roald Amundsen, completed the first trip from the Atlantic to the Pacific by the Arctic passage in a small ship. Between 1940 and 1944, a tough little ship belonging to the Mounted Police traversed the Northwest Passage in both directions.

The severe Arctic winters and the heavy Arctic ice may prevent the Northwest Passage from ever being used for commercial purposes. But in 1969 a huge U.S. oil tanker, the S.S. *Manhattan*, helped by the Canadian ice-breaker *Macdonald*, made the passage from the Atlantic as far as the oil fields of northern Alaska. The voyage proved that specially built ships might one day open up the Northwest Passage to regular trade.

ALSO READ: AMUNDSEN, ROALD; ARCTIC OCEAN; EXPLORATION; HUDSON, HENRY.

▲ *A map of northwest Europe showing the North Sea's location.*

▲ *Sir Martin Frobisher, an English mariner of the 1600's who made three unsuccessful voyages to discover the Northwest Passage. However, he did discover and name Frobisher Bay, an arm of the Atlantic on the Northwest Territory.*

▲ *Rae is a small, peaceful town located on the Great Slave Lake in the Northwest Territories.*

There are so few people in the vast area of the Northwest Territories that there is on average only one person for every 25 square miles (65 sq. km).

The oldest fossil of an animal is of a clamlike creature that lived more than 720 million years ago. It was found on Victoria Island in Canada's Northwest Territories.

NORTHWEST TERRITORIES

The northern third of Canada consists of a vast wintry domain of forest, tundra, and ice. It is the largest frontier in North America.

The land and islands north of Canada's ten provinces are divided between the Yukon Territory, next to Alaska, and the three districts of Mackenzie, Keewatin, and Franklin, which together form the Northwest Territories.

Eskimos were the first people to live here. Explorers from Europe, looking for the Northwest Passage from the Atlantic to the Pacific, visited the area from the 1500's to the 1900's. Samuel Hearne became the first white person to cross the territories by land in 1770 and 1771.

Half of the Northwest Territories is located north of the Arctic Circle. Much of this northern half is low-lying, but in the far north, barren, stony mountains rise to more than 7,000 feet (2,130 m). On the Canadian-mainland part are two of Canada's largest lakes, Great Bear and Great Slave, and Canada's longest river, the Mackenzie.

The territories are a land of midnight sun in summer and a three-month night in winter. In summer, the sun never rises very high above the horizon, and the temperature never becomes really warm. The northernmost islands are covered with ice and snow that never melts. The largest islands are Baffin, Victoria, and Ellesmere. Ellesmere Island is only about 500 miles (800 km) from the North Pole.

Farther south, temperatures reach about 50° F (10° C) in summer, and the growth of small bushes and moss permits caribou and reindeer to live in the region. The soil always stays frozen a few inches below the surface.

Still farther south, below what is called the "tree line," the ground does not freeze and trees grow.

Fish and fur-bearing animals were the only known resources in the Northwest Territories for the first 300 years after its discovery by white people. The trees were not big enough to be used for lumber. But the value of this wood for making paper transformed the northern forest into an important resource.

Then oil was discovered along the Mackenzie River. Other vast oil reserves probably exist along the Arctic Ocean. Radium, gold, and uranium were discovered. There is so much copper in the ground around the tiny Arctic seaport of Coppermine that the soil is green from rusting copper particles. There is very little farming, so agriculture is not an important industry.

In 1670, England granted a fur-trading company, the Hudson's Bay Company, control over all the area drained by rivers and streams emptying into the Hudson Bay and the Arctic Ocean. This land was placed under control of the Canadian government in 1869.

The Northwest Territories Act of 1875 gave the area its present name and created a government for it. Land was taken from the territories to form parts of the Canadian provinces. In 1920, the remaining land was divided into the three present districts, which today are governed by a commissioner and a council.

The vast area of the Northwest Territories has a smaller population than that of a small city in southern Canada or in the United States. The capital and largest city, Yellowknife, has a population of 10,300—not much larger than that of a large village. About half of the people of the Northwest Territories are of English descent, and about a quarter are Eskimos. There are also some native Indians and some French Canadians. Some of the people are *Métis*—mixed French and Indian. Mining of various ores is the main industry.

ALSO READ: CANADA, NORTH AMERICA, NORTHWEST PASSAGE.

GREENLAND

ARCTIC OCEAN

QUEEN ELIZABETH ISLANDS

ELLESMERE ISLAND

Baffin Bay

BAFFIN ISLAND

AVAUYUITTUG N.P.

VICTORIA ISLAND

Inuvik

Great Bear Lake

Cambridge Bay

Frobisher Bay

Mackenzie

Hudson Strait

YUKON

NAHANNI N.P.

Great Slave Lake

Yellowknife

Rankin Inlet

QUE.

Hudson Bay

Eskimo Point

Hay River

Pine Point

Fort Smith

B.C.

WOOD BUFFALO N.P.

ALB.

SAS.

MAN.

Churchill

© RAND MC NALLY & CO.

0   100   200   300
Miles

NORTHWEST TERRITORIES

Capital and largest city
Yellowknife (12,000 people)

Area
1,271,422 square miles (3,292,968 sq. km)

Population
53,000

Created
1870

Principal river
Mackenzie River

Highest point
Mount Sir James McBrien
9,062 feet (2,762 m)

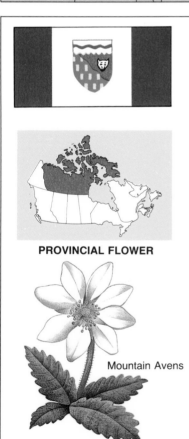

PROVINCIAL FLOWER

Mountain Avens

▲ *Forests of spruce, pine, poplar, and birch trees grow near the Mackenzie River region of the Northwest Territories.*

▲ *Norway is a land of high mountains and deep valleys, many of which were cut by glaciers during the last ice age. Where these valleys reach the sea, long narrow saltwater lakes called* fiords *appear.*

NORWAY The country of Norway is part of the Scandinavian peninsula in northern Europe. It has a long, broken coastline. Scattered along Norway's coast are about 150,000 islands, many of which are only bits of rock.

The coast of Norway was carved by glaciers that scraped along the rocks during the last ice age. Glaciers cut deep inlets, *fiords*, into the coastline. The fiords twist inland between steep walls of rock. While most fiords are short, some of them are more than 100 miles (160 km) long and are so wide that big ocean liners can enter them. Oslo, the capital city, lies at the head of a large fiord.

Norway is bordered on the east by Sweden, Finland, and the Soviet Union. The North Sea is on the south of Norway, the Norwegian Sea on the west, and the Barents Sea on the north.

Norwegians are generally a hardy people. Many are blonde and blue-eyed. Popular sports among Norwegians are outdoor pastimes such as skiing and hiking.

In the far north of Norway live the dark-haired Lapps. Some Lapps are still nomads who follow herds of reindeer.

For at least one day a year in the summer, the sun never sinks below the horizon in the "Land of the Midnight Sun," the part of Norway that is mostly north of the Arctic Circle.

There is light 24 hours a day. But in winter, this northern part of Norway is dark, and the sun does not rise above the horizon. Reindeer, polar foxes, Arctic hares, wolves, and lemmings live in northern Norway.

About one-fourth of Norway is covered with forests of spruce, pine, and birch. Much timber is made into pulp and paper. The country has little good farmland, most of which is used to grow feed for livestock. Fishing is a major business in Norway, with large numbers of cod, capelin, haddock, and herring being caught. Large amounts of oil are extracted from Norway's North Sea oil fields. Oil-refining is an important industry.

Norway's people are the descendants of the bold Vikings who raided and explored the coasts of Europe and North America about 1,000 years ago. They were known as great warriors. They settled colonies along the North Atlantic and Arctic Ocean coasts.

During the A.D. 800's, the country was united under one ruler, King Harold the Fairhaired. Later, Norway was again divided into small kingdoms. In 1397, the kingdoms of Norway, Sweden, and Denmark were united under the rule of Denmark. After centuries of rule by Denmark, Norway was controlled by Sweden from 1814 to 1905. Norway had its own constitution and legislature. In August 1905, the Norwegians voted to separate from Sweden and become

NORWAY

Capital City: Oslo (455,000 people).

Area: 125,182 square miles (324,219 sq. km).

Population: 4,225,000.

Government: Constitutional monarchy.

Natural Resources: Oil and natural gas, iron ore, copper, lead, zinc, nickel, pyrites.

Export Products: Petroleum and petroleum products, natural gas, ships, fish, aluminum, pulp and paper.

Unit of Money: Krone.

Official Language: Norwegian.

an independent country. In 1907, Norway became the first country in Europe to give women the right to vote. Norway is a constitutional monarchy with a king, prime minister, and a parliament, or *Storting*.

ALSO READ: FISHING INDUSTRY, ICE AGE, LAPLAND, LEMMING, MYTHOLOGY, NORTH SEA, POLAR LIFE, SCANDINAVIA, SCANDINAVIAN LANGUAGES, VIKINGS.

NOSE Your nose aids in breathing, and it is the organ of smell. The outer nose, or external nose, is the part you see on your face. The two openings of the nose are called *nostrils*. The dividing wall between them is called a *septum*. The lower part of the septum is made up of cartilage, which is softer than the bone in the upper part of the nose. The inner nose, or internal nose, is a hollow above the roof of the mouth. It is divided into two parts by a septum of bone. The internal nose opens at the rear into the *pharynx*, which is part of the throat.

The nose acts as a filter that removes almost all the dust from the air you breathe. The larger particles of dust are caught by the hairs at the lowest part of the nose. Lining the nose is a *mucous membrane*, which gives off a sticky fluid called *mucus*. The smaller particles of dust stick to the mucus. When you blow your nose, you get rid of the dust.

The mucous membrane has a very large number of tiny blood vessels, which are called *capillaries*. The blood passing through the capillaries keeps the membrane at the temperature of the rest of the body. Air passing through the nose is warmed by contact with the mucous membrane.

In the upper part of the internal nose, there is a group of cells that makes up the organ of smell. These cells are connected by nerves to the brain. Molecules enter your nose in the air you breathe. When they come

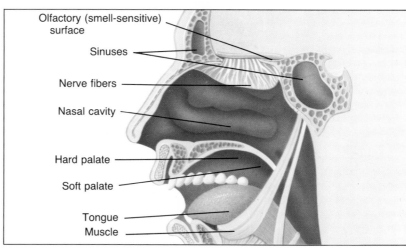

in contact with the "smelling" cells, messages go through the nerves to the brain, where they are interpreted as the odor of the substance.

ALSO READ: BREATHING, SMELL.

NOUN see PARTS OF SPEECH.

NOVA see STAR.

NOVA SCOTIA Nova Scotia is a province on the east coast of Canada. Most of Nova Scotia is a peninsula jutting out into the Atlantic Ocean, with part of the province, Cape Breton Island, at its northern end. The peninsula is connected with the Canadian province of New Brunswick by a narrow *isthmus* (strip of land). The isthmus is bounded on the north by the Northumberland Strait and on the south by the Bay of Fundy. Nova Scotia has a rugged, rocky coastline with many deep harbors. Inland are several fertile valleys and a number of rivers and lakes. The surrounding sea gives Nova Scotia a more moderate climate than that of most of eastern Canada.

Fishing has long been a major occupation in the province. Nova Scotia cod, lobsters, and haddock are sold all over the world. Apples and other fruits are grown in the sheltered inland valleys. There is a substantial

▲ *When you breathe in through your nose, the air first travels up the nostrils, where many tiny hairs stop most dust and other particles. The air goes into the nasal cavity, which connects with the breathing tube and with the sinuses, two cavities in the skull above the nose. At the back of the nasal cavity is a surface containing* olfactory *(smell-sensitive) cells. These pass information along nerves to the brain, which interprets the smells.*

Noses come in many shapes and sizes, varying with race as well as from one individual to another. A nose is Roman if it is straight, Grecian if it is straight and continues to the forehead without any depression, aquiline if it curves out like an eagle's beak, and retroussé if it turns up at the end.

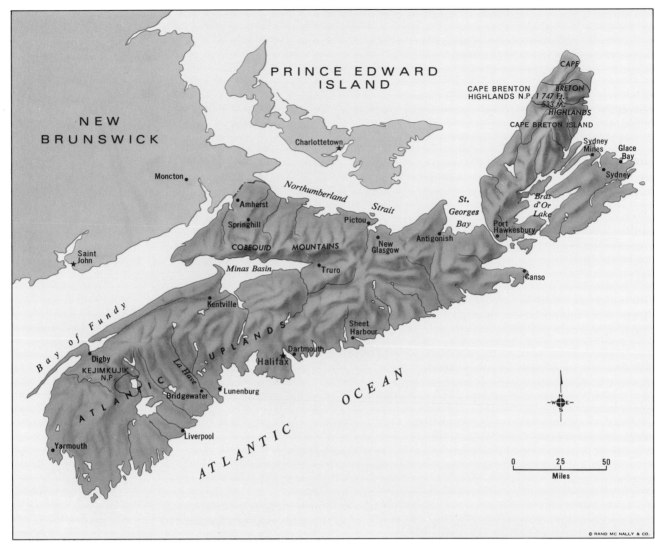

PRINCE EDWARD
ISLAND

NEW
BRUNSWICK

CAPE BRENTON
HIGHLANDS N.P. 1 747 Ft.
533 M

CAPE
BRETON
HIGHLANDS

CAPE BRETON ISLAND

Charlottetown

Sydney
Mines

Glace
Bay

Moncton

Northumberland

Sydney

Amherst

Strait

St.
Georges
Bay

Bras
d'Or
Lake

Springhill

Pictou

COBEQUID

MOUNTAINS

New
Glasgow

Antigonish

Port
Hawkesbury

Saint
John

Minas Basin

Truro

Canso

Bay of Fundy

Kentville

UPLANDS

Sheet
Harbour

Digby

KEJIMKUJIK
N.P.

La Have

Dartmouth

Halifax

ATLANTIC

Bridgewater

Lunenburg

ATLANTIC   OCEAN

Liverpool

N
W E
S

Yarmouth

0   25   50
Miles

© RAND MC NALLY & CO.

NOVA SCOTIA

Capital and largest city
Halifax (114,000 people)

Area
20,402 square miles
(52,840 sq. km)

Population
885,000

Entry into Confederation
July 1, 1867

Principal river
Annapolis River

Highest point
Cape Breton Highlands
1,747 feet (532 m)

Famous people
Sir Robert Borden, Sir
John Dawson, George
Dawson, Joseph Howe,
Hugh MacLennan

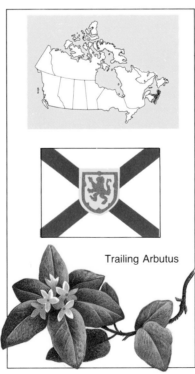

Trailing Arbutus

▲ *A small fishing village in Halifax
County, on the south of Nova Scotia.*

coal industry in Nova Scotia.

The mine tunnels at Sidney, on Cape Breton Island, stretch out for miles under the sea. Large deposits of oil exist offshore in the Atlantic. Nova Scotia's capital city, Halifax, is one of Canada's major Atlantic ports.

The Viking, Leif Ericson, is believed to have seen the coast of Nova Scotia about A.D. 1000. The English explorer, John Cabot, supposedly landed on Cape Breton Island in 1497. The French established a colony in 1605 and later fought against the British for control of the area. Nova Scotia was one of the four original provinces that joined together to form the Dominion of Canada in 1867.

The name "Nova Scotia" means "New Scotland." Almost one Nova Scotian in three is of Scottish ancestry. Nova Scotia is famous for its Scottish festivals, when the people dress in gay tartans and listen to the music of bagpipes.

ALSO READ: CANADA, NORTH AMERICA.

NOVEL A novel is a long story. Some novels are exciting adventure stories set in faraway places with unusual and fascinating characters. Other novels may tell of things that happen every day to ordinary people in ordinary places. Some novels are set in the future. But all novels, like most other forms of literature, are written to entertain you and to give you new understanding of people and the experiences they go through.

The novel developed gradually from ancient forms of storytelling, such as the *epic poem*, a long poem that told stories of brave heroes and their glorious deeds. During the 1300's, the Italian writer, Giovanni Boccaccio, combined a number of loosely related stories into a long work called the *Decameron*. This book inspired Geoffrey Chaucer, an English poet, to write *The Canterbury Tales*,

which are a similar group of loosely related stories.

Picaresque novels (*picaro* means "rascal" in Spanish) were realistic stories concerning events in everyday life. They were popular in Italy, France, and Spain. Picaresque tales were about clever, adventurous heroes who traveled from place to place, looking for—and finding—trouble. *Don Quixote* (1605–1615), by Miguel de Cervantes, was an early novel based on such tales. The English novel as it is known today began in the 18th century. During this period, Daniel Defoe and Samuel Richardson wrote the first novels in which the many adventures of the hero or heroine were really connected into a plot.

A *novelist* (a writer of novels) combines many elements in creating an entertaining, thought-provoking story. One element, the *plot*, is the series of events that makes up the action of the book. The plot may be very long and complicated, as in adventure stories and novels about a person's life. The novel *Great Expectations* (1860–1861), by Charles Dickens, has a long, involved plot covering a number of events over many important years—from childhood to adulthood—in the life of the main character. Other novels may have simple plots dealing with only a few events over a short period of time. The novel *Franny and Zooey* (1962), by J. D. Salinger, takes place in one day and consists primarily of three conversations a young man has, one with his mother and two with his sister.

The people in a novel are called *characters*. There may be many of them in one novel, but the story usually revolves around one or two main characters. The novelist tries to make the characters as believable as possible by giving them recognizable human traits (or even by modeling them on real people). Some characters, such as Elizabeth Bennett in Jane Austen's *Pride and Prejudice* (1813),

▲ Some bestselling 20th-century novels.

▶ *The old miser Ebenezer Scrooge is visited by the ghost of his former partner Marley, in the novel* A Christmas Carol *by Charles Dickens. Dickens combined many of the key ingredients that make up a fine novel: humour, pathos, mystery, social observation, and wicked versus kind characters.*

▼ *November's flower is the chrysanthemum.*

seem as real and fully developed to readers as actual people. Other characters are purposely made not to seem like real people because the novelist has chosen them to represent a certain idea or quality in human nature. The character named Fagin in *Oliver Twist* (1837–1839), by Charles Dickens, represents an exaggerated, evil kind of cleverness.

The novelist combines the elements of plot, character, *setting* (place where the action or plot occurs), and *point of view* (the character through whose eyes the author tells the story). The author combines them in order to present the *theme*—the statement about life or people that he or she wishes to make with the book. The author may want to present an idea about love, youth, religion, society, or human nature. For example, *The Scarlet Letter* (1850), by Nathaniel Hawthorne, explores the problem of sin, guilt, and punishment among Puritans in New England. The novel *The Grapes of Wrath* (1939), by John Steinbeck, concerns problems faced by poor people during the Depression in the 1930's.

Authors write many kinds of novels. *Historical* novels, such as Tolstoy's *War and Peace* (1863–1869) and Dickens's *A Tale of Two Cities* (1859), are fictional stories set in the past, usually in an exciting, glamorous period of history. *Suspense* novels, such as Doyle's *The Hound of the Baskervilles* (1902) and Collins's *The Woman in White* (1860), are detective stories and mysteries. In these the reader—and the characters—try to solve a sinister crime or a mysterious happening. *Realistic* novels are written to be as true to life as possible. They nearly always have a serious theme. Realistic novels may concentrate on social problems, personal problems, or relationships between people. Some, called *psychological* novels, concentrate on personalities of characters.

It would be impossible to list all the good novels that have been written, but your public library and school library contain many of them. Try one or two, and you will discover how reading a novel is an exciting way to pass the time!

ALSO READ: LITERATURE, SHORT STORY.

NOVEMBER The 11th month of the year is November. Its name means "nine" in Latin. November was the ninth month of the first calendar of the ancient Romans. The Roman emperor, Julius Caesar, gave November 31 days, but the emperor Augustus later changed this to 30 days. November still has 30 days.

November is bleak and gray in much of the Northern Hemisphere. The rich, bright season of autumn is coming to an end. Earth is beginning the long sleep of winter. Most of the leaves have fallen from the trees, and many animals are beginning to hibernate. Farmers have harvested their crops and the fields are bare. The weather grows colder during this month. In some areas, the first snows begin to fall. However, during November, much of the Southern Hemisphere is enjoying spring.

The birthstone for November is the tawny-colored topaz. Thanksgiving is celebrated in November. Thanksgiving began in 1621, when the Pilgrim Fathers gave thanks for their first harvest in a strange new world. Many people in the United States eat roast turkey, sweet potatoes, and pumpkin pie on Thanksgiving Day. Election Day in the United States is also held in November.

ALSO READ: AUTUMN, CALENDAR, SEASON, THANKSGIVING.

NUCLEAR ENERGY
Atoms are the "building blocks" of which everything in the world is made. It is almost impossible to imagine how small these tiny particles are. It is even more difficult to imagine that each atom is made up of smaller particles—protons, neutrons, electrons, and others. Most of every atom is empty space. At the center is the *nucleus*, made up of protons and neutrons. Then there is a great empty space. Then come the electrons that travel in *orbits* (paths) around the nucleus. We can imagine the atom to be like a tiny solar system, with the planets (electrons) orbiting the sun (nucleus). (This is not what the atom is really like, but it is as near as we can picture it.)

The tiny nucleus at the atom's center contains the most powerful force ever discovered. This force—the *strong nuclear force*—provides nuclear energy (sometimes called atomic energy).

What Makes the Energy Chemical elements differ because their atoms have different numbers of protons. The nucleus of an atom of *hydrogen*, the lightest element, is the simplest—it contains one proton. The most complicated—and the heaviest—element that occurs in nature is *uranium*. Its atom has 92 protons and 143 neutrons in its nucleus. Scientists add these numbers—92 + 143—and call this atom uranium 235, or U-235 for short.

A tremendous force locked inside

DATES OF SPECIAL EVENTS IN NOVEMBER

1 • U.S. exploded world's first hydrogen bomb (1952).

2 • Daniel Boone, American frontiersman, was born (1734)
• President James K. Polk was born (1795).
• President Warren G. Harding was born (1865).
• World's first public television broadcasting service began in London, England (1936).

4 • Will Rogers, U.S. humorist, was born (1879).
• First wagon train of emigrants reached California from Missouri (1841).

5 • Guy Fawkes and fellow conspirators tried to blow up the British Parliament (1605). The day is now celebrated in Great Britain as Guy Fawkes Day with fireworks and burnings of Guy Fawkes's effigy on bonfires throughout the nation.
• First transcontinental airplane flight landed at Pasadena, flown by C. P. Rogers (1911).
• Sinclair Lewis became the first U.S. writer to win the Nobel Prize for Literature (1930).

7 • Battle of Tippecanoe, in which General William Henry Harrison and his soldiers defeated the Indians (1811).
• The Communist Revolution began in Russia (1917). The day is now a national holiday in the Soviet Union.

8 • X rays were discovered by the German scientist, Wilhelm Roentgen (1895).

10 • Martin Luther, Protestant religious leader, was born (1483).

11 • First U.S. telescope was patented (1851).
• Armistice Day, commemorating the end of World War I, was celebrated until 1954. The day is now called Veterans Day.

13 • Robert Louis Stevenson, British author of *Treasure Island* and other exciting stories, was born (1850).

15 • Second Continental Congress approved the Articles of Confederation, uniting the 13 colonies in their struggle against British rule (1777).
• League of Nations Assembly met for the first time in Geneva, Switzerland (1920).

16 • Space shuttle *Columbia* completed first operational flight (1982).

17 • Congress met in Washington, D.C. for the first time (1800).
• Suez Canal was opened (1869).

18 • United States and Panama signed a treaty to allow building of the Panama Canal (1903).

19 • President James A. Garfield was born (1831).
• Abraham Lincoln delivered the Gettysburg Address (1863).
• *Mayflower* reached Virginia coastline (1620).

22 • President John F. Kennedy was assassinated in Dallas, Texas (1963).

23 • President Franklin Pierce was born (1804).

24 • President Zachary Taylor was born (1784).

26 • First national Thanksgiving Day proclaimed by George Washington (1789).

29 • First flight over the South Pole by Richard E. Byrd and his crew (1929).
• Samuel Clemens (Mark Twain), U.S. author, was born (1835).
• Winston Churchill, British statesman, was born (1874).

(Election Day held first Tuesday of the month.)

▼ The fuel used in simple nuclear reactors is uranium-235, which is radioactive (its atoms split very easily). Neutrons (smaller subatomic particles) split the uranium atoms, and small particles move around at great speed, hitting and splitting other atoms. This is a chain reaction: If it were allowed to go on, there would be an explosion. However, control rods, made of substances that absorb neutrons, can be used to slow things down so that the fuel is "just" very hot. The hot fuel is used to heat a liquid (such as water), and the hot liquid is pumped to a boiler. A heat exchanger (a tube) carries water through the boiler. This water is heated and turns into steam. The steam can be used to power steam turbines, which in turn power electric generators.

every atom keeps all the protons and neutrons pressed tightly together. In a complicated atom, such as that of U-235, a neutron sometimes shoots away from the nucleus. No one knows what causes this, but it does happen. Because the U-235 atom slowly loses pieces of itself, scientists say it is *unstable*, or *radioactive*.

Every time a neutron flies away from the nucleus, the atom loses energy—this is nuclear energy.

One neutron, however, does not produce enough energy to be useful. But the neutron may crash into another U-235 atom and knock loose another neutron. The second atom also loses some energy. The problem is to keep the collisions going—to start a *chain reaction*. When the piece of U-235 is big enough, a great many neutrons fly about at once. They crash into atoms and knock more neutrons loose, and many atoms give up their energy at once. The result is a tremendous explosion—an atomic bomb. You can get an idea of its power if you realize that one pound (0.454 kg) of U-235 has as much energy as 3 million pounds (1,360,000 kg) of coal!

▲ *A nuclear reactor being built. We are looking right down into the reactor's core.*

Putting Nuclear Energy to Work
An atomic bomb is a terrible weapon—one that can kill many people and destroy large cities. But the chain reaction can be controlled in a nuclear power station.

A nuclear power station does not use pure U-235. When uranium is dug from the ground most of it consists of the type U-238, which has three extra neutrons in its nucleus. This natural uranium does not explode because the fast-moving neutrons escaping from the U-235 are absorbed by the U-238. To make a chain reaction happen in natural uranium, extra U-235 atoms must be added and the escaping neutrons must be slowed down. If they are moving slowly enough they are not absorbed by the U-238. This slowing down is done by adding a substance such as carbon—called a *moderator*—to the uranium. Some of the neutrons then lose energy bouncing off the carbon atoms.

The first nuclear reactor, built by Enrico Fermi and a group of other scientists in 1942, was called a pile. To control it, the scientists used cadmium rods, which work something like the accelerator pedal of an automobile. When the rods are pushed

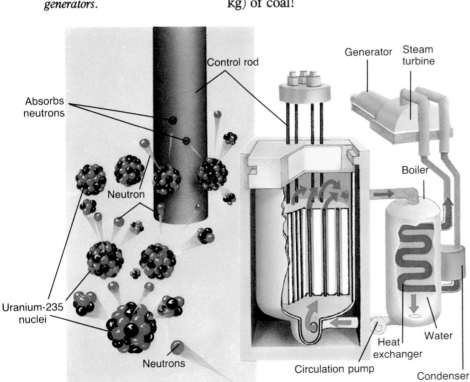

Absorbs neutrons

Control rod

Neutron

Uranium-235 nuclei

Neutrons

Generator

Steam turbine

Boiler

Water

Heat exchanger

Circulation pump

Condenser

into the reactor, they soak up most of the free neutrons and slow down or stop the chain reaction. When the rods are pulled out, the reaction speeds up. In some modern reactors other substances, such as boron, are used for the rods.

Even a controlled nuclear reaction is so hot that nuclear reactors would melt if they were not cooled. The cooling system consists of water-filled pipes that run through the reactor. As the cold water in the pipes passes through the reactor, the water absorbs (takes up) heat and turns to steam. The steam is carried through the pipes to a large turbine—a special kind of fan. The steam squeezes out of the pipes and turns the fan, which is connected to an electric generator. In this way, nuclear energy is used to produce electricity.

Small nuclear reactors are used to drive submarines and ships. By 1985 there were more than 340 large nuclear power plants in use in the world. Although it is expected that the use of nuclear energy will increase, many people became afraid of it following two major disasters—at Three Mile

▼ *The Prototype Fast Reactor (P.F.R.) at Dounreay in northern Scotland, one of the first reactors to start operating.*

USING NUCLEAR POWER

A reactor is at the center of every nuclear power system. It can produce plutonium or radioisotopes directly. Otherwise, the reactor's heat is used via a heat exchanger.

Plutonium

Radioisotopes

Reactor

Fresh water

Heat exchanger

Steel making

Steam

Generator

Turbine

Electricity

Power

▲ *Nuclear energy can be used for peace, to bring low-cost power to the peoples of the world. But it can also be used for war. This is the mushroom cloud rising above the test explosion of a nuclear weapon like the ones dropped on Hiroshima and Nagasaki in 1945.*

Island near Harrisburg, Pennsylvania, in 1979, and at Chernobyl in the Soviet Union in 1986. It is still not known how many people will die from radioactive fallout from these disasters. However, scientists are working to make nuclear power safer.

Existing nuclear reactors gain energy from *fission*, the splitting of atoms. Many scientists are now working to try to gain energy from *fusion*, the joining of atoms. Fusion power, if it can be harnessed, should be a lot safer than fission power.

ALSO READ: ATOM; ELECTRIC POWER; ELEMENT; ENERGY; EXPLOSIVES; FALLOUT; FERMI, ENRICO; HYDROGEN.

In their efforts to master fusion power, scientists at Princeton University produced a temperature of 360 million degrees Fahrenheit (200 million degrees Celsius). This temperature is ten times hotter than that at the center of the sun, but it was kept at this level for only a third of a second.

NUCLEIC ACID see BIOCHEMISTRY, CELL, GENETICS.

NUMBER It is as important to be able to use numbers as it is to read and write. Numbers are used everywhere—on calendars, clocks, telephones, price tags, and labels. Numbers are used for keeping the scores of games and for keeping track of money. Houses and streets are numbered. Scientists and engineers make constant use of numbers. All businesses must use numbers for keeping records of their products, their workers, and their money.

The words "number" and "numeral" are different in meaning. A *numeral* is a written mark or sign that stands for a number. The numeral that looks like this—2—stands for two. The numeral that looks like this—8—stands for eight. The numeral ½ stands for one-half.

The word "number" is often used to mean numeral, but number is actually the amount that the numeral stands for. You can write down a number using different kinds of numerals. For example, let's say you have 17 pencils. You could write this down as seventeen, 17, or //////////////////. If you were an ancient Roman, you would have written it as XVII. No matter which *numerals* you use, the *number* (the amount) stays the same.

Numerals and Counting All ancient civilizations had ways of counting. They had to keep track of their animals and crops, and they had to keep track of how much they bought and sold things for. The earliest way of counting was to use *counters*. Pebbles, sticks, shells, or other small objects were used as counters. Farmers with flocks of sheep kept bags of pebble counters—one pebble for each sheep. When they counted their flocks they would take the pebbles from the bag. For each sheep they saw, they would put one pebble back into the bag. If they had a pebble left over, they knew that a sheep was missing. If they had no pebbles left and there was still another sheep to be counted, then they knew there was an extra sheep from somewhere. The ancient Incas used to tie knots in a rope, called a *quipu*. Each knot stood for an animal or for an amount of grain.

Fingers were also used as counters. Since a person has ten fingers, many people based their numbering on 10. When they had to count higher than ten, they used "one-more-than-ten," "two-more-than-ten," until they reached 20 ("two-tens"). Fingers are fine for telling the number of days in a week, but how could you tell someone with your fingers that there are 365 days in a year? People had to find a way to show larger numbers.

The first kind of writing was picture writing. "Three cows" would be written as a picture showing three cows. "Five days" was a picture of five suns. Pictures worked for smaller numbers, but it would be very hard to show in picture writing that there are 100 billion stars in the Milky Way! To solve this problem, people began making short lines to stand for numbers one through nine, and then using other marks for 10, 100, 1,000, and larger numbers. The ancient Greeks used alphabet letters to stand for numbers. The Romans also used numerals that look like alphabet letters—I=1, V=5, X=10, L=50, C=100, D=500, and M=1,000. The numbers 1, 2, 3 were written I, II, III

▼ *The numbers from 1 to 10, as written in some ancient civilizations. You can see the Roman numbers. They had an advanced system for their time. The system we use is based on the Indian one. You can recognize 2 and 3. But look at the Indian for 10. The small round symbol at bottom right is zero, or 0, which the Indians invented. (The curved lines used by the Maya showed a number was to be multiplied 20 times.)*

1	2	3	4	5	6	7	8	9	10	
1	2	3	4	5	6	7	8	9	10	Arabic
▼	▼▼	▼▼▼	▼▼▼▼	▼▼▼▼▼	▼▼▼▼▼▼	▼▼▼▼▼▼▼	▼▼▼▼▼▼▼▼	▼▼▼▼▼▼▼▼▼	◄	Babylonian
A	B	Γ	Δ	E	Z	H	Θ	I	K	Greek
I	II	III	IV	V	VI	VII	VIII	IX	X	Roman
一	二	三	四	五	六	七	八	九	十	Chinese
·	··	···	····	▬	·	··	···	····	◯	Mayan
۱	۲	۳	۴	۵	۶	۷	۸	۹	۱۰	Indian

in Roman numerals. Number 4 was written IV (the I on the *left* of V meant "one *less* than five"). Number 6 was VI (the I on the *right* meant "one *more* than five").

Roman numerals were used throughout the Roman Empire and in most of Europe during the Middle Ages, but there was one serious problem with them. It is very difficult to do arithmetic problems using Roman numerals. People used an *abacus* (an ancient device for calculating using beads) to add, subtract, multiply, and divide. Numerals were used only to write the answer.

About A.D. 800, Europeans discovered that the Arabs had a better way of writing numbers. Europeans called these numerals "Arabic numbers," although the Arabs actually learned them from the Hindu traders of India. Arabic numerals are the ones we use today. It took a long time for the Arabic numerals to become popular, but eventually they replaced Roman numerals.

Arabic numerals were better than Roman numerals because any number could be written by using only ten numerals (0, 1, 2, 3, 4, 5, 6, 7, 8, 9). Also, it was easy to do arithmetic problems with Arabic numerals. The trick in using Arabic numerals is their *position* in a number. The position at the far right of a number stands for *ones*. The next positions to the left stand for *tens, hundreds, thousands, ten-thousands, hundred-thousands, millions*, and so on. In the number 76, the 6 stands for "six ones" and the 7 stands for "seven tens." In 743, the 3 is "three ones," the 4 is "four tens," and the 7 is "seven hundreds."

Counting Systems The counting system (also called numeration system) used in most countries today is the *decimal system*. The word "decimal" comes from the Latin word *decem*, meaning "ten." This means the decimal system is based on ten and uses only ten numerals (0, 1, 2, 3,

4, 5, 6, 7, 8, 9). You can check this yourself by studying the decimal system in the chart that shows kinds of counting systems. Each square is a number position. The first position is "ones." The next position to the left is "tens" (1 × 10). The next position is "hundreds" (10 × 10), and the next is "thousands" (100 × 10). Each position is *ten times* higher than the one before. As you can see on the chart, 76 is 7 tens and 6 ones.

The *binary system* is based on two and uses only two numerals (0 and 1). The position of each numeral shows that it is *two times* higher than the one before. The chart shows that in the binary system, 76 is written as 1001100 (1 sixty-four, 0 thirty-twos, 0 sixteens, 1 eight, 1 four, 0 twos, 0 ones).

The *quinary system* is based on five and uses only five numerals (0, 1, 2, 3, 4). The position of each numeral shows that it is *five times* higher than the one before. In the quinary system, 76 is written as 301 (3 twenty-fives, 0 fives, 1 one).

The *duodecimal system*, based on 12, uses 0–9 and *a* and *b* (the letters *a* and *b* standing for the two-figure numerals 10 and 11). The position of each numeral shows that it is *twelve times* higher than the one before; thus, 76 is written as 64 (6 twelves, 4 ones).

Kinds of Numbers The simplest kind of number is the *counting num-*

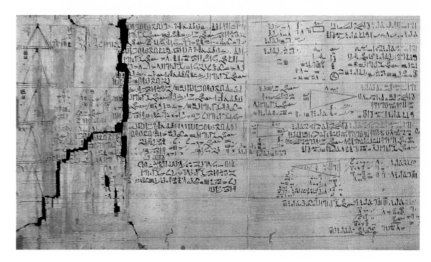

▲ *Part of a long roll of papyrus (a sort of paper) found in Thebes, Egypt. It is full of mathematical problems for students, which are similar to the ones we do today. For example: "A cylindrical granary is of diameter 9 and height 6. How much grain goes into it?"*

COUNTING SYSTEMS

The number 76 in four different systems

Decimal System (base 10)

10s	ones
7	6

76

Binary System (base 2)

64s	32s	16s	8s	4s	2s
1	0	0	1	1	0

ones
| 0 |

1001100

Quinary System (base 5)

25s	5s	ones
3	0	1

301

Duodecimal System (base 12)

12s	ones
6	4

64

▲ *A nurse checks her patients' records. Nursing is an administrative as well as caring job.*

When the American Civil War broke out there were no trained nurses. Most of the nursing for both armies was done by untrained volunteers.

ber, also called a *whole number* or *integer*. They are the numbers we use to count things.

The *fraction number* is used when we want to count *part* of something, such as *half* an hour or *two-thirds* of the world. A fraction is written with two numerals—$\frac{1}{2}$ is one-half, $\frac{2}{3}$ is two-thirds. The bottom number tells how many parts an object has been divided into. The top number tells how many parts you have. Fractions can also be written as *decimal numbers*.

Negative numbers are used in algebra and other kinds of mathematics. They are always written with a minus sign in front of them (-5, -26, -35). Negative numbers are used to stand for numbers that are lower than zero. You have probably heard of temperatures such as "16 degrees below zero" or "22 degrees below zero." These temperatures are written $-16°$ and $-22°$.

Even numbers are those than can be divided by two (2, 4, 6, 8, and so on). *Odd numbers* can also be divided by two, but not evenly (1, 3, 5, 7, and so on). *Prime numbers* are those that can only be divided evenly by themselves and by the number one (1, 2, 3, 5, 7, 11, 13, 17, and so on).

For further information on:
Instruments That Make Use of Numbers, *see* ABACUS, BAROMETER, CALCULATOR, COMPASS, COMPUTER.
Numbers in Everyday Life, *see* CALENDAR, CLOCKS AND WATCHES, LATITUDE AND LONGITUDE, MAP, MEASUREMENT, MONEY, SCALE, TEMPERATURE SCALE, THERMOMETER, TIME, WEIGHT.
Occupations That Make Use of Numbers, *see* ACCOUNTING AND BOOKKEEPING, BANKS AND BANKING, ECONOMICS, STATISTICS, SURVEYING.
School Subjects That Make Use of Numbers, *see* ALGEBRA, ARITHMETIC, CHEMISTRY, GEOMETRY, MATHEMATICS, MECHANICAL DRAWING, MUSIC, PHYSICS, SCIENCE.
Working with Numbers, *see* ANGLE,

BINARY SYSTEM, CHANCE AND PROBABILITY, DECIMAL NUMBER, GRAPH, INTEREST, PERCENTAGE, SET, SYMMETRY.

NURSING The profession of providing care to the sick, injured, and helpless under the direction of doctors and of teaching disease-prevention and health-care is called nursing. In the United States, you must be licensed to work as a nurse. There are two kinds of licenses. One allows you to work as a *registered nurse* (RN). The other permits you to work as a *licensed practical nurse* (LPN) or a *licensed vocational nurse* (LVN).

In order to be licensed as a registered nurse, you must pass a course of training in an approved school and then pass a state board examination. Most nursing students are trained in a three-year course at a nursing school run by a hospital. Another way to become a registered nurse is to take a four-year college course, which leads to the degree of Bachelor of Science in Nursing. Training includes classroom and laboratory work. Student nurses also work in hospitals.

Most professional nurses are *hospital* nurses, who are full-time employees in hospitals or related institutions. Most hospital nurses do "general duty" work, following doctors' instructions about the care that each hospital patient must have. They keep charts of each patient's treatment, condition, and progress. They give any medicine prescribed by the doctor. They keep constant checks to see that equipment, such as oxygen tents, is working properly.

A hospital nurse may have special training in addition to the basic nursing courses. This training prepares the nurse to perform special jobs or care for certain kinds of patients. *Pediatric* nurses are especially trained to care for infants and young children. *Psychiatric* nurses receive special training to care for patients with mental and emotional disorders. *Surgical* nurses are trained to help surgeons in operating rooms and to care for patients who have had surgery. A *private-duty* nurse is employed by sick persons or their families to give nursing care at home or extra care in a hospital.

Practical and vocational nurses take a briefer and much simpler course of training than that taken by registered nurses. They also work in hospitals, allowing registered nurses to have time for the more difficult duties for which they have been trained. Practical and vocational nurses may perform such jobs as taking patients' temperatures and pulses, giving baths, and making beds. (If necessary, registered nurses also perform these tasks.)

An occupation that has become important in recent years is that of *nurses' aide*. A nurses' aide does not have to have any special training and does not have to be licensed. He or she just needs the ability to work with people and a strong desire to help others. Aides working in hospitals help not only nurses, but also doctors and patients. Nurses' aides may make beds, serve patients' meals, read to or play with children in the hospital, or even help a patient to write a letter.

Nurses may be employed in many places other than hospitals. *Office* nurses work in doctors' private offices. They make appointments for patients to see the doctor, receive patients, and take care of the patients' records. They may also assist the doctor in examining a patient or give special tests under the doctor's supervision. *Public-health* nurses work for national, state, or local governments. *Industrial* nurses are hired by companies to care for employees.

Once, almost all nurses were women, but now there are many male nurses, too. Nursing is a fulfilling profession for people who enjoy taking care of others. Perhaps you may become a nurse one day.

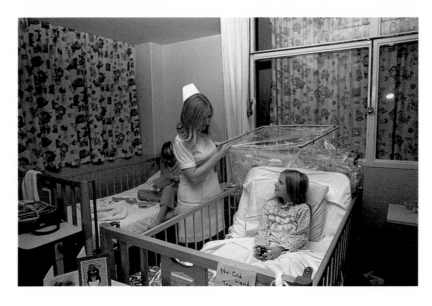

ALSO READ: BARTON, CLARA; CAREER; CAVELL, EDITH; HOSPITAL; NIGHTINGALE, FLORENCE.

NUT A nut is the fruit of a plant. Each nut has an outer covering, or shell, containing the *kernel*, or seed—the part of the nut that you eat.

Peanuts are the most popular nuts in the United States. Peanuts are not true nuts but are related to the pea family. They grow under the ground, and each shell (which is really a pod) usually contains two nuts. Peanuts are eaten roasted, salted, or dried. They are used in making cookies and, of course, peanut butter. Peanuts are crushed to get peanut oil, which is an important oil that is used in cooking.

Pecans are one of the hickory family of trees. Raising pecans is an important industry in Southern states, such as Georgia and Louisiana. Pecan trees are large and fast-growing, and the nuts are very nourishing. Some nutritionists say that a pound (454 g) of shelled pecans gives as much nutrition as five pounds (2.27 kg) of beef.

Chestnuts are scarce in the United States. There have not been chestnut trees in the United States since 1911, when a plant disease killed them all. (There are many *horse chestnut* trees in the United States, but horse chestnuts are not good to eat.) All of the edible

▲ *A young girl has her oxygen tent adjusted by a nurse in this children's ward. Caring for sick children requires sensitive nursing skills.*

▼ *Horse chestnut trees can grow to heights of about 80 feet (about 25 m). Their seed is contained in a fleshy, spiky, green case.*

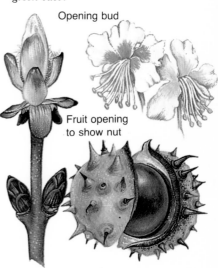

Opening bud

Fruit opening to show nut

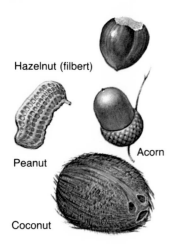

Hazelnut (filbert)

Peanut

Acorn

Coconut

▲ *Nuts come in all shapes and sizes. The hazelnut (filbert) and acorn are small and seem very different from the large coconut. The peanut is not really a nut at all, being related to the pea.*

chestnuts sold in the United States are imported from Europe. The prickly outer covering of a chestnut is called a *burr*. Inside the burr is the brown chestnut shell, and inside the shell is the meat of the chestnut. Chestnuts should be cooked before they are eaten.

The *black walnut* is a native American nut. The *English walnut* is native to Europe but is also grown in the United States. Black walnuts grow wild in the United States, but English walnuts do not. Both types of walnuts have very hard shells.

Filberts (or *hazelnuts*), *beechnuts*, *hickory nuts*, and *almonds* are also grown in the United States, but many nuts you buy in the store come from faraway lands. *Brazil nuts* come from the valley of the Amazon River in South America. Mozambique is the world's largest producer of *cashews*. *Pistachio nuts* come mainly from the Middle East. *Macadamia nuts* are from Australia but are also raised in Hawaii. *Coconuts* are grown in many tropical lands. They provide food and oil, and their fibers are used for matting.

ALSO READ: CARVER, GEORGE WASHINGTON; FRUIT; NUTRITION; PALM; PLANT PRODUCTS; SEEDS AND FRUIT.

NUTRITION Some health experts call the human body a machine, but machines do not change once they are built. Human beings never stop changing. Every moment some part of you changes. Old cells die, and new ones take their place. New cells can only be made because of the food you eat.

The United States produces thousands of kinds of food. Some fruits, vegetables, and meats are sold fresh, but much of our food is processed. *Processed food* is changed in some way at a factory. Cake mixes, potato chips, canned and frozen foods, puddings, ice cream, hot dogs, bread, and soft drinks are examples of processed foods. Processed foods give people a greater variety of things to eat, and they usually do not take much time to prepare, but processing removes many of the *nutrients* (vitamins and minerals) from foods. People may enjoy the taste of processed foods, but most of these foods are not giving people enough of the body-building nutrients they need. Without proper nutrients, cells throughout the body must struggle very hard to do their work. Your body may constantly feel tired. You become impatient, depressed, or "crabby," and unable to pay attention to anything. These are some of the first signs of *malnutrition*.

Malnutrition is a weakening of the body caused by eating too little food, or eating food that lacks enough of the nutrients that keep your body strong and healthy. A team of doctors studied two groups of people in India. One group lived on food rich in nutrients. These people developed strong bones and powerful muscles. They were intelligent, fast workers. The other group ate food without enough nutrients. The people in this group developed weak bones, did not grow as tall, and were not as active or strong. Their children were poor at schoolwork. These people were suffering from malnutrition.

Important Nutrients A very important nutrient is *protein*. Not all proteins are equally valuable. They all have *amino acids* (substances found in all living cells), but some proteins have more than others. Meat has 18. Dried peas and beans and nuts have just a few, but if you eat the right mixture of these foods, your body will get all the amino acids it needs.

A person could survive by eating only protein, but he or she would not feel well and would have no energy. Most energy is provided by *carbohydrates* (starches and sugars). Bread, potatoes, cookies, and cakes contain carbohydrates. They "burn" quickly and give you pep. People in the United States eat many carbohydrates. If too many are eaten, the body changes them to fats. Too much fat is harmful.

Early in the 1900's, scientists discovered vitamins. Now we know that vitamins are important in various ways to good health.

The human body needs *minerals* for strength and healthy tissues. The most important minerals are *calcium*, *phosphorus*, *iron*, and *iodine*. Besides these, *trace minerals* (minerals found in very small amounts), such as manganese, copper, zinc, and cobalt, are needed. A well-balanced diet provides enough minerals of each kind.

Diet Protein, carbohydrates, fats, vitamins, and minerals should be eaten every day. To help people plan, buy, and prepare nutritious meals, experts have a Daily Food Plan.

1. *Milk and milk products.* Children need a quart (950 ml) of milk every day. Either natural cheese or ice cream may substitute for part of the milk. Milk contains calcium, which is vital for your bones to grow. One to three servings of butter or margarine supply enough vitamin A.

2. *Fruits and vegetables.* A citrus fruit and a leafy vegetable should be eaten each day. Fresh fruits and vegetables are the best. Frozen ones are next best.

3. *Breads and cereals.* These should be eaten at least twice a day. The ones made of whole grains and left unbleached contain the most nutri-

ents. Most white breads contain very few nutrients. The nutrients in wheat lie just under the hull of the kernel. These nutrients are lost when wheat is milled into flour. Bleaching removes even more nutrients. Many manufacturers add some vitamins and call the product "enriched," but they have wasted the natural vitamins. Vitamins added later are not enough. Breads and cereals are also rich in *fiber*, which helps your body to digest foods more easily.

4. *Protein.* Everyone needs two servings of protein every day. The best proteins are in meat, fish, and eggs. Other, less costly, proteins are in nuts, peas, and dried beans.

Wheat germ (the rich center of the wheat grain) can be added to many foods, for both vitamins and flavor.

Cooking can destroy some nutrients. Vegetables have the most nutrients when eaten raw (although some, like potatoes, should *never* be eaten raw). If you cook vegetables, use only a little water, heat them fast, and do not cook them long.

Malnutrition is a worldwide problem. Some countries have a variety of foods, but they cannot produce enough of them to feed all the people. Also, they have too little money to buy foods from other countries. In some areas of the world, only a limited number of foods can be grown, and so the people do not get certain necessary nutrients. Some countries produce a great amount of food, but people often eat the wrong things.

For further information on:
Diet, *see* DAIRY PRODUCTS, FISH, FOOD, FRUIT, MEAT, NUT, VEGETABLES, VEGETARIAN, WATER.
Human Body, *see* BLOOD, BONE, BRAIN, CIRCULATORY SYSTEM, DIGESTION, GLAND, GROWTH, HUMAN BODY, MUSCLE, NERVOUS SYSTEM, RESPIRATION, SKELETON.
Nutrients, *see* CARBOHYDRATE, FATS AND OILS, PROTEIN, VITAMINS AND MINERALS.

▲ *Milk, vegetable oil, butter, and meat are rich in* fat.

▲ *Fruits and vegetables are especially rich in* vitamins.

▲ *Bread, potatoes, and sugary foods are rich in* carbohydrates.

▲ *Fish, meat, eggs, nuts, and milk are rich in* protein.

Fiber is an essential part of a healthy diet. Fiber, as found in bread, helps you digest food more easily.

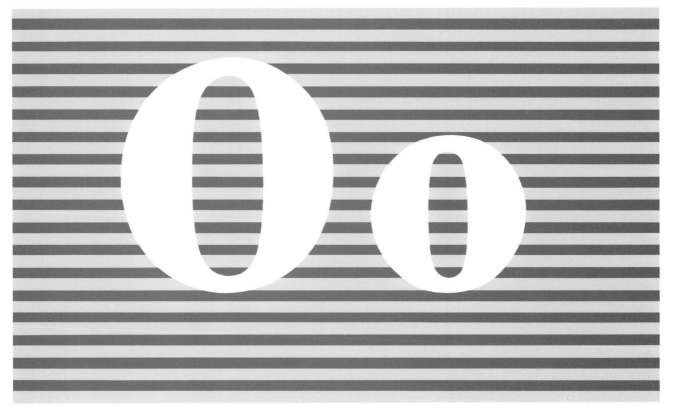

▲ *A photograph made in 1899 of sharpshooter Annie Oakley.*

OAKLEY, ANNIE (1860–1926) Annie Oakley was only six years old when she began helping to support her family by selling rabbits, pheasants, and quail she had shot with her father's rifle. She was born Phoebe Anne Oakley Mozee in a log cabin in Darke County, Ohio. She became a crack shot with rifles, pistols, and shotguns. At age 15, Annie entered a shooting contest and defeated the well-known marksman and vaudeville star, Frank Butler. Five years later she married Butler, who became her partner in stunt-shooting, and then her show-business manager.

In 1885, Annie became a star in Buffalo Bill's Wild West Show, giving shooting exhibitions throughout the United States. She gave many performances before the kings and queens of Europe. Annie thrilled audiences at Queen Victoria's Diamond Jubilee in 1887 in London.

Only five feet (1.5 m) tall, Annie was nicknamed "Little Sure Shot." She could throw a playing card into the air and shoot five or six holes in it before it hit the ground. She once shot 4,772 glass balls out of 5,000 thrown into the air on one day.

Irving Berlin's musical comedy, *Annie Get Your Gun*, is based on her life.

ALSO READ: BUFFALO BILL, RODEO.

OASIS see DESERT.

OBESITY see HEALTH.

OBSERVATORY An observatory is a place for studying the stars, planets, and other bodies in space. Weather stations are sometimes called observatories, but "observatory" usually means a place for observing (watching) the skies. Most observatories are built on high hills in the countryside, where the air is clear.

The first observatory was built in China in 2600 B.C. This observatory, like most early observatories, was used for measuring and calculating time. Early *astronomers* (scientists who study the bodies in space) kept careful records of when certain stars and planets were at certain places in the sky. They particularly watched the moon and saw how it changes "shape." By doing this they were able to come up with a calendar.

Early observatories did not have telescopes. But early astronomers, just by watching the sky and keeping records of what they saw, were able to map the visible part of the universe and discover some important astronomical laws.

The first astronomer to use a telescope was Galileo Galilei, in 1610. From then on, almost every observatory had a telescope. Galileo's telescope was a *refracting* telescope—the light passes through two or more glass lenses that collect the light and magnify the object observed. The largest refracting telescope is located at Yerkes Observatory in Wisconsin. Its lens is 40 inches (102 cm) in diameter.

Most of the large telescopes built after 1900 have been *reflecting* telescopes. In a reflecting telescope, the light is reflected (bounced) off a huge curved mirror, and then into a lens. The world's largest reflecting telescope is at Zelenchukskaya, Soviet Union. Its mirror is 236 inches (6 m) across and weighs 78 tons (71 metric tons). Reflecting telescopes can be much larger than refracting telescopes, because the mirror can have a solid support on one side. The large lens of a refracting telescope can be supported only around its edges, so it sags because of its own weight.

Telescopes need large lenses or mirrors because large ones collect more light than small ones. Most telescopes today are used to study distant bodies in space. Little of the light given off by these bodies reaches the Earth, so the usefulness of a telescope depends more on how much light it can collect than on how much it can magnify an object.

Today, most observatories are used

SOME IMPORTANT OBSERVATORIES

Name	Location	Opened	Interesting Feature
Jodrell Bank Observatory	Jodrell Bank, England	1949	Has the world's first radio telescope capable of pointing in any direction
Kitt Peak National Observatory	Tucson, Arizona	1962	Has the world's largest solar telescope
Mount Palomar Observatory	Mount Palomar, California	1948	Has the largest reflecting telescope in the United States
National Radio Astronomy Observatory	Socorro, New Mexico	1981	Has the world's largest radio telescope
Special Astrophysical Observatory	Zelenchukskaya, Soviet Union	1974	Has the world's largest reflecting telescope
Yerkes Observatory	Williams Bay, Wisconsin	1897	Has the world's largest refracting telescope

for *astrophysics*, the science of the physical make-up of stars, star clusters, and galaxies (groups of billions of stars).

The nearest star is so far away from Earth that the star's light, moving at 186,000 miles (300,000 km) a second, takes about four years to get here. Other stars are much farther away. Scientists find out what a body is made of by studying the electromagnetic radiation (light, radio waves, X rays, and so on) it gives off.

Light can be studied with an optical telescope and a *spectroscope*. The telescope picks up light from a star, and the spectroscope splits the light into different colors (wavelengths). By studying the different wavelengths of light given off by a star, scientists can tell what the star is made of.

Radio waves can be studied in about the same way but, since radio waves cannot be seen, they must be picked up by a radio telescope. A radio telescope is not at all like an optical telescope. It is more like a huge radar antenna, shaped like a dish or the blade of a bulldozer. The antenna picks up the radio waves and a *radiometer* measures their intensity (strength). To catch the longer radio waves, several antennas are put side by side in a long row. A radio telescope with several antennas is one type of *interferometer*. Some radio-

▲ *The dome of one of the world's largest telescopes. The mirror of the Mayall reflector at Kitt Peak Observatory, Arizona, is over 13 feet (4 m) across.*

▲ *The world's largest refracting telescope is at Yerkes Observatory, near Chicago. It is 62 feet (18.9 m) long, and its large (objective) lens is 40 inches (102 cm) across.*

▼ *These two views of the earth help us realize that ocean covers nearly three-fourths of the Earth's surface.*

astronomy interferometers are more than a mile (1.6 km) long.

In 1990 the Hubble Space Telescope was launched, enabling scientists to look even further into space.

ALSO READ: ASTRONOMY, LENS, RADIATION, RADIO ASTRONOMY, STAR, TELESCOPE.

OCEAN For centuries the oceans were vast, mysterious places. Explorers such as Christopher Columbus sailed across the oceans in fear and ignorance. Gradually people mapped the oceans and learned what their boundaries are and what winds blow across them. But our knowledge of what lies underneath the ocean surface is very recent. A great deal of it has been learned in the last 40 years. We now know that the oceans are a far more fantastic part of the Earth than the early explorers could ever have guessed. Very recently, we have realized that the oceans are really all just parts of one big ocean, the "world ocean."

The world ocean is a large body of salt water that covers 71 percent of the Earth's surface. The Earth is the only planet in the solar system with such a large quantity of water. The continents divide the ocean into the Atlantic, the Pacific, the Indian, the Antarctic, and the Arctic Oceans. Smaller bodies of water, such as the Mediterranean Sea, the Gulf of Mexico, and Hudson Bay, are all part of the ocean, but they are largely closed in by land. Seas that are completely surrounded by land, such as the Caspian Sea (between the Soviet Union and Iran), are not part of the world ocean.

Ocean Water Seawater is said to have a high *salinity* (saltiness) because at least 80 elements are dissolved in it. The large amounts of chlorine and sodium, which combine to form sodium chloride (common salt), make the ocean water taste very salty.

Water pressure in the ocean increases by 14.7 pounds per square inch every 33 feet (1.03 kg per sq. cm every 10 m). As people go deeper down in the ocean, their equipment needs to be stronger. Scuba divers can go down only about 100 feet (30 m). Wearing pressurized suits, divers have been able to descend to 600 feet (180 m) below the surface. In 1960, the *Trieste*, a U.S. Navy bathyscaphe (a deep-sea research vessel similar to a submarine), made the deepest dive on record—35,800 feet (10,900 m). This was at the Marianas Trench in the Pacific Ocean. The *Trieste* withstood a pressure of 16,000 pounds per square inch (1,125 kg per sq. cm)!

Ocean Movements *Waves* are the most easily seen kind of ocean movement because they happen at the surface. Waves are caused by wind blowing over the water, making it move in a circle (downward and upward). When waves from out at sea travel from deep water to shallow water, the

▼ *The surface waters of the ocean are whipped into waves by the wind.*

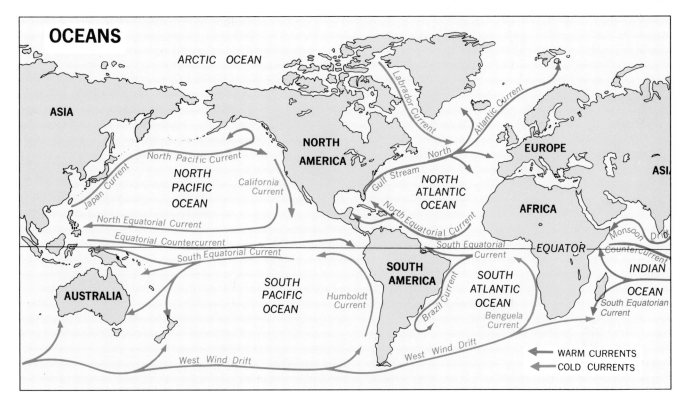

OCEANS

ocean bottom interferes with the downward motion of the wave, so the wave rises higher above the surface. When it gets too high, the top of the wave falls forward, forming a breaker. A very dangerous kind of wave, called a *tsunami*, is caused by undersea earthquakes or volcanoes that start a huge wave rolling at speeds up to 500 miles an hour (800 km/h). Boats at sea do not notice this wave because it is only about 3 feet (1 m) high, but by the time it reaches land it may, with little warning, have built up to 100 feet (30 m) high, causing great damage. Tsunamis are sometimes called *tidal waves*, but they are not caused by tides.

Less easily observed movements of water are *currents*. Currents are streams of water that flow through the ocean along well-mapped routes. There are two kinds of currents: *surface currents*, which extend from the surface down to about 700–1,000 feet (200–300 m), and *deep-sea currents*, which flow much farther below sea level.

Currents that flow toward the poles from the equator are *warm currents*.

They come from hot, tropical regions where the sun beats down and heats up the surface waters. Currents that flow from the poles toward the equator are *cold currents*. Their waters come from icy regions in the north and south. Cold water sinks because it is denser and heavier than warm water, so cold currents flow beneath the warm currents.

Tides are the regular rise and fall of sea level. At high tide the water reaches farther up the coast than at low tide. Tides occur because the gravity of the moon and the sun pulls on the Earth's waters. Most parts of the world have high and low tides twice a day. Enclosed seas, such as the Mediterranean, hardly have tides at all.

The Ocean Floor People used to think that the ocean floor was flat, but this is not true. Along most coastlines is a *continental shelf*. This is a wide, flat area extending in places 40 miles (65 km) seaward and sloping gently downward to 360–600 feet (110–180 m). The ocean floor then plunges steeply downward. This steep descent

▲ The "oceans" of the world are really only a single ocean, as we can see from this map. Under the ocean's surface, large-scale currents cross thousands of miles. Some bring warm waters; others bring cold. The currents affect the weather of the countries they reach. The currents exist because the Earth is not stationary, but spinning.

▼ On average one pound (0.45 kg) of ocean water contains half an ounce (15 g) of dissolved minerals. The two main elements are chloride and sodium.

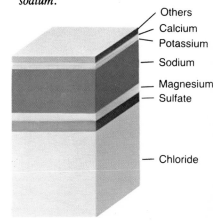

Others
Calcium
Potassium
Sodium
Magnesium
Sulfate

Chloride

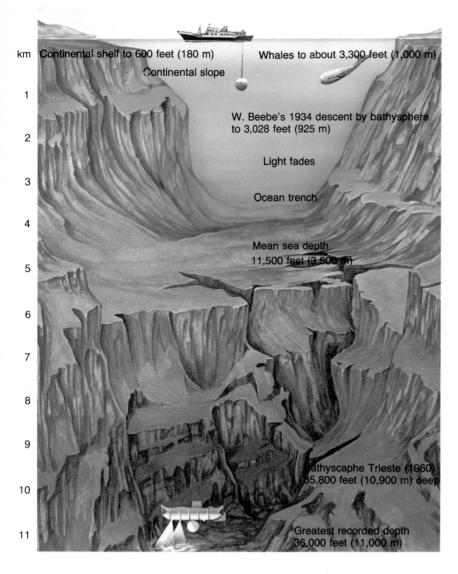

clefts that plunge to depths far below the ocean floor. Trenches are usually found along the edges of continents.

Mid-ocean ridges and oceanic trenches mark the divisions between the giant rigid plates that form the Earth's crust. Mid-ocean ridges are called *constructive margins*. Here, molten rock rises from great depths into the gap between the plates, adding to the sea floor as the plates move apart. Oceanic trenches are found at *destructive margins*, where one plate is sliding under another.

Submarine canyons are narrower than trenches and not so deep. Canyons are found near the mouths of rivers that pour into the ocean. Canyons were probably formed by river water that eroded (wore away) the ocean floor when the sea level was lower.

The ocean floor is covered by layers of *sediment* (soil particles and other matter) that has sunk to the bottom. Sediment has been building up over millions of years, covering the rock beneath it, and in time becoming solidified itself. In bringing up samples of sediment, scientists have discovered the fossils of very ancient plant and animal life.

▲ *It is hard to imagine how deep the ocean really is, but this illustration gives you some idea.*

▼ *Echo-sounders measure the ocean's depth by sending a sound toward the bottom and measuring the time it takes for the echo to return.*

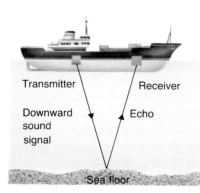

is called the *continental slope*. At the bottom of the slope is the *abyss*, the deep ocean floor.

The ocean bottom is very rugged in places. Mountain ranges, volcanoes, canyons, and great *abyssal plains*, the flattest places on Earth, can all be found under the ocean. One mountain range, the Mid-Atlantic Ridge, stretches from Iceland to Antarctica. Ranges like this are called *mid-ocean ridges*. Mountains that rise above sea level are called *seamounts*. Some islands are the tops of seamounts. Underwater volcanoes spew red-hot lava into the sea. The lava quickly cools when it comes into contact with the cold water to form dark, glassy *pillow lavas*.

Ocean trenches are narrow, steep

Oceanic Life As on land, all life in the oceans depends on plants. The plants in the sea are often very small, and some are almost like particles of dust. They live near the surface, where they can use the energy from sunlight to make their own food from the minerals in the seawater. Deep in the ocean it is completely dark.

The plants float about wherever the currents in the ocean take them. Floating with them are billions of little animals. Some are almost as small as the plants. Others are the young of larger animals, such as fishes. All these tiny plants and animals are known as *plankton*, which means "drifters." The smallest animals feed on the plants of the plankton, and larger animals eat the small animals. Strangely enough, the biggest animal in the world, the great blue whale, feeds on *krill*, tiny shrimplike creatures that are part of the plankton.

Some of the most fantastic ocean life has been discovered not on the surface but 1½ miles (2.4 km) under the Pacific in the Galápagos Rift. A number of bacteria and animals live there, far from the light of the sun. They get their energy from *hydrothermal vents*, fountains of hot water and gases spouting from the deep ocean floor. The creatures found there include huge blood-red worms and large clams.

Ocean Resources   People are just beginning to discover the vast natural resources of the ocean. Fish and other sea animals are the most used resources. They are plentiful, and, if people use great care in how they fish, they can increase the numbers of fish. Most whales, however, are in danger of extinction because people have killed so many of them. The world supply of lobsters and shrimps may also be decreasing.

Aquaculture means "seafarming," raising marine plants and animals in the same way a farmer raises crops and animals on land. People have been raising oysters, clams, and seaweed for a long time. Now scientists are experimenting with ways to raise and harvest a large variety of seafood.

The ocean contains deposits of useful minerals. Many lie in sand and gravel near coasts. They include gold, tin, titanium, and magnetite (an ore of iron). Shallow deposits are already being mined by dredgers, and there are plans to work in deeper water. These deposits have come from the land, washed down by rivers, but in the deep ocean there are other minerals that have apparently come up from deeper in the Earth's crust.

Lying on part of the ocean floor are lumps called *manganese nodules*.

These nodules are rich in minerals, particularly manganese, nickel, cobalt, and copper. In the mid-1980's people were planning to mine these nodules in the northern Pacific.

Under the continental shelf there are rich deposits of oil and natural gas. These deposits are being exploited off the coasts of the United States, Australia, Indonesia, Malaysia, and Nigeria, and in the North Sea.

Exploring the Ocean   Interest in the bottom of the ocean began when people started laying telegraph cables across the ocean floor in the 1850's. One of the people helping to lay cables was a U.S. naval officer, Matthew Fontaine Maury. Maury collected information on winds, currents, and water temperatures to help navigators at sea. He studied the ocean bottom using *sounding lines*. These were ropes weighted with cannonballs and having hollow tubes at the ends. The tubes were driven into the sea bottom by the weight of the cannonballs, and samples of the sediments were trapped in the tubes. Maury was then able to study the microscopic sea life embedded in the ocean bottom, as well as make discoveries about its formation.

Scientific exploration of the ocean developed even more in 1872 when the British warship H.M.S. *Chal-*

▲ *A glimpse of ocean life, including clams, mussels, snails, and a starfish, can be seen in this coastal pool at low tide.*

The flattest plains on Earth lie beneath the oceans at depths of 2 to 4 miles (3 to 6 km). These plains are so flat that any lump more than 3 feet (1 m) high is a mountain.

As you go down beneath the surface of the ocean, colors begin to change. Not only is there less light the deeper you go, but also colors are filtered out. The colors of the rainbow slowly disappear, starting with the reds and working through the yellows and greens. A hundred feet (30 m) down, there is no color left except blue. Below a depth of 3,000 feet (1,000 m), there is complete darkness. The only light in these depths comes from fish that make their own light.

▼ *A typical cross-section of the ocean floor, showing where different types of mineral resources are found.*

▶ *A map showing the global distribution of seabed oil, gas, and other mineral resources.*

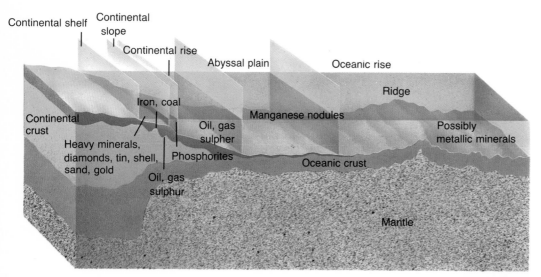

Continental shelf
Continental slope
Continental rise
Continental crust
Iron, coal
Heavy minerals, diamonds, tin, shell, sand, gold
Phosphorites
Oil, gas sulphur
Abyssal plain
Oil, gas sulpher
Oceanic crust
Manganese nodules
Oceanic rise
Ridge
Possibly metallic minerals
Mantle

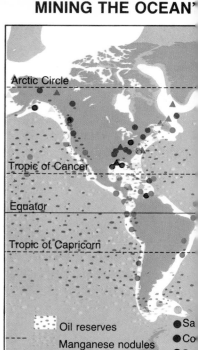

Arctic Circle
Tropic of Cancer
Equator
Tropic of Capricorn

Oil reserves
Manganese nodules
Sa
Co
Ga

▼ *Contents of a manganese nodule.*

Cobalt 0.3%
Titanium 0.5%
Barium 0.5%
Others 0.7%
Calcium 3.8%
Aluminum 6.3%
Manganese 11.5%
Water 15.3%
Iron 20%
Oxygen 20.4%
Silica 20.7%

▶ *Manganese nodules like these occur in abundance on the floor of deep oceans. They are a rich source of many vital metals that will soon be in short supply.*

▼ *Metals in the form of dissolved minerals abound in seawater but are sparsely distributed, and with one vital exception they will probably never be exploited. That exception is magnesium, of which there is some 6 million tons per cubic mile (1.4 metric tons per cubic km). Much of our magnesium is already extracted from seawater. The concentration of other metals in seawater is very much lower, as the table shows.*

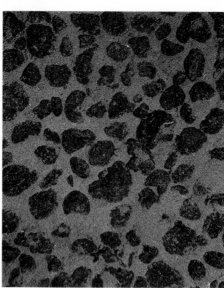

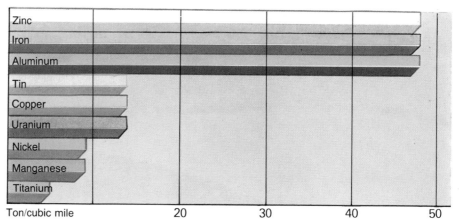

Zinc
Iron
Aluminum
Tin
Copper
Uranium
Nickel
Manganese
Titanium

Ton/cubic mile   20   30   40   50

1 ton/cubic mile = 0.22 metric tons/cubic km

MINERAL RESOURCES

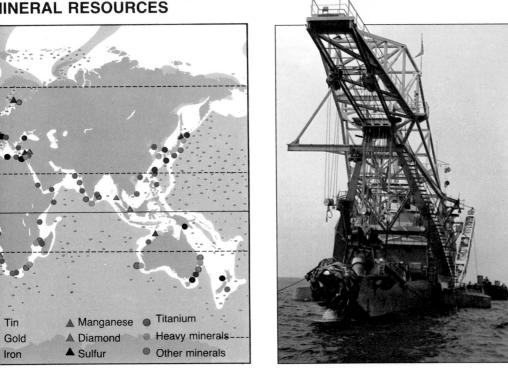

◀ A sea dredger at work. Dredgers like this are used for mining sand, gravel, and mineral-rich sands in shallow coastal waters as well as for excavating navigational channels.

▼ Three methods of extracting manganese nodules from the deep ocean floor. The ship on the left "vacuums" them off the bottom. The two ships in the middle pull the continuously moving series of dredge buckets that scoop up the nodules. The system on the right relies on remote-controlled collectors that shuttle between the ocean floor and the surface platform.

Tin	▲ Manganese	● Titanium
Gold	▲ Diamond	● Heavy minerals
Iron	▲ Sulfur	● Other minerals

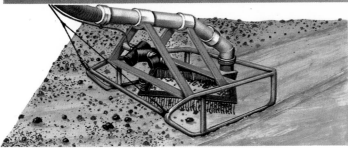

▲ There are several ways of collecting manganese nodules by suction. This sledge has a rake to scrape the nodules off the seabed before they are sucked to the top.

▲ This remote-controlled vehicle moves on screws. It is guided by a sonar homing beacon. A factory platform processes the nodules brought up by these shuttles.

▲ *This Pisces submersible (vessel for underwater exploration) has robot arms and a videotape system to help its crew find out more about the ocean depths.*

The deeper you dive in the ocean, the more the weight of water presses down on you. In the deepest part of the Pacific Ocean, nearly 7 miles (11 km) down, the pressure is more than 7 tons on every square inch (a metric ton on every square cm). Yet people in special vessels have been this deep and lived.

lenger began a 3½-year voyage around the world. Techniques of undersea exploration were developed during World War II, when people spent time and effort trying to detect submarines.

In 1968, the United States joined with five other countries—France, Great Britain, Japan, the Soviet Union, and West Germany—in the Deep Sea Drilling Project. This was carried out by the drilling ship *Glomar Challenger*. The ship has been roaming the oceans ever since, drilling holes deep into the seabed to find out what the Earth's crust is like under the oceans.

People Under the Sea Divers have been exploring the sea for hundreds of years. More than 5,000 years ago people used to dive for pearls and sponges in the Mediterranean Sea, holding their breath when they dived. Diving suits came into use in the 1800's. Divers wearing these suits are supplied with air pumped from the surface. Diving suits are very heavy and cumbersome, but people still use them for some kinds of underwater work.

Skin diving, in which the diver carries his or her own air supply, was made possible by a Frenchman, Jacques-Yves Cousteau. He invented a portable air supply, the *aqualung*, in the 1940's. With aqualungs divers have been able to explore and photo-

graph in shallow seas.

Exploration of the deeper parts of the ocean is carried on in special diving vessels. In 1934, two U.S. scientists, William Beebe and Otis Barton, were lowered 3,028 feet (925 m) down into the Atlantic in a *bathysphere*. The bathysphere was a round chamber with windows and lights that could be directed out into the blackness of deep ocean waters. But the bathysphere was dangerous because, if the cable lowering it had snapped, the vessel would have plunged straight to the bottom.

A far safer vessel was the *bathyscaphe*, invented by a Belgian named Auguste Piccard. The bathyscaphe was made up of a large float tank and a small observation sphere. Piccard's bathyscaphe was the first vessel in which scientists could study the ocean for long periods of time at great depths.

A later diving vessel is the U.S. research submarine *Alvin*, which is built specially strong to withstand great pressure. It has been tested to a depth of 22,000 feet (6,700 m). It carries a crew of three. Scientists aboard it discovered the strange underwater worms in the Galápagos Rift.

Scientists have been trying to find ways in which people can live in homes built under the sea. In 1962, Cousteau led an experiment called *Conshelf I*, in which two *aquanauts*

FACTS ABOUT THE OCEANS

AREA The total area covered by the earth's oceans is about 140,000,000 square miles (362,000,000 sq. km). This is just over 70 percent of the earth's surface area. The largest ocean is the Pacific, with an area of about 63,800,000 square miles (165,000,000 sq. km). The smallest is the Arctic Ocean, with an area of about 5,440,000 square miles (14,100,000 sq. km).

VOLUME The total volume of the earth's oceans is about 310,000,000 cubic miles (1,292,000,000 sq. km). The total weight of the water is about 1,450 thousand million million tons (1.32 million million million metric tons).

DEPTH The average depth of the oceans is about 11,700 feet (3,566 m). The Pacific is the deepest ocean, with an average depth of about 14,000 feet (4,267 m). The deepest part of the oceans is the Marianas Trench, in the Pacific; it is about 36,000 feet (10,970 m) deep.

(undersea explorers) lived for a week in a steel chamber on the sea floor. It was anchored in the Mediterranean 40 feet (12 m) below the surface. *Conshelf II* was an experiment in 1963 in which five persons lived 36 feet (11 m) below sea level for a whole month. Two years later, Cousteau built *Conshelf III*, a large underwater house in which six aquanauts lived for three weeks at a depth of 330 feet (100 m). Similar experiments were carried out in 1964, 1965, and 1968 by the U.S. Navy with *Sealab I*, *Sealab II*, and *Sealab III*, in the Pacific Ocean. The aquanauts in these underwater stations studied currents and temperatures and experimented with methods of raising sunken ships. In 1969, another underwater station, *Tektite II*, was submerged off the U.S. Virgin Islands. Some scientists think that one day people may be able to live permanently under the sea.

For further information on:
Exploration and Use of the Ocean, *see* AQUACULTURE; BOATS AND BOATING; BYRD, RICHARD E.; COUSTEAU, JACQUES-YVES; DIVING; DRILLING RIG; FISHING INDUSTRY; MAURY, MATTHEW; NATURAL RESOURCES; NAVIGATION; PETROLEUM; SAILING; SCUBA DIVING; SHIPS AND SHIPPING; SUBMARINE; SWIMMING.
Geography and Geology of the Earth, *see* ANTARCTICA, ARCTIC, CONTINENTAL DRIFT, EARTH, EARTH HISTORY, EQUATOR, GEOGRAPHY, GEOLOGY, MAP, MINERAL, PLATE TECTONICS.
Ocean Life, *see* ALGAE, BIOLUMINESCENCE, CLAMS AND OYSTERS, CORAL, DEEP SEA LIFE, DOLPHINS AND PORPOISES, ECHINODERM, ELECTRICAL FISH, FISH, FOSSIL, GULLS AND TERNS, HYDRA, JELLYFISH, LICHEN, MARINE LIFE, MOLLUSK, OCTOPUS AND SQUID, PROTOZOAN, SEABIRDS, SEAHORSE, SEALS AND SEA LIONS, SHARKS AND RAYS, SHELL, SPONGE, TROPICAL FISH, WALRUS, WHALES AND WHALING.
Ocean Surface and Depths, *see* ATLANTIC OCEAN, CLIMATE, GLACIER, GULF STREAM, ICEBERG, INDIAN OCEAN, PACIFIC OCEAN, SALT, SAND, SEACOAST, TIDE, WAVE, WIND.
Water, *see* WATER, WATER CYCLE, WATER POLLUTION, WATER SUPPLY.

O'CONNOR, SANDRA DAY (born 1930)

Sandra O'Connor was the first woman justice to sit on the bench of the U.S. Supreme Court. She was born in El Paso, Texas, on March 26, 1930, but spent her childhood on the Day family ranch near Duncan, Arizona. She studied law at Stanford University, where she met her husband, John Jay O'Connor III.

As a young lawyer, she practiced in Arizona, and from 1965 to 1969 she served as assistant attorney general for the state. In 1969, she was elected to the Arizona Senate as a Republican and became majority leader, the first woman ever to hold such a position. She became a judge in 1974.

In 1981, President Ronald Reagan chose Sandra O'Connor as his first appointee to the U.S. Supreme Court. Known as a conservative, Justice O'Connor won respect for her independent judgments, particularly in regard to constitutional questions about religion. She is a strong supporter of police and prosecutors. In 1986, Justice O'Connor supported a Supreme Court ruling that sought to prevent racial discrimination in the selection of juries.

ALSO READ: SUPREME COURT.

OCTOBER October is the tenth month on our calendar. It was the eighth month on the ancient Roman calendar. *Octo* means "eight" in Latin. It once had only 30 days, but in 45 B.C. Julius Caesar added another day. October's flower is the calendula, often called the pot marigold. October has two birthstones. One is the tourmaline, a gem of many colors. The other is the opal, which glows with firelike brilliance.

▲ *Sandra Day O'Connor, the first woman to become a U.S. Supreme Court judge.*

▼ *Calendula is the flower for the month October.*

DATES OF SPECIAL EVENTS IN OCTOBER

1 • First U.S. jet plane was flown (1942).
2 • Mahatma Gandhi, Indian political leader, was born (1869).
  • Thurgood Marshall sworn in as first black U.S. Supreme Court justice (1967).
3 • Ethiopia was invaded by Italy (1935).
  • The reunification of Germany (1990).
4 • President Rutherford B. Hayes was born (1822).
  • *Sputnik I*, the first space satellite, was launched by the Soviet Union (1957).
5 • President Chester A. Arthur was born (1830).
  • President Harry Truman made the first televised address from the White House (1947).
  • The Great Chicago Fire began (1871).
6 • First showing of part-talking movie *The Jazz Singer* starring Al Jolson, in New York (1922).
10 • U.S. Naval Academy was opened at Annapolis, Maryland (1845).
  • Spiro Agnew resigned as Vice-President of the United States (1973).
11 • Eleanor Roosevelt, the wife of President Franklin D. Roosevelt and a tireless worker for rights of minorities, was born (1884).
12 • Christopher Columbus reached the island of San Salvador in the Bahamas (1492).
14 • William the Conqueror invaded England from France (1066) and became king of England.
  • President Dwight D. Eisenhower was born (1890).
  • John Brown led a daring raid on the U.S. arsenal at Harpers Ferry, West Virginia (1859).
  • Eugene O'Neill, U.S. dramatist, was born (1888).
17 • John Burgoyne, British general, surrendered at Saratoga to American Revolutionary forces (1777).
18 • World's largest permanent circus was opened in Las Vegas, Nevada (1968).
19 • British surrendered to the American Revolutionary forces under General George Washington at Yorktown, Virginia (1781).
20 • Christopher Wren, great British architect, was born (1632).
  • John Dewey, U.S. philosopher and education pioneer, was born (1859).
21 • Ferdinand Magellan entered the present-day Strait of Magellan at the tip of South America (1520).
  • Battle of Trafalgar was won by the British (1805).
22 • Sam Houston was inaugurated as the first president of the Republic of Texas (1836).
  • Metropolitan Opera, one of the world's greatest operatic centers, opened in New York City (1883).
23 • Hungarian Revolution began (1956).
24 • United Nations Day. Church bells ring and special prayers of peace and brotherhood are said all over the world.
25 • The English won the Battle of Agincourt, a decisive victory over the French during the Hundred Years' War (1415).
  • Pablo Picasso, great modern artist, was born (1881).
26 • Erie Canal was opened to traffic (1825).
27 • Federalist Papers first published in *New York Independent Journal* (1787).
  • President Theodore Roosevelt was born (1858).
28 • Harvard College in Cambridge, Massachusetts, was founded (1636).
29 • Great stock market crash in the United States (1929).
30 • President John Adams was born (1735).
  • Actor Orson Welles created nationwide invasion scare during radio broadcast of science fiction drama, *War of The Worlds* (1938).
31 • Martin Luther nailed his 95 theses to a church door in Wittenberg, Germany (1517).
  • Halloween. Children dress up in fancy costumes and play "trick or treat" on the neighbors.

October is crisp and cool in most of the northern parts of the world. Its days are golden with sunshine and bright with red and yellow autumn leaves. Large orange pumpkins lie in the fields, ready to be picked. Children carve them into scary jack-o'-lantern faces for Halloween, October 31. Columbus Day is celebrated in October, too. Christopher Columbus, sailing across the ocean, landed in the Americas on October 12, 1492.

Sometimes in early October mornings, there is an icing of frost on the grass and on the windowpanes. A few late flowers still brighten the gardens. Cider and crunchy red apples are sold at roadside stands. In the southern part of the world, beyond the equator, gentle springtime is bursting into bloom in October.

ALSO READ: AUTUMN, CALENDAR, HALLOWEEN, MONTH.

OCTOPUS AND SQUID Both octopuses and squids are highly developed *mollusks*. They live in the sea and have soft bodies.

The octopus has a large, football-shaped head and enormous eyes that are very similar to those of higher animals. It has excellent vision and a good nervous system. Its strong, hard, beaklike jaws are used to crush and tear apart its prey—usually crabs. Eight *tentacles*, or arms, extend from around the head of the octopus. The tentacles help the octopus to creep along the rocks and coral deposits of

▼ *Each of the octopus's arms* (tentacles) *has two rows of suckers.*

the ocean bottom. Each arm has two rows of suckers underneath, which act like suction cups. With these the octopus can grip its prey and other objects.

The octopus has cells in its skin filled with color pigments. When the octopus is frightened or excited, the cells change shape. This changes the distribution of color pigments and the color of the skin. The octopus at times appears to be blushing!

Contrary to popular belief, most octopuses are small creatures, less than one foot (30 cm) across from the tip of one arm to the tip of the opposite arm. Several kinds of octopuses may be up to 28 feet (8.5 m) across, but such giants are rare. Adult octopuses are preyed on by eels, fish, seals, and many other marine animals. People eat octopuses, too.

The squid has ten tentacles, a long, pointed body, and two triangular fins. It uses the fins to move through the water. A squid may be from 2 inches (5 cm) to 30 feet (9 m) in length. Giant squids are the largest of all animals without backbones. Squids feed on fish, which they grasp with two of the longest tentacles, called "grasping arms."

Both octopuses and squids usually creep along slowly. If danger comes, they move quickly by shooting streams of water out of a *siphon* on the body—just as a jet plane is propelled forward by the streams of hot gas from its engines. When moving in this way, the squid shoots backward! Squids and octopuses can also shoot an inky fluid into the water. The ink not only confuses the enemy by hiding the octopus or squid, but also dulls the enemy's sense of smell.

Many tales have been told about fierce attacks by octopuses on human beings. Most of these stories are exaggerated. The age-old tales of "man-eating" octopuses have probably given them their name of "devilfish."

ALSO READ: MARINE LIFE, MOLLUSK.

OGLETHORPE, JAMES see GEORGIA.

OHIO Ohio's admission to the Union was complicated by a very unusual mistake. Ohio was admitted as a state in 1803. But by some strange error, Congress did not ratify (approve) the state's admission. This error was not discovered until 1953!

Ohio is unusual in another way. It has given this country more Presidents than any other state except Virginia. Ulysses S. Grant, Rutherford B. Hayes, James A. Garfield, Benjamin Harrison, William McKinley, William H. Taft, and Warren G. Harding were born in Ohio. For this reason, the state is called the "modern mother of Presidents."

The Land and Climate Ohio is a north-central state. Michigan and Lake Erie are north of it. The winding Ohio River forms the southern and southeastern borders. Across the straight western boundary is Indiana. Pennsylvania is on the other side of Ohio's eastern boundary. The Scioto River divides Ohio into two parts. The state capital, Columbus, is on this river.

A gently rolling plain lies west of the Scioto. It is part of the plains that are west and south of the Great Lakes. In Ohio, most of these plains are called Till Plains. But the north-

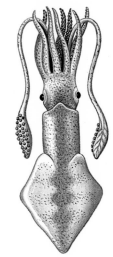

▲ *The common squid has a slender body with two triangular tailfins.*

The octopus is the most intelligent of the animals without backbones. It can be trained to find its way through a maze and to solve simple problems, such as removing the stopper from a sealed jar containing food.

▼ *Cleveland, one of the most important cities of Ohio, lies on the shores of Lake Erie at the north of the state.*

▲ *A statue of Christopher Columbus stands, appropriately enough, in the state capital—Columbus.*

One of Ohio's nick-names is the "Buckeye State." It received this name because many buckeye, or horse chestnut, trees grow there.

ern tip is called the Great Lakes Plain. Campbell Hill, northwest of Columbus, is the highest point in the state.

East of the Scioto, the land rises. This area is called the Allegheny Plateau. Most of the plateau is hilly, but a strip of flat plain lies close to Lake Erie. A small part of the hilly, fertile bluegrass region is in south-central Ohio.

Winters in Ohio are cold, and summers are warm and humid.

History Indians called Mound Builders were some of the earliest inhabitants of the region. The Mound Builders had disappeared long before European explorers arrived in the 1600's. But some of the mounds they built remain undamaged.

In the early 1700's, French fur traders found a number of Indian tribes living in Ohio's wooded river valleys. The Iroquois were in the northeast and center. The Delawares had moved into the southeast. In western Ohio lived the Ottawa, the Shawnee, and the Miami.

France claimed a large area that included Ohio because of French explorations there. But Britain claimed the same region. British fur traders from Pennsylvania and Virginia had built trading posts in the region. Ohio was one of the prizes that France and Britain fought for in the French and Indian War. Some tribes helped the British, and some helped the French. When the British won, they took practically all the French-claimed land east of the Mississippi.

But the region south of the Great Lakes was not British for long. The United States gained it as a result of winning the American Revolution. Settlers began moving into this area, then called the Northwest Territory, in 1788. Some former soldiers came down the Ohio River by boat. Where the Muskingum River joins the Ohio, they started a town that they named Marietta, after Marie Antoinette. She was queen of France at the time the

French helped the United States win the Revolution. Cincinnati was founded the next year, in 1789. It also was built on the Ohio River. When the settlers moved into Ohio, forest covered nearly all of the land. They cleared whatever land they wanted.

Settlers took away more and more Indian land for their towns and farms. The Indians tried to defend their land by uniting to fight the white people. In 1794, General Anthony Wayne marched a small army to northwestern Ohio. He met the Indians in a place where a windstorm had felled many trees. Wayne and his soldiers won the Battle of Fallen Timbers. With this defeat the Indians lost Ohio.

Many more settlers then moved in. In 1800, Congress divided the Northwest Territory into two parts. Ohio was made a state in 1803.

Waterways have meant a great deal to Ohio's development. The first steamboat west of the mountains reached the state in 1811. Steamboats made the rivers more useful than ever. And soon canals linked Ohio with the East. Ohioans could then ship goods by water all the way to the Atlantic Coast.

Ohio was settled mostly by people from the northeast of our country. Most were strongly against slavery. Some Ohioans helped slaves escape from the South. Troops from Ohio played a big part in winning the Civil War.

Ohioans at Work The location of the state has much to do with its success in manufacturing. It is situated in the middle of the most densely populated part of the United States. Ohio factories, therefore, have millions of customers close at hand. A network of airlines, railroads, and highways carries Ohio's products to customers. The state has access to two major water routes—the Ohio River and Lake Erie. Ohio's location makes it a convenient meeting place for the

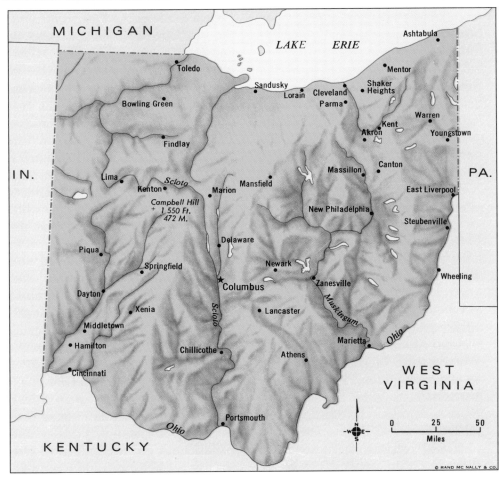

MICHIGAN

LAKE ERIE

Ashtabula

Toledo

Mentor

Sandusky

Lorain

Cleveland

Shaker
Heights

Bowling Green

Parma

Warren

Findlay

Kent

Akron

Youngstown

Lima

Scioto

Massillon

Canton

IN.

Kenton

Marion

Mansfield

East Liverpool

Campbell Hill
+ 1,550 Ft.
472 M.

New Philadelphia

PA.

Piqua

Delaware

Steubenville

Springfield

Newark

Scioto

Muskingum

Dayton

Columbus

Zanesville

Wheeling

Xenia

Lancaster

Middletown

Marietta

Ohio

Hamilton

Chillicothe

Athens

Cincinnati

WEST
VIRGINIA

Portsmouth

Ohio

N
W E
S

0   25   50
Miles

KENTUCKY

© RAND MC NALLY & CO.

OHIO

Capital and largest city
Columbus (574,000 people)

Area
41,222 square miles
(106,764 sq. km)
Rank: 35th

Population
10,908,000
Rank: 6th

Statehood
March 1, 1803
(17th state admitted)

Principal rivers
Great Miami River
Scioto River
Ohio River

Highest point
Campbell Hill
1,550 feet (472 m)

Motto
"With God, All Things are Possible"

Song
"Beautiful Ohio"

Famous people
Neil Armstrong, Thomas Alva Edison, John Glenn, Orville Wright

STATE EMBLEMS

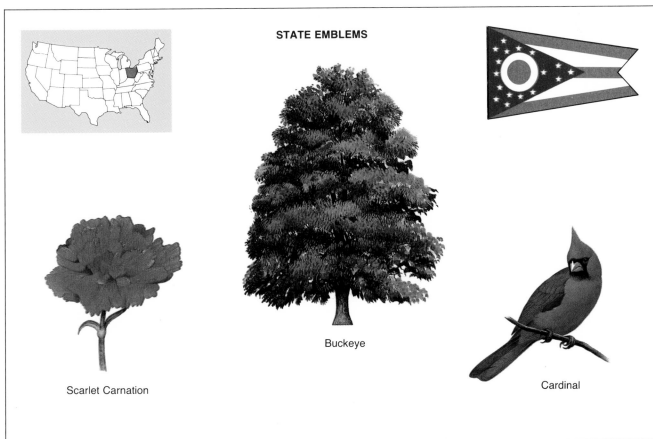

Buckeye

Scarlet Carnation

Cardinal

Seven United States Presidents were born in Ohio: Ulysses S. Grant, Rutherford B. Hayes, James A. Garfield, Benjamin Harrison, William Howard Taft, William McKinley and Warren G. Harding. Garfield, Hayes, McKinley and Harding are buried there also, as are Presidents Henry Harrison, and Grover Cleveland.

▲ *Red Blanket, an Ojibwa Indian, had this photograph taken in 1899 in Minnesota.*

two things that manufacturing must have—raw materials and fuel. The principal raw material is iron ore, which comes from mines in Minnesota and Wisconsin. Heavy freight like this can be moved most cheaply by water. Iron ore comes most of the way by ship on the Great Lakes. The principal fuel is coal. Some is mined in Ohio, but much comes from West Virginia and Pennsylvania. The manufacturing centers of Ohio grew up close to the coal fields.

Ohio ranks third in the country for money earned in manufacturing. It has thousands of manufacturing plants. Much equipment for transportation (cars, buses, and trucks) is made in Cleveland, Dayton, and Toledo. Akron is known for its rubber manufacturing; Cincinnati, for its jet engines; and Canton, for its roller bearings. Steel, glass, chemicals, and office machines are also made in Ohio.

Mining is a significant source of income for the state. Coal, gravel, sand, salt, petroleum, and natural gas are mined in Ohio.

Fertile soil and a good climate help Ohio's agriculture. Corn is the state's biggest crop. Wheat, tomatoes, and soybeans are other money-making crops. Much of the corn is fed to the hogs and cattle raised in Ohio. Dairy farms all over the state provide many products. Tourism is another important industry in the state.

ALSO READ: FRENCH AND INDIAN WAR, FUR, GREAT LAKES.

OIL see FATS AND OILS, PETROLEUM.

OIL SHALE see PETROLEUM.

OJIBWA INDIANS The Ojibwa tribe was once one of the largest Indian tribes in North America. These people lived in the Great Lakes regions of what are now the states of Minnesota, Wisconsin, and Michigan, and the Canadian provinces of Ontario and Manitoba. The Ojibwa Indians speak the Algonkian language. Their name, "Ojibwa," meant "to roast until puckered up" in Algonkian. This name referred to the puckered seams they sewed on their moccasins. Early European settlers found it hard to pronounce the word "Ojibwa" and called the tribe the "Chippewa."

The Ojibwa Indians hunted and fished in the forests, marshes, and lakes. They gathered wild fruit and made sugar and maple syrup from the sap of the maple trees. In the autumn, the Ojibwa would go in their birch-bark canoes to the shallow places of the Minnesota lakes, where huge patches of wild rice grew. They would lean the tall rice stalks over their canoes and beat them with a paddle until the rice grains fell into the canoes.

The Ojibwa families lived in dome-shaped *wigwams*. These houses had wooden frames and were covered with long strips of birch bark. The Ojibwa also used birch bark as writing paper. They drew small pictures on the birch bark to represent different events and, in this way, kept a record of tribal affairs. The Ojibwa helped the French fight the British in the French and Indian War, but they sided with the British in the American Revolution and in the War of 1812. They signed a peace treaty with the United States government in 1815 and later sold most of their territory to the government. More than 55,000 Ojibwa Indians now live on reservations in Michigan, Minnesota, Wisconsin, North Dakota, and Ontario. Those living in Minnesota have special rights to the wild-rice crop.

ALSO READ: ALGONKIAN; FRENCH AND INDIAN WAR; INDIANS, AMERICAN; SIOUX INDIANS; WAR OF 1812.

OKLAHOMA

A race for free land! Western Oklahoma was opened up to settlement in an exciting way. Thousands of homesteaders came on foot, on horseback, and in covered wagons to dash for the free land. They were to start at the signal of a shot being fired. Some people went ahead of time and claimed their land sooner than they should have. They gave Oklahoma its nickname, the "Sooner State." It is also sometimes called the "Boomer State."

The first *land run*, or *land rush*, in Oklahoma was held on April 22, 1889, when government land was opened to any settler who wanted it. Small farms were staked out and tent villages sprang up. Other land runs were held in later years. The land had been territory set aside by the government for Indians.

The Land and Climate Oklahoma lies west of Arkansas, south of Kansas, and north of Texas. It looks like a hand with a finger pointing west. The finger, a strip only 34 miles (55 km) across, reaches as far as Colorado and New Mexico. This strip is called the *panhandle*.

Western Oklahoma is in the Great Plains. The plains are almost level but slope toward the southeast. East of the Wichita Mountains, another plain begins. It is a branch of the plains that curve around the Great Lakes. Here, also, the land slopes toward the southeast. Two highlands rise on the state's eastern border and extend into Arkansas. The northern highland is the Ozark Plateau. The southern one is the Ouachita Mountains. The Arkansas River flows between the highlands.

Oklahoma summers are long and sometimes very hot. The air is dry and winds sweep over the plains. Winters are cold but usually short. Great differences in *precipitation* (rain and snow) are found in the state. Oklahoma lies across the line where the dry western part of the United States meets the moist eastern part. The Great Plains section of Oklahoma has less than 28 inches (71 cm) of precipitation in an average year. The panhandle is extremely dry. More rain falls in the eastern part of the state.

History Many Indian tribes used the land that is now Oklahoma as a hunting ground for buffalo. Wichita, Caddo, Quapaw, Plains Apache, and Osage were some of the tribes who hunted there. Spanish explorers were the first Europeans in Oklahoma. Later, French fur traders came. All of Oklahoma except the panhandle was part of the Louisiana Territory claimed by France. The United States bought the territory in 1803.

In the early 1820's, the U.S. Government decided to send most of the southeastern Indian tribes west to Oklahoma so that white settlers could have their land in the East. During the next 20 years, many Indians died on this "Trail of Tears" to the West. They suffered from hunger, cold, and disease on the long journey.

The "Five Civilized Tribes" were the first Indian tribes sent west. They were the Creek, Choctaw, Chicasaw, Cherokee, and Seminole Indians. They were called "civilized" because many had been to mission schools in the East and had become teachers,

Oklahoma City is one of the largest cities in area in the United States. It covers about 650 square miles (1,680 sq. km).

▼ *The great Oklahoma land rushes gave settlers a chance to race for land that they could get for nothing.*

▲ *Oklahoma's state capitol building was built in 1917.*

▼ *Oil rigs pierce the evening sky as the sun sets over Oklahoma City. This city owes much of its livelihood to the oil industry of the nearby region.*

lawyers, and owners of farms and businesses. A Cherokee named Sequoya had invented an alphabet for his people. The Cherokee printed a newspaper that had columns both in their language and in English. After they settled in Oklahoma, these tribes founded towns and set up governments.

Some Indians had adopted the white people's custom of farming with slave labor. They brought black slaves to Oklahoma. When the Civil War broke out, many Indians took the Confederate side. After the war, the government took about half of the land belonging to these Indians and settled other Indian tribes on some of it. The government also bought land from the tribes. During the 1860's and 1870's, cattle ranchers, coal miners, and railroad workers began to move onto Indian land. Then lands were opened to settlers in 1889 through the land runs.

Oklahoma was divided into two territories, *Indian Territory* and *Oklahoma Territory*. The territories soon asked to be made states. The Indians wanted to name their state "Sequoya." But in 1907, both territories were admitted to the Union as a single state, Oklahoma.

Oklahomans at Work At first, nearly all Oklahomans lived by agriculture. Some raised cattle, but most grew crops. Cotton and corn were the main crops raised for sale. But wheat grows better than either of these crops where there is little rain. In the 1930's, wheat became the main crop. Much of Oklahoma's land turned into a "dust bowl" in the 1930's when there were long, dry spells. The topsoil turned to dry powder and wind blew it away. Thousands of Oklahoma families were forced to leave their farms. Many went to California in search of work. Some people became migrant workers, moving from place to place with the crops. This was the time of the Great Depression

in the country, when jobs were scarce.

Livestock now brings in more money than all the crops put together. More than 5 million head of cattle graze in Oklahoma today. Near the cities, dairy cows and chickens are kept.

Besides agriculture, the other big businesses in Oklahoma are manufacturing and the mining of oil and natural gas. Either oil or natural gas is found in most of Oklahoma's counties. Often the two are found together. Many oil companies have their headquarters in Tulsa, which is known as the "Oil Capital of the World."

The rivers of Oklahoma were the routes of early explorers and fur traders. The Arkansas River Navigation System, completed in 1971, made it possible for boats and barges from the Mississippi River to reach Oklahoma ports on the Arkansas River. To keep the water deep enough for boats all year, 17 dams were built across the Arkansas River. *Locks* allow boats to pass the dams. Catoosa, Oklahoma, is now a port, handling freight for nearby Tulsa.

Visitors to Oklahoma can see a history of the West at the National Cowboy Hall of Fame and Western Heritage Center in Oklahoma City. The center is sponsored by 17 western states. Indian City, U.S.A., near Anadarko, displays villages typical of Plains Indians. Frontier City, U.S.A., near Oklahoma City, is a copy of a frontier town of the late 1800's. Oklahoma has other museums and craft centers showing pioneer and Indian life. The Will Rogers Memorial in Claremore honors the cowboy-humorist, Will Rogers, who was born in Oklahoma.

ALSO READ: CHEROKEE INDIANS; CHOCTAW INDIANS; CREEK INDIANS; GREAT PLAINS; PRAIRIE; ROGERS, WILL; SEMINOLE INDIANS; SEQUOYA; WESTWARD MOVEMENT.

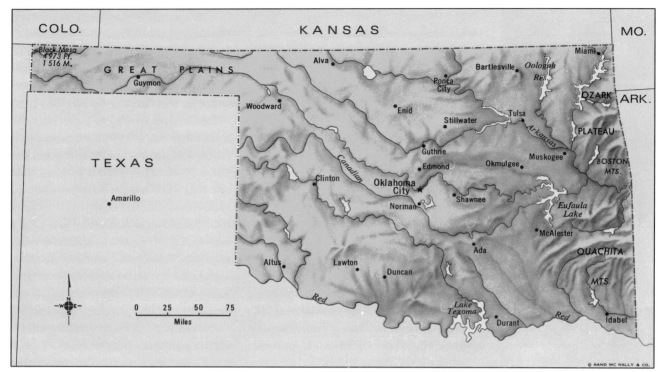

OKLAHOMA

Capital and largest city
Oklahoma City (436,000 people)

Area
69,919 square miles
(181,089 sq. km)
Rank: 18th

Population
3,268,000
Rank: 26th

Statehood
November 16, 1907
(46th state admitted)

Principal rivers
Arkansas River
Canadian River
Red River

Highest point
Black Mesa
4,973 feet (1,516 m)

Motto
Labor Omnia Vincit
("Labor Conquers All Things")

Song
"Oklahoma!"

Famous people
Woody Guthrie, Will Rogers, Maria Tallchief, Jim Thorpe, David L. Payne, Lynn Riggs, Frederick Remington

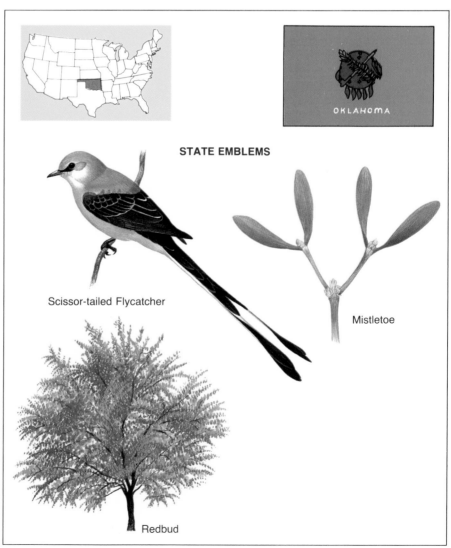

OKLAHOMA

STATE EMBLEMS

Scissor-tailed Flycatcher

Mistletoe

Redbud

▲ *Pierre de Coubertin, who revived the idea of the Olympic Games.*

Only nine nations took part in the first modern Olympics, held at Athens in 1896. Now more than a hundred nations compete, and there are over thirteen thousand competitors.

▶ *An aerobatic display team creates the Olympic symbol using smoke above the Los Angeles Stadium, for the 1984 Games. The five rings link together to represent the sporting friendship of all peoples and also symbolize the five competing continents.*

OLYMPIC GAMES In the year 776 B.C., a religious festival was held by the ancient Greeks to honor their chief god, Zeus. Such festivals had probably been held since about 1370 B.C. The site of the festival of 776 B.C. was in the southwestern part of Greece, in a place called Olympia. The Greeks decided to hold the Olympian games every four years at the sanctuary (holy place) of Zeus. The games were held every four years until the Roman emperor Theodosius in A.D. 393 ordered them to be discontinued because they had become corrupt.

The Olympian games were almost forgotten until 1894, when interest in them was revived by a Frenchman, Baron Pierre de Coubertin. He succeeded in establishing the International Olympic Committee, which enlisted the aid of sports organizations and individuals from various countries. The committee organized the first modern Olympic Games, held in Athens, Greece, in April 1896. The Olympics are held every four years in different cities around the world, but because of World Wars I and II, no Games were held in 1916, 1940, and 1944.

Amateur athletes (those who receive no money for their athletic skill) of all nations can participate in the Olympics. The various events are intended as contests among athletes, rather than among nations.

It is a great honor for a country to be selected to host the Olympics. The host cities for Summer Olympic Games have been Athens (1896), Paris (1900), St. Louis (1904), London (1908), Stockholm (1912), Antwerp (1920), Paris (1924), Amsterdam (1928), Los Angeles (1932), Berlin (1936), London (1948), Helsinki (1952), Melbourne (1956), Rome (1960), Tokyo (1964), Mexico City (1968), Munich (1972), Montreal (1976), Moscow (1980), Los Angeles (1984), and Seoul (1988).

Winter sports became a part of the Olympic Games in 1924. While almost any temperate climate is suitable for the Summer Olympics, the Winter Olympics can be held only in a nation with mountains and much snow. The 1964 and 1976 Winter Olympics, for example, were held at Innsbruck in the Austrian Alps. In 1980, they were held in Lake Placid, New York, and in 1984, in Sarajevo, Yugoslavia. Calgary, Canada hosted the 1988 event.

In the Olympics, as in almost every international sports competition today, distances are measured by meters, instead of by feet or yards. (The marathon, a long running race, is, however, 26 miles, 385 yards—about 42 km.) Well-trained athletes from all over the world compete for individual and team honors. The winner of each event receives a gold medal. A silver medal is awarded for second place, and a bronze medal is awarded for third place.

In the Winter Olympics, most of the medal winners have come from those nations that have long, cold winters. The Netherlands, Norway, and the Soviet Union usually have the best speed skaters. Winning bobsled and toboggan teams have come from the snowy mountainous regions of Austria, Germany, Italy, and Switzerland. Athletes from Austria, France, Germany, Italy, Switzerland, and the

▲ *The English ice-dance couple Jayne Torvill and Christopher Dean won the "Grand Slam" of Olympic, European, and World titles in 1984.*

Scandinavian countries generally excel in the skiing contests. The Soviet Union always offers tough competition in figure-skating.

Most track and field event medalists come from the Soviet Union, Germany and the United States. Many champion gymnasts have been Romanians or Soviets. Champion swimmers have often been American or Australian. American athletes have won the most medals of any country. The greatest U.S. Olympic athlete was Jesse Owens, who won four gold medals in one day in 1936.

Today, the Olympic Games are highly organized. Many countries have national Olympic Committees that hold tryouts among qualified athletes for membership on the country's Olympic team. The United States Olympic Committee (U.S.O.C.) supervises the selection of the U.S. Olympic team. The U.S.O.C. also organizes a nationwide campaign for contributions to pay for the travel and living expenses of the U.S. team. In some nations, the expenses of the Olympic team are paid for by the government.

Since the first modern Olympic Games, performances by athletes have markedly improved. This is usually due to better training methods and sophisticated, new equipment. But sometimes, sportsmen use drugs to help build up muscle in their bodies. This is illegal, and athletes are given random checks to see if they have used drugs. During the 1988 Olympics in Seoul, South Korea, a routine check revealed that the Canadian sprinter Ben Johnson had used drugs.

The Olympics are often affected by politics. In 1936, Hitler used the Berlin Olympics to promote Nazism. The Moscow Olympics of 1980 were not attended by more than 60 nations who opposed the Soviet invasion of Afghanistan. South Africa was once banned from the Olympics for its apartheid policies. After abandoning these policies in 1991, the ban was lifted, and South Africa was welcomed to the 1992 Olympics in Barcelona.

ALSO READ: MARATHON RACE; OWENS, JESSE; SPORTS; TRACK AND FIELD.

OMAN see ARABIA.

O'NEILL, EUGENE (1888–1953)
Eugene Gladstone O'Neill was the first U.S. playwright to be awarded a Nobel Prize for Literature. Four of his plays won Pulitzer Prizes.

O'Neill was born in New York City. His father was a famous actor, and O'Neill worked as an actor, too. He also worked as a sailor and a newspaper reporter. He searched for gold briefly in the country of Honduras in Central America.

While O'Neill was recovering from tuberculosis in 1912, he began writing for the theater. O'Neill's early plays were performed by the Provincetown Players in Provincetown, Massachusetts, and in Greenwich Village, part of New York City.

Several of O'Neill's plays concern

OLYMPIC FACTS

- The 1900 Games were so badly organized that it was only in 1965 that one cyclist discovered he had won a silver medal at them.
- In 1904, the first man home in the marathon race was disqualified when it was discovered that he had been carried for nearly half of the course by car.
- When the 1976 Olympics opened in Montreal, several of the sports complexes were still not fully built.
- The Olympic Oath taken by all the athletes is "In the name of all competitors I promise that we will take part in the Olympic Games, respecting and abiding by the rules which govern them, in the true Spirit of sportsmanship for the glory of sport and the honor of our teams."
- Tennis and 10,000 meters for women were added as Olympic sports in the 1988 Seoul Games.

▼ *Don Quarrie, gold medalist in the men's 200-meter dash at the 1976 Olympics.*

▲ *Eugene O'Neill, U.S. playwright.*

family problems and are based on his own tragic family life. *Long Day's Journey Into Night*, published after O'Neill's death, is a tragic play about the unhappy life his parents had and its effects on their children. *Ah, Wilderness!* is also based on O'Neill's own family, but this play is not tragic. Other outstanding plays include *Desire Under the Elms*, about a conflict between father and son, and *The Iceman Cometh*, about the illusions (false beliefs) of people.

ALSO READ: DRAMA, LITERATURE.

ONTARIO Ontario is the second largest province in Canada (the province of Quebec is larger). Ontario is about the size of Texas and California combined. More than a third of Canada's people live in Ontario.

Geography The name "Ontario" probably came from two Huron Indian words meaning "beautiful lake." More than half of northern Ontario is a low, rolling, rocky plateau covered with forests, lakes, and rivers. The land in the north is too rocky and the soil is too thin for farming, but it is a treasure house of natural resources. Most of Canada's nickel, uranium, and platinum is mined in this area, as is a major share of its gold, copper, and iron ore. Wood products from the extensive forests provide a major export. On the north, Ontario has a saltwater coastline along Hudson Bay.

The southern part of Onatrio has borders on four of the five Great Lakes. Canada's richest farmlands lie in southern Ontario. Tobacco and vegetables are major crops in the southwest. The Niagara peninsula is famous for fruits and wines.

History The first white person to visit parts of what is now Ontario was Henry Hudson. In 1611, Hudson claimed the Hudson Bay area for Brit-

ain. French explorers Samuel de Champlain and Etienne Brulé arrived in 1613 and 1615. The French built several forts and fur-trading posts, but they made no attempts to colonize the region. Strong competition developed between the British and the French over the valuable fur trade. In 1763, at the end of the Seven Years' War between France and Great Britain, the Treaty of Paris established the region as British territory.

During and after the American Revolution, large numbers of colonists in the United States who wished to remain British subjects settled in Ontario. By 1791, the colony had its own government. During the War of 1812, U.S. troops invaded Ontario and burned its capital to the ground. British forces retaliated by setting fire to Washington, D.C.

Ontario was one of the four provinces that joined together in 1867 to form the new nation of Canada.

People Three of every four residents of Ontario live in cities or towns. Toronto, the capital of the province, has a population of about 700,000 people—although about 3 million people live in the Toronto conurbation (group of cities). The city of Hamilton, 30 miles (48 km) from the capital, is also growing rapidly.

Other major cities include Ottawa, Canada's capital, and Windsor, which, like its neighbor Detroit, is a major automobile-manufacturing center. Sudbury is famous for its nickel mines. An annual Shakespeare festival is held in the city of Stratford.

About nine out of ten people in Ontario speak English as their first language, and about six out of ten people are of British descent. Germans, Italians, Dutch, Poles, and Ukrainians also form important groups in Ontario. Many Indians live in the province, mostly on 170 reservations.

Ontario's businesses and industries

Ontario is a province of rivers and lakes. It has about 250,000 lakes, covering nearly a sixth of the province.

There is a huge stone sculpture of Alexander Graham Bell at Brantford, Ontario. The inventor of the telephone lived there for a few months between leaving Scotland and moving to Boston.

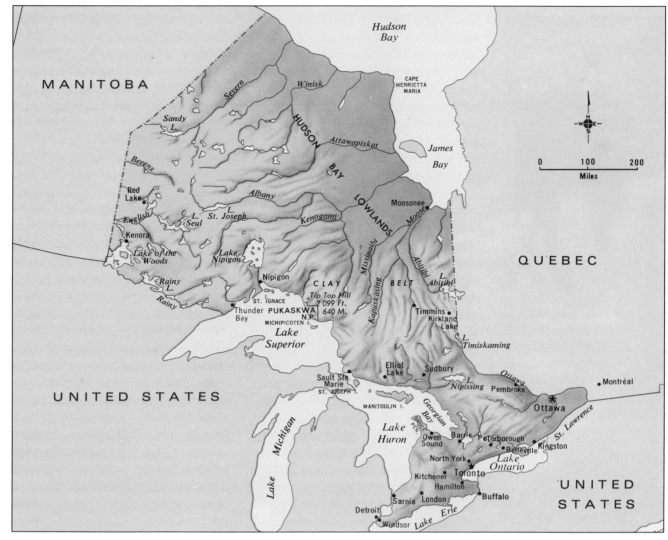

ONTARIO

Capital and largest city
Toronto (3,680,000 people)

Area
344,090 square miles (891,090 sq. km)

Population
9,125,000

Entry into Confederation
July 1, 1867

Principal river
Albany River

Highest point
Timiskaming District 2,275 feet (693 m)

Famous people
Mazo de la Roche, John Diefenbaker, W. L. Mackenzie King, Agnes Campbell MacPhail, Lester Pearson

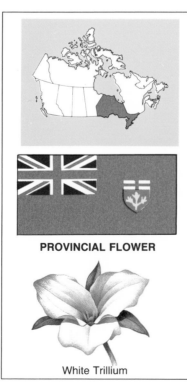

PROVINCIAL FLOWER

White Trillium

▲ *Sightseers wear raincoats against the massive spray of Ontario's Niagara Falls.*

▲ *Sir Arthur Sullivan, British composer most famous for the operettas he wrote with W.S. Gilbert.*

The world's largest opera house is the Metropolitan Opera House, at Lincoln Center, in New York City. It can seat 3,800 people.

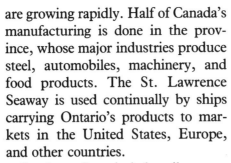

▼ *People go to the opera not only to hear the music but also to watch the drama and spectacle.*

are growing rapidly. Half of Canada's manufacturing is done in the province, whose major industries produce steel, automobiles, machinery, and food products. The St. Lawrence Seaway is used continually by ships carrying Ontario's products to markets in the United States, Europe, and other countries.

Southern Ontario is heavily populated. Someday, there may be one solid city from Detroit to Montreal! The northern part of Ontario will probably offer a frontier for exploration and development for many years to come.

ALSO READ: CANADA, FATHERS OF CONFEDERATION, TORONTO.

OPERA Imagine you are in a darkened theater. On stage are actors. Behind the actors you can see the scenery. Down in front of the stage, in what is called the *pit*, are an orchestra and a conductor. As the orchestra plays, the actors on stage do not speak their lines—they sing them!

This is opera—a combination of drama and music. Operatic dramas are usually serious, but there are several comic operas and funny scenes in tragic operas. The music is usually complicated and difficult to sing well. Only the most skillful singers can handle it. The cast is usually made up of a few main characters (the soloists)

and a chorus (a group of singers who act as a crowd of people involved in the action of the plot). Some operas have scenes in which dancing is performed by a small ballet group.

Operas usually begin with an *overture*—an introduction played by the orchestra alone. Once the curtain goes up, the soloists and chorus sing throughout most of the drama. *Arias* (songs sung by soloists) are the important points in an opera. In an aria, a character sings about his or her feelings and thoughts, or about what he or she is going to do. Between arias, the soloists may sing back and forth to each other in a kind of musical discussion called *recitative*. Besides singing arias, soloists often join together to sing *duets, trios, quartets, quintets, or sextets* at various points in the opera. The chorus usually has several songs to sing, either alone or with the soloists. The music follows the action and mood of the plot.

Operas are usually performed in special buildings called *opera houses*. A *choreographer* creates the dances, and the *chorus master* rehearses the singers. The *conductor* leads the entire opera performance from his or her place in the pit. The soloists, chorus members, and dancers all follow the directions of the conductor.

The ancient Greeks blended drama and music, but opera as we know it today developed in Italy in the late 1500's. At first, the music was used mainly for background. But by the end of the century, the drama and the music were equally important. In the late 1600's, opera became extravagant, with magnificent scenery and huge casts of people. Arias were written into the plots, and the dramas demanded more acting. Women were trained to sing the female roles. Previously, the women's parts had been sung by men or boys. Some composers began writing full-length comic operas. Before 1750, comic operas were short, funny little scenes performed for audiences as entertainment

▲ *The British soprano Janet Baker in a performance of the opera* Dido and Aeneas *by the 17th-century composer, Henry Purcell.*

between the acts of a serious opera.

During the 1800's, *grand opera* developed. Grand operas are gigantic productions, full of powerful singing. The vocal parts are extremely difficult to sing and are a real test of a vocal musician's skill. Giuseppe Verdi was one of the great composers of grand opera. Richard Wagner, who was composing at about the same time as Verdi, had his own ideas about opera. He thought the music, the words, and the acting should all work together as a music-drama. Wagner wrote his own *libretto* (the story and words of an opera), unlike most composers who used words from plays or hired poets to create the lines. Wagner also used a short melody (called a *leitmotiv*) to stand for each important character, idea, or object in the drama. When a particular character came on stage or was mentioned in the lines, that character's *leitmotiv* could usually be heard in the music.

Since the 1850's, many operas have been based on true-to-life stories or experiences. And operas are being staged in many different ways. The Italian-born U.S. composer, Gian-Carlo Menotti, has written operas espe-cially for radio and television. Menotti's opera *Amahl and the Night Visitors* is usually broadcast at Christmastime.

Famous popular operas include Mozart's *The Magic Flute*, *The Marriage of Figaro* and *Don Giovanni* (1780's); Rossini's *The Barber of Seville* (1816); Verdi's *Aida*, *La Traviata*, *Otello*, and *Rigoletto* (1850's–1870's), Puccini's *Madame Butterfly* (1904), and Bizet's *Carmen* (1875) to list just a few. Famous recording opera stars include Enrico Caruso, Maria Callas, Dame Joan Sutherland, Kiri Te Kanawa, Placido Domingo, Luciano Pavarotti, and José Carreras.

Operetta Operettas are sometimes called "light operas." They are like operas but are lighthearted. The settings are often make-believe, with colorful scenery and elegant costumes. The plot of an operetta is always based on romance, in which the good characters win and the evil characters are punished. Operetta music is full of happy tunes, and the dancing is light and gay.

Franz von Suppé was probably the first composer to create real operettas. He made romance the main part of the plot and made the waltz an important part of the music. After von Suppé, most operettas had a big waltz scene that was an important part of the plot.

Some of the most successful European operettas were written by Franz Lehár, Johann Strauss, Jr., and the team of Gilbert and Sullivan. In the United States, operettas included both comedy and romance. Victor Herbert was the first great U.S. operetta composer. His works, such as *Babes in Toyland* and *Naughty Marietta*, have been performed all over the world.

ALSO READ: BALLET; CARUSO, ENRICO; DRAMA; GILBERT AND SULLIVAN; HANDEL, GEORGE FREDERICK; MOZART, WOLFGANG AMADEUS; MUSIC; MUSICAL COMEDY; OPERA; SINGING; STRAUSS, JOHANN; STRAVINSKY, IGOR; VERDI, GIUSEPPE; WAGNER, RICHARD.

▲ *Pamina, the heroine of Mozart's opera* The Magic Flute. *She falls in love with an Egyptian prince, Tamino.*

Although opera only developed about 400 years ago, more than 42,000 operas and operettas have been composed, and more are being created all the time.

▲ *Sigmund Romberg, the Hungarian-born U.S. composer who wrote the music for such popular operettas as* The Student Prince *and* The Desert Song.

▲ *George Gallup, founder of the famous Gallup political polls.*

OPINION POLL People's opinions can influence governments, industries, and other organizations. Research firms are hired to conduct opinion polls (ask questions and analyze answers) on a great many subjects. A political party might want to know what the voters of a certain state think about the party's candidate. A manufacturer might want to know if people prefer its product in a green or a red box.

It would take too long to ask the opinions of everyone, everywhere, so a carefully selected group of people, called a *sample*, is chosen to represent a larger group. The sample may be only 5 percent of the larger group, but it must represent the make-up of the larger group. For example, if 30 percent of the larger group are teenagers, 30 percent of the sample must be teenagers. The people in the sample are then questioned. The questions may be asked by a trained interviewer (who must be careful not to influence the answers), or they might be printed on a *questionnaire*. It is very important that the questions be worded in a fair way. They must also be worded so that they can be answered with "yes," "no," or "undecided." It is easier to add up simple answers.

The answers received from the sample are analyzed in order to determine the opinions of that group. The sample may be broken down into smaller groups—for example, teenagers, housewives, Democrats, teachers, or high-school graduates. The results are used as an indication of opinions of the larger group.

■ LEARN BY DOING

You can take your own opinion poll. Decide on some questions that people might be interested in. Pick a sample group, such as everyone in your class. You do not have to record people's names, only whether they are boys, girls, third-graders, fourth-graders, and so on. When you have

QUESTION: Do you like long hair?		
YES	20	(50 percent)
NO	10	(25 percent)
UNDECIDED	10	(25 percent)
Total polled	40	(100 percent)
Boys		
YES	15	(75 percent)
NO	0	(0 percent)
UNDECIDED	5	(25 percent)
Total polled	20	(100 percent)
Girls		
YES	5	(25 percent)
NO	10	(50 percent)
UNDECIDED	5	(25 percent)
Total polled	20	(100 percent)

According to this poll, 75 percent of the boys like long hair. But only 50 percent of the *entire* sample agree. What does this mean?

received all the answers, make a chart like this to analyze the results. ■

Public-opinion research began in the 1920's. Elmo Roper, Louis Harris, and George H. Gallup are three well-known U.S. poll takers (*pollsters*). The Gallup Poll is famed for its political predictions.

ALSO READ: STATISTICS.

OPOSSUM More than 80 species (kinds) of opossums live in North and South America, from the Canadian woods to the Andes Mountains. Opossums are *marsupial* mammals. Other marsupials, such as the kangaroo, live in Australia. Some opossums live only on land, while others live on both land and water. Some will eat nearly anything, others eat only insects, and still others eat only marine animals. Most opossums sleep during the day and hunt for food at night.

Opossums are not completely developed when they are born. Four to 14 babies may be born at one time. Each baby is no bigger than a thumbnail! The newborn opossum crawls into a pouch on the mother's abdomen and stays there until it is fully developed. After about three months,

▼ *A mother opossum and her babies. Newborn babies live in their mother's pouch. Later she carries them on her back.*

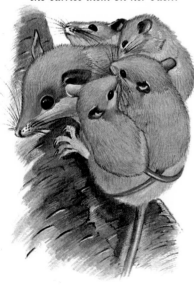

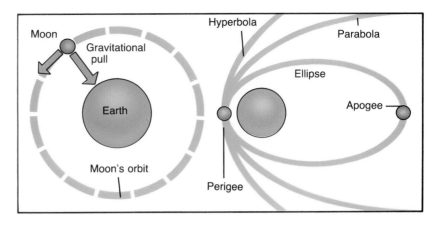

the babies come out and ride around on the mother's back. Eventually, they are big enough to go off by themselves.

The largest opossum is the common species of the eastern United States. It is about 30 inches (76 cm) long, including its long, hairless tail. The opossum is covered with long, gray hair with an undercoat of soft, woolly fur. It sometimes hangs upside-down by wrapping its tail around the branch of a tree. When frightened, the opossum lies completely still and appears to be dead. This habit is the source of the expression "playing possum," describing someone who is pretending to be dead or injured.

ALSO READ: MAMMAL, MARSUPIAL.

___

OPTICAL FIBER see FIBER OPTICS.

___

OPTICAL INSTRUMENTS see LENS, MICROSCOPE, TELESCOPE.

___

ORATORIO see CHORAL MUSIC.

___

ORBIT The moon moves in an orbit around Earth, and Earth moves in an orbit around the sun. The moon is a satellite of the Earth. The Earth is a satellite of the sun. An orbit is the path of an object in space around its center of attraction. How is the Earth the center of attraction for the moon? How does the Earth attract the moon?

The Earth attracts the moon by the force of *gravitation* or *gravitational pull*. This is the same force that makes an object fall toward the ground or floor if you drop it. The object is attracted to the Earth in the same way the moon is attracted to the Earth. In fact, every object attracts every other object by gravitation. Gravitational force between two objects depends on

their masses (quantities of matter they are made of) and on how close together they are.

The moon doesn't fall in to the Earth because the Earth's gravitational pull is not the only force acting on it. The moon has *inertia*. This inertia is the tendency of an object to keep on moving at the same speed in a straight line unless some other force acts on it. If inertia were the only force acting on the moon, the moon would shoot off into space in a straight line. But gravitation pulls it toward the Earth with just enough force to balance the outward push of inertia. And the moon keeps moving around the Earth in an orbit that is almost a perfect circle. The inward pull of gravity is a *centripetal* force—a force that pulls on an object that is trying to move in a straight line and makes it move in a curve. The outward push of inertia is sometimes called *centrifugal* force, but there isn't really any centrifugal force. There is just the straight-ahead force of inertia and the inward pull of gravity.

An orbit is not a circle, although it can be very nearly a circle. The shape of an orbit depends on the difference between the force of gravitation and the force of inertia. Artificial (manmade) satellites are put into orbit at a precise height above the Earth, and with a precise speed, to ensure that gravity and inertia exactly balance each other. If gravitation is stronger than inertia, the satellite will be pulled closer to the Earth and sooner

▲ *The illustration (left) shows how the shape of an orbit depends on the difference between the force of gravitation and the force of inertia. The illustration (right) shows open and closed orbit curves.*

Scientists use machines called *centrifuges*. These spin very quickly and are used to separate liquids of different densities. As it spins, a centrifuge throws the dense liquids to the sides with more force than it does the less dense liquids. The liquids are separated.

Cosmonaut Yuri Gagarin completed the first manned orbit around the Earth on April 12, 1961. It took his spacecraft *Vostok 1* just under 90 minutes to complete the orbit.

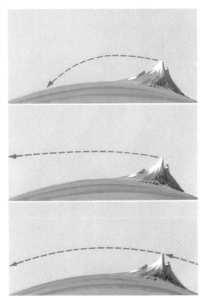

▲ *Imagine a fantastically powerful gun on the top of a very high mountain, firing bullets at different speeds. Three things could happen. The bullet could land on the ground far below (1). It could fly off into space (2). Or it could curve exactly around (go into orbit around) the Earth and become a satellite (3).*

The speed at which the planets orbit the sun depends on their distance from it. The sun's closest planet, Mercury, orbits at a lightning-fast 30 miles (48 km) per second. Far-away Pluto only travels at 3 miles (5 km) per second.

or later will crash into it. If the force of inertia is too strong, the satellite will curve past the Earth in what is called an "open" curve. This means it will curve around the Earth once, then escape into space. If gravity and inertia are balanced, the satellite will keep on orbiting the Earth—that is, it will travel in a "closed" curve.

In a closed curve, or *ellipse*, which is like a flattened circle, the satellite flies back out into space until its inertia becomes weaker than the force of gravitation. Then it curves around and begins falling back toward the Earth. As it gets closer, the satellite goes faster, and this increases its inertia again. Its inertia becomes stronger than gravitation, and it curves around the Earth and back out into space for another trip through the same orbit. The satellite is at its *perigee* when it is closest to the Earth, and at its *apogee* when it is farthest away. The orbit of an artificial satellite can be changed by slowing or speeding the satellite with small rockets.

An open curve may be either a *parabola* or a *hyperbola*. A parabola is a curve that is "almost closed." Most comets, for example, have parabolic orbits, but a few come around the sun regularly. Halley's comet is one of these. Its orbit is an ellipse, but so flattened that it is almost a parabola. In a parabolic orbit, a satellite has just enough inertia to completely escape the Earth's gravitational pull, but its distance from Earth gets bigger more and more slowly. In a hyperbola, the satellite has enough inertia to escape, and it also has some extra inertia. Satellites that are sent from the Earth to Mars must leave the Earth's gravitation in a hyperbolic orbit. If they have only a parabolic orbit, they will have enough inertia to escape the Earth's gravitation, but it will take them a vastly longer time to reach even the nearest planet.

The basic movements of objects in orbit were discovered by Johannes Kepler, a German astronomer, around 1600. He accepted Copernicus' idea that the sun is the center of the solar system. Kepler studied the observations made by his teacher, Tycho Brahe, of the orbit of Mars around the sun. From this study, he developed three laws concerning the motion of planets in orbits. These laws are true also for the movement of satellites and other spacecraft. Strangely enough, Kepler did not know about gravitation.

ALSO READ: COMET; GRAVITY AND GRAVITATION; KEPLER, JOHANNES; MOTION; SATELLITE; SOLAR SYSTEM.

ORCHESTRAS AND BANDS

Many schools and community groups have orchestras or bands. If you play an instrument or plan to learn music, you would probably enjoy playing in one of these groups. Young people's bands often perform at concerts and in parades. Junior high and high school orchestras and bands also play for football games, musical plays, dances, and other events. The earlier you start playing with an orchestra or band, the more skilled you will become.

Orchestras "Orchestra" comes from an ancient Greek word meaning "dancing place." In ancient Greek theaters, the dancing place was the area between the audience and the stage. Today, that area is known as the *pit*. Orchestras that accompany stage performances (operas, musicals, and operettas) are located in the pit and are called *pit orchestras*. Other kinds of orchestras include *jazz* or *rock orchestras* that specialize in playing jazz or rock music. *Chamber orchestras* are small groups of string and woodwind players.

The *symphony orchestra* is the largest and most varied instrumental group, having anywhere from 60 to 120 musicians. About half of a symphony orchestra is made up of *strings*—violins, violas, cellos, double basses, and harps. The violins are the most prominent instruments. They are divided into *first violins* (which carry the main melodies) and *second violins* (which play secondary or accompanying melodies). The *woodwind* section contains flutes, oboes, clarinets, bassoons, and often other instruments—for example, a piccolo, an English horn, or a contrabassoon (the lowest-pitched instrument in the orchestra). The *brass* instruments include trumpets, French horns, trombones, and tubas. Among the various *percussion* instruments are the timpani (kettledrums), snare drums, bass drums, cymbals, gongs, bells, chimes, xylophones, triangles and tambourines. Pianos, organs, and harpsichords are also used in symphony orchestras.

The *conductor* leads the orchestra. He or she must direct the musicians in *rehearsals* (practice sessions) and make sure the music is played correctly. The conductor guides the musicians so that the entire orchestra plays as if it were one great instrument. The conductor sets the *tempo* (speed) at which the music is played and determines the interpretation (or style) in which the music will be played. Most conductors use a *baton* (a short, white stick) when directing. Others use only their hands. With facial expressions as well as hand and body movements, the conductor gives signals to the musicians. Each signal has a meaning that the musicians transfer to their playing.

Orchestras were first organized in Italy during the 1600's to accompany operas. Through the years, many improvements were made in the various instruments. Their pitch and tone quality became more exact, and their flexibility and tonal range became greater. Composers began writing music for symphony orchestras, such as symphonies, tone poems, concertos, and overtures.

Bands *Marching* or *military bands* and *concert bands* are the two basic kinds of bands. *Jazz, rock,* and *dance bands* are smaller bands that specialize in playing certain types of music. Bands have always been important in circus performances. *Rhythm bands* of simple instruments (wood blocks, triangles, tambourines, and so on) are

Actor and comedian Danny Kaye directed 1,342 majorettes leading some 4,500 players in what is the record for the largest marching band. This was at the Dodgers Stadium, Los Angeles in 1985.

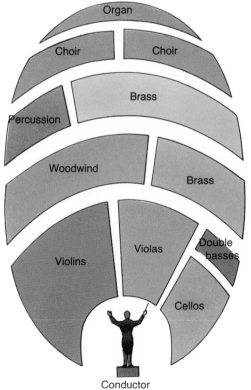

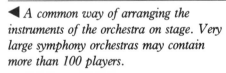

◀ *A common way of arranging the instruments of the orchestra on stage. Very large symphony orchestras may contain more than 100 players.*

Organ

Choir

Choir

Brass

Percussion

Woodwind

Brass

Violins

Violas

Double basses

Cellos

Conductor

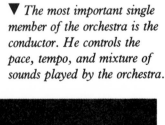

▼ *The most important single member of the orchestra is the conductor. He controls the pace, tempo, and mixture of sounds played by the orchestra.*

▲ *Chamber orchestras are much smaller than symphony orchestras. They may have as few as 20 players, sometimes even less.*

flower

tubers

▲ *Like most ground-dwelling orchids, the early purple orchid grows from tubers.*

widely used in schools to teach music.

Concert and marching bands have the same brass, woodwind, and percussion instruments as an orchestra, with the addition of baritone cornets and saxophones. In marching bands, the sousaphone replaces the tuba because it is easier to carry, and the glockenspiel replaces the xylophone for the same reason. Members of marching bands dress in colorful uniforms. The leader is called a *drum major*. He or she walks at the head of the band carrying a long staff that extends far above the head. The drum major directs the music and the marching by moving the staff in various ways. Marching bands are most often seen at parades, football games, and military events. Well-trained bands often march in complicated patterns that form letters or pictures to show their skill at drill.

Some bands contain only certain instruments. *Brass bands* have only brass instruments. *Drum and bugle bands* and *bagpipe bands* are others of this type. *Steel bands* are popular in the West Indies; all the instruments in these bands are made from steel oil drums or barrels.

Concert bands perform seated on a stage. The conductor directs with a baton. Concert bands often play orchestral music that has been arranged so that stringed instruments are not

needed. Perhaps the best-known composer of band music was John Philip Sousa. His many exciting marches, such as *The Stars and Stripes Forever*, are still popular with audiences. Modern composers are now writing more music especially for bands.

Popular music or rock bands are quite different from traditional bands. Most of them use electric guitars (one of which is usually a bass guitar, to play the lowest notes), a set of drums, and various other instruments.

ALSO READ: BAGPIPE; BRASS INSTRUMENTS; CIRCUS; HARP; JAZZ; MUSIC; MUSICAL COMEDY; MUSICAL INSTRUMENTS; MUSICIAN; OPERA; PERCUSSION INSTRUMENTS; PIANO; POPULAR MUSIC; SOUSA, JOHN PHILIP; STRINGED INSTRUMENTS; WOODWIND INSTRUMENTS; XYLOPHONE.

ORCHID Orchids are beautiful, showy flowers often used by florists in corsages. They belong to one of the largest plant families. About 6,000 kinds of orchids grow in moist climates in many parts of the world. Most orchids grow in the tropics, but some are found as far north as Greenland. About 140 kinds of orchids grow in the United States. One of the most common is the *lady's-slipper*.

Orchids grow on the ground in temperate regions. Tropical orchids may grow high up in trees. Tree orchids attach themselves to the tree and send their roots into the air to take in food and water. Orchid seeds are so small that you can barely see them. One plant may produce 3 million seeds.

Plant breeders have developed about 9,000 different kinds of orchids, in addition to the natural varieties. Breeders in temperate climates grow tropical orchids in greenhouses and sell them to florists.

ALSO READ: GREENHOUSE, PLANT, PLANT BREEDING.

OREGON The pioneers who made the long, dangerous journey to Oregon in the 1800's had to cross hot, dry deserts and dusty prairies. Water was scarce. These people were pleasantly surprised at the mild, rainy climate of Oregon's western valleys. They began to say that they would need webbed feet to get through the rainy winter season. Because of this joke, Oregonians are often called "Webfoots."

The Land and Climate Oregon lies near the northwest corner of the United States. The state of Washington is north of Oregon, and California and Nevada lie south of it. The waves of the Pacific Ocean break along the coast of the state. Across its eastern border is Idaho. Oregon's shoreline is bordered by mountains. The Coast Range, the lowest part of the state's mountain ranges, covers three-fourths of the coastline. Cows graze here in pastures among the forested hills. The Klamath Mountains are below the Coast Range, in the southwestern corner of the state. The state's richest mineral deposits are found in the Klamath Mountains. East of the Coast Range is a beautiful valley. The Willamette River flows north through it to the Columbia River. Early settlers liked this valley better than any other part of Oregon. Today, the state's largest cities are here. Most of Oregon's factories are located in and around the cities. Between the cities are dairy farms, orchards, and green fields of crops. The high Cascade Range lies on the eastern side of the Willamette Valley. This rugged mountain range has some of the tallest peaks in North America. Much of the land east of the Cascades is desert or almost so. The northern half is a highland. Part of it is a dry plateau. This plateau is the wheat-growing region of Oregon. The grain has to be grown by what is called *dry farming*. A crop is planted only every two years. Between plantings, the soil collects water. The moisture of two years is needed to produce a single crop. The Blue Mountains cover the rest of the northern half of the state. They are mostly covered with forest.

The southern half of eastern Oregon is part of the Great Basin. It has short mountain ranges with flat valleys between them. The land is so dry that most rivers end by soaking into the ground or evaporating. Lakes are very shallow, and they shrink in size in summertime.

The differences between western and eastern Oregon are due largely to differences in precipitation. West winds bring moisture from the Pacific Ocean. As the winds rise to cross the Coast Range and the Cascades, the air becomes chilled. It drops most of its moisture in the form of rain or snow. Winter snows are very heavy in the Cascade Range. The climate of western Oregon is mild as well as wet. Ocean winds cool the land in summer and warm it in winter.

It is easy to see why eastern Oregon is different. The Cascades wall it off from the ocean. Winds from the water cannot cool it very much in summer or warm it in winter. It is hotter in summer and colder in winter than western Oregon is. It is much drier, too. By the time the winds have crossed the Cascades, they have lost most of their moisture. Most of the

▲ *A ranch in Oregon, one of the three Pacific Coast states. Cowboys are needed to look after the cattle, which can wander vast distances on the ranches.*

▼ *Part of the old Oregon Trail in Oregon. The trail, which was used by pioneering migrants, was often water-logged and hazardous to cross.*

▲ *Succor Creek Canyon is typical of the desert land in southeastern Oregon.*

▲ *Members of a mountain-climbing club making their way up a hogback ridge toward the summit of Mount Hood, near Portland, in northwestern Oregon.*

rain that does fall in the east comes down on its mountains.

History The first Europeans to see Oregon saw it from the water. Sailor-explorers from Spain and Britain began coming in the 1500's. From the decks of their ships, they saw only the beautiful wooded coast. They learned nothing about the Indians who lived in Oregon.

The Indians of western Oregon were the Tillamook, Kalapuia, and Chinook tribes. They caught salmon in the rivers and gathered shellfish on the beaches. Elk and deer provided them with meat and skins. These Indians hollowed out tree trunks to make canoes. They chopped logs into thick boards. They built houses from the boards. East of the Cascades, the Indians did not live nearly as well. Their food was scarce. For this reason, they were wanderers (*nomads*) and had to go where food could be found. Some fished for salmon in the rivers. Others gathered roots and seeds to eat.

Captain Robert Gray of Boston sailed the *Lady Washington* into an Oregon bay in 1787. This was the first time U.S. citizens landed in Oregon. Five years later, Gray sailed another ship, the *Columbia*, to Oregon. He sailed up a great river and named the river after his vessel. In 1805, Meriwether Lewis and William Clark traveled to the mouth of the Columbia River from the east.

A U.S. citizen named John Jacob Astor built the first fur-trading post in Oregon at Astoria in 1811. A period of trade began. The Indians exchanged furs with the white people for guns, kettles, nails, and cloth. In the 1830's, settlers began coming to the area in covered wagons. At that time, both Britain and the United States claimed the Oregon region. In 1846, the two nations signed a treaty dividing British and U.S territory in North America at the point where Washington's northern boundary is today.

When Oregon became a territory in 1848, it included what is now the state of Washington. Later, Washington became a separate territory. Oregon became a state in 1859. More and more settlers arrived. The white settlements alarmed the Indians, and war broke out. Indians and soldiers fought each other as late as the 1870's. The tribes were finally forced to move to reservations.

By this time, railroads had been built across the continent. It was now easy for easterners to reach Oregon. Soon all the land in the Willamette Valley had been taken. Farmers went into the dry lands east of the Cascades to grow wheat. Lumberjacks pushed into the mountains to fell timber.

Oregonians at Work Lumbering is now Oregon's most important industry. The state's leading manufactures are lumber, paper, and other wood products. Agriculture comes second. Livestock and crops are about equal in value. Hay and wheat are the two largest crops. Fruits and vegetables are grown and processed in large quantities in the Willamette Valley. Oregon's natural beauty attracts many visitors, making tourism the state's third most important industry. Crater Lake, a brilliant-blue lake formed in the crater of an extinct volcano in the Cascade Range, is a favorite attraction. So is Mount Hood, a snow-covered peak in the Cascades, where people can ski all year round.

ALSO READ: CHINOOK INDIANS, FUR, LEWIS AND CLARK EXPEDITION, OREGON TRAIL, WESTWARD MOVEMENT.

OREGON TRAIL Long lines of covered wagons rumbled along the Oregon Trail in the 1800's, carrying pioneers from the Mississippi Valley to the Pacific Coast. The trail extended about 2,000 miles (3,200 km) from Independence, Missouri, to the

OREGON

Capital
Salem (96,000 people)

Area
96,981 square miles
(251,180 sq. km)
Rank: 10th

Population
2,800,000
Rank: 30th

Statehood
February 14, 1859
(33rd state admitted)

Principal river
Columbia River

Highest point
Mount Hood
11,235 feet (3,424 m)

Largest city
Portland (445,000
people)

Motto
"The Union"

Song
"Oregon, My Oregon"

Famous people
Chief Joseph, Joaquin
Miller, Linus Pauling

STATE EMBLEMS

Western Meadowlark

Douglas Fir

Oregon Grape

▲ *The volcanic mass of Mount Hood towers above the surrounding scenery of the Cascade Range. It is the highest point in Oregon.*

▼ *If you blow into a whistle, the sound is produced because the air inside the whistle vibrates (moves in a regular way). The same thing happens in the pipes of an organ. Pressing a key allows air from a fan to enter a pipe or set of pipes. The air is split by a brass "reed," which vibrates and makes the air in the pipe vibrate, too.*

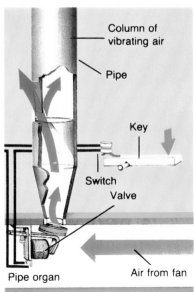

Column of vibrating air

Pipe

Key

Switch

Valve

Pipe organ

Air from fan

Columbia River in Oregon. (See the map with the article on WESTWARD MOVEMENT.) It followed the Platte and Sweetwater rivers, crossing the Green River to the Bear River in Idaho. Then it crossed the Snake River and the Blue Mountains and came down to the Columbia River near the Umatilla. For a time, the Oregon Trail ended at that point, and wagons were floated on rafts to Fort Vancouver from there. But to avoid rapids in the river, the trail was later extended another 100 miles (160 km) to the Willamette Valley.

Paths made by fur trappers and Indians were the beginnings of the trail. The Lewis and Clark expedition blazed a section of it in 1804. In 1811, a group of fur traders employed by John Jacob Astor followed the Lewis and Clark trail to Oregon to set up fur-trading posts. They returned by way of the Platte River instead of the Missouri, tracing another section of the trail. An explorer named John Charles Frémont traveled westward in 1843 and added new information about the trail. That year also saw the first large wave of settlers along the trail.

The Oregon Trail was well established by 1846 and was heavily traveled by settlers seeking new lands in the West.

ALSO READ: LEWIS AND CLARK EXPEDITION, OREGON, WESTWARD MOVEMENT.

ORGAN The organ has been called the "king of musical instruments" because of its great power and wide range of tones. The word "organ" most often refers to a *pipe organ*, although there are several other kinds. A pipe organ is made up of a console, hundreds of pipes, and a wind-chest. The *console* is where the organist sits to play. The console has several *manuals* (keyboards) played with the hands, and a set of 30 or more foot pedals. Above and around the manuals are rows of knobs and levers, called *stops*. The organist uses stops to open up the pipes.

The pipes of an organ are usually shaped like cylinders, ranging from seven inches (18 cm) to more than 60 feet (19 m) in length. All pipes are connected to a *wind-chest*—a large chamber that is kept full of air. Air is pumped into the chest by *bellows* (air pumps) or by great electric fans. The air presses against the mouths of the pipes. By pressing keys or foot pedals, the organist opens the mouths of various pipes. Air rushes into the opened pipes, making the pipes sound their tones until the keys or

▼ *Really large organs can have as many as 40,000 pipes, of lengths from a few inches up to 60 feet (19 m). This organ is in Salisbury Cathedral, England.*

pedals of the organ are released.

The pipes are arranged in *ranks*. Each rank is a complete set of tones of a certain quality. For example, one rank may make flutelike sounds and contain pipes for all the tones a flute can play. Another rank may make cellolike sounds and contain pipes for all the tones a cello can play. Some ranks of pipes can make tones that are lower than on any other musical instrument. When an organist wants to use a particular rank of pipes, he or she pulls out one of the stops on the console. This removes the covers on the mouths of the pipes and makes them ready to be played by pressing the keys and foot pedals.

The *electric organ* was invented by Laurens Hammond in 1935. The tones of an electric organ are made electronically: A very small vibration in an electronic component is amplified (made louder) to produce the sound.

ALSO READ: CALLIOPE, CATHEDRAL, ELECTRONIC MUSIC, HARMONICA, MUSIC, MUSICAL INSTRUMENTS, MUSIC BOX.

ORGANIC COMPOUND see CHEMISTRY.

ORGANIZATION OF AMERICAN STATES
In 1826, the liberator of Latin America, Simón Bolívar, dreamed of an organization of North and South American nations. More than 120 years later, in 1948, such an organization was created at a meeting in Bogotá, Colombia. It is called the Organization of American States (OAS). Its purpose is to promote the unity and welfare of the American nations and to defend their independence. The members are Antigua, Argentina, Bahamas, Barbados, Bolivia, Brazil, Chile, Colombia, Costa Rica, Cuba, Dominica, the Dominican Republic, Ecuador,

El Salvador, Grenada, Guatemala, Haiti, Honduras, Jamaica, Mexico, Nicaragua, Panama, Paraguay, Peru, St. Kitts-Nevis, St. Lucia, St. Vincent, Surinam, Trinidad and Tobago, the United States, Uruguay, and Venezuela. Cuba was excluded from OAS activities in 1962 because it was thought to be "exporting revolution," but it still retains its membership.

The Inter-American Conference meets every five years. A council handles problems between these sessions. When an emergency arises, the foreign ministers of the countries meet to decide what to do. In 1965, for example, the OAS met and decided to send a peace commission to the Dominican Republic to help end fighting there.

The OAS plans projects to improve the health and living conditions of people, and to make farmland better so that more crops can be grown.

ALSO READ: BOLÍVAR, SIMÓN.

ORGAN TRANSPLANT see MEDICINE, SURGERY.

ORIENTAL ART
The art objects pictured with this article are examples of the art of China, Japan, India, Persia, and other lands of the East. The art of these Oriental countries has a rich and beautiful history. A few museums and galleries in the United States—such as the Freer Gallery of Art in Washington, D.C.—are devoted to the art of the Orient. Shown on the next two pages are glimpses of a great history of art on the world's largest continent.

To a great extent, Oriental art is religious in inspiration. It is seldom made to be useful. More frequently it is made for beauty—to inspire thoughts of love, peace, and the finer things of life in people who view it.

Among the oldest surviving pieces of Oriental art are those from the

▲ *Flag of the Organization of American States.*

▲ *A Chinese bronze vessel, or* kuang, *from the Shang Dynasty.*

▲ *A seated statue of Buddha, from a temple in Bangkok, Thailand.*

Shang Dynasty. The Shang people lived on the central plains of China, beginning about 1500 B.C. They discovered how to make an alloy called bronze (a blend of copper and tin). They began making beautiful objects using it. They made ceremonial vessels, possibly for use in religious rites. Since the Shang period in China, there have been many great periods of Chinese art.

Sculptors in many Oriental countries have been inspired by Buddha, a great and good man of India who founded one of the world's important religions. He is often shown sitting in what is called the lotus position, with his legs folded, contemplating (thinking about life). It was after Buddha had died that many sculptors began making statues of him. Some beautiful ones were made in the Gupta period, the greatest time of art in India. Sculpture in the Gupta period used rounded and refined figures. From India the influence of Buddha spread to the east—through central Asia to China and Japan, southeast to Thailand. As Buddhism spread to various countries, sculptors in each country adapted the statue of Buddha to the art and costume of their land. For example, a statue of him made in Thailand often shows him wearing a type of headdress that befits a leader in Thailand.

One kind of Japanese art that has had an influence on Western artists is the Japanese print. From the 1600's to the 1800's, a succession of Japanese printmakers developed printmaking from a very simple form to a highly complicated art using several colors. One great printmaker was Ando Hiroshige, who died in 1858. He was the last of the great printmakers of Japan. By Hiroshige's time, an art that had started with simple black-

◀ *A T'ang Dynasty figure made of glazed earthenware. It shows a lady carrying a little dog. Chinese potters made many small figures like this to be buried in tombs.*

▲ *Painting miniatures has long been popular in India. This scene shows the Hindu god Krishna on the left.*

and-white woodblocks 300 years earlier had become a highly developed art, involving several blocks. Each of these blocks was used to print a different color onto the sheet of paper. When all the areas of different color had been printed, the result was a picture that looked as if it had been painted in lots of colors.

But there is no use of shadow in a Japanese print. There are large, flat planes (areas) of solid colors. These two characteristics of Japanese prints were imitated by Western artists, including Edgar Degas, Mary Cassatt, and Winslow Homer. Japanese printmakers were skilled also in the use of "negative space"—that is, space on the print where the bare paper shows.

Another of the many kinds of Oriental art is the Oriental carpet. From Turkey eastward through central Asia, into the southern part of the Soviet Union and northern India, the making of beautiful carpets has long been an art. Particular designs have been traditional among certain groups of people. One kind of carpet, the *prayer carpet*, has long been a religious art of the Muslims—of whom there are about 600 million in Asia. The prayer carpet is important to a Muslim because he or she must kneel five times a day and face Mecca to pray. Many Muslims take a prayer rug with them wherever they go. The Muslim kneels on the rug with the point of the arch facing Mecca. The design of the prayer niche, or *mihrab*, is traditional, with the keystone arch at one end and the columns on each side of the carpet. Red and blue are the colors traditionally used in such rugs. A very famous carpet-making center is Anatolia, in Turkey.

■ LEARN BY DOING

Perhaps this glimpse at some of the treasures of Oriental art will whet your curiousity to see more. China, India, Japan, Iran, Thailand, Turkey, and many other countries of Asia have long and rich art histories in painting, sculpture, prints, miniatures, porcelain-making, and other visual arts. You might pick one country and see how much you can find out about its art. ■

ALSO READ: ART HISTORY, BUDDHA, HINDUISM, ISLAM, MINIATURE, POTTERY AND CHINA, TAJ MAHAL.

▼ *A 17th-century Japanese screen print showing the arrival of the Portuguese in Japan.*

ORIGAMI SEE PAPER SCULPTURE.

ORTHODOX CHURCH The Eastern Orthodox Church is the third largest branch of Christianity. It has about 80 million members. Most of them live in Greece, the countries of Eastern Europe, including Bulgaria, Yugoslavia, Romania, as well as Cyprus, the U.S.S.R., the Middle East and southwest Asia. Almost four million believers in the Orthodox Church live in the United States. "Orthodox" is Greek for "true belief." Members of the Orthodox Church believe that it was founded by Jesus Christ and his apostles.

For 1,000 years, Christianity was undivided. But then disagreements arose. Emperor Constantine moved the capital of the Roman Empire from Rome to Constantinople (now Istanbul, Turkey) in A.D. 330. The Roman Empire was divided into the Western Empire, ruled from Rome, and the Eastern Byzantine Empire, ruled from Constantinople. In 1054, Christianity split in two. The *pope* headed the western Roman Catholic Church. A *patriarch* in Constantinople ruled the Eastern Orthodox Church.

Today, the Eastern Orthodox Church has four *patriarchates*. They are large religious groups, headed by

▲ *One of a set of 12 prints made by the Japanese artist Kuniyoshi. This is called* View of the Post-stations of Hodogaya *and dates from about 1835.*

▲ *A Muslim prayer carpet, made in Turkey in the 1700's.*

▲ *At mass in this Eastern Orthodox church, incense is burned in front of the Bible as a sign of respect before a passage is read from the Bible.*

▲ *Patriarch Athenagoras. The Patriarch of Constantinople is the most honored leader of the Eastern Orthodox Church.*

▲ *George Orwell, British writer.*

patriarchs in Istanbul, Jerusalem (in Israel), Antioch (in southern Turkey), and Alexandria (in Egypt). There are also self-governing Orthodox churches in the United States, the Soviet Union, Greece, Albania, Cyprus, Finland, Bulgaria, Czechoslovakia, Romania, and Yugoslavia. The patriarch of Constantinople is the spiritual leader of all the Orthodox churches. He governs only the Istanbul patriarchate, however.

Orthodox church services are sung, often by the whole congregation. Beautiful religious paintings, called *icons*, decorate the churches and are sometimes used in the services. Easter is the most important feast in the Orthodox Church. It is usually celebrated later than in other Christian churches, because the Orthodox Church uses the old Julian calendar. The feast is highlighted by a midnight candlelight resurrection service. Orthodox priests are allowed to marry. In recent years, the Orthodox and Roman Catholic churches have become friendlier.

ALSO READ: CALENDAR, CHRISTIANITY, EASTER.

ORWELL, GEORGE (1903–1950) George Orwell was the pen name of an English author and social critic. His real name was Eric Arthur Blair. Orwell was born in Motihari, India.

He was educated in England and then returned to India. In 1927, Orwell moved to Europe and devoted his time to writing. His first book, *Down and Out in Paris and London* (1933), is based on his experiences in those cities. *Homage to Catalonia* (1938) describes fighting in the Spanish Civil War.

Orwell was deeply interested in politics. He hated dictatorship. He was afraid that people's individual freedoms were being taken away. His two most famous books, *Animal Farm* (1945) and *Nineteen Eighty-four* (1949) are Orwell's efforts to warn the world of what might happen. *Animal Farm* is a story about animals who take over their farm and try to establish a Communist government. But the pigs become dictators, and the other animals lose their freedom. This book is based on what Orwell thought had happened to Communism in Russia.

Nineteen Eighty-four is set in a terrifying future where no privacy or freedom exists. A few dictatorships, constantly at war with each other, rule the world. Children are encouraged to spy upon their parents, and to report them to the "Thought Police" if they say anything against the state's rulers. Some people think Orwell predicted the future accurately in this book.

ALSO READ: DICTATOR, LITERATURE, NOVEL.

OSTRICH see FLIGHTLESS BIRDS.

OTTAWA Ottawa, the capital of Canada, stands on the Ottawa River in the province of Ontario. The city has over 300,000 people. Facing Ottawa on the north bank of the river is the industrial city of Hull in the province of Quebec. Hull is part of the metropolitan area of Ottawa, whose population totals 718,000. The city of Ottawa includes the lower

Rideau River, which flows into the Ottawa River over the 37-foot-high (11-m-high) Rideau Falls. The Rideau River is part of the Rideau Canal, a waterway linking Ottawa with Lake Ontario.

Some Ottawans speak only English or French, but many speak both languages. Ottawa is a major commercial and financial center. Its largest industry is the lumber, wood-pulp, and paper industry.

The first settlement on the site of Ottawa was made in 1826 by British soldiers. The town that grew up there was called Bytown until 1855, when it was renamed Ottawa, the English version of an Algonkian Indian word, *adawe*, meaning "to trade." It became Canada's capital in 1857. Ottawa's most striking landmark is Parliament Hill, which overlooks the Ottawa River. The hill is dominated by Peace Tower, commemorating Canada's war dead. The tower rises above the Parliament buildings. A fire destroyed most of these buildings in 1916, but they were rebuilt by 1920. Other notable buildings include Rideau Hall—the official residence of Canada's Governor General—and the Anglican and Roman Catholic cathedrals.

▼ *Ottawa's Parliament building dominates the Ottawa River and surrounding city.*

OTTER The otter belongs to the same animal family as the badger, skunk, and weasel. The head of the otter is broad and flat, with short, rounded ears. Its legs are short but strong. Its feet are clawed as well as webbed. Its long, smooth body, covered with chestnut-brown fur, enables it to swim through water quickly. It may stay underwater for several minutes. The otter feeds on fish, crabs, frogs, birds, and other small animals that live in or near the water.

The *freshwater otter* lives in an underground burrow along the bank of a river or stream. Since the entrance to the burrow is underwater, the otter must swim underwater to enter its home. The burrow provides good protection from other animals.

Otters are very playful animals. In the winter, they sometimes like to make slides in the snow, taking turns sliding down a hill on their stomachs. They will often enter the water by sliding down slippery mudbanks.

A female otter has from two to five babies at one time. The baby otters are called kittens. The mother takes care of the kittens for about a year. She teaches them to hunt and swim. Also known as river otters, freshwater otters hunt fish, frogs, and crayfish. They tend to be smaller than sea otters.

Otters are found all over the world except in Australia. Large numbers of

▲ *A sea otter floating on its back. Lying comfortably like this, the animal will batter a sea shell against a stone laid on its chest until the shell breaks. Then the otter eats the shell's contents.*

▼ *Otters are well adapted to living both on land and in the water. On land they will hunt rabbits and voles.*

The endangered South American giant otter can be more than 6 feet (2 m) in length. There are not many of these otters left because they have been hunted for their valuable fur.

them once lived in North America. Hunters killed many thousands of otters for their valuable fur, reducing their number considerably.

Sea otters live in the waters along the coast of California and the Aleutian Islands. Sea otters spend most of their time in the water, often swimming on their backs.

The sea otter feeds on crabs, fish, and shellfish, such as clams and oysters. When the sea otter catches a fish, it returns to the surface of the water. It eats the fish while floating on its back, using its chest as a table. If a sea otter finds an oyster or clam, it will lay the shellfish on its chest. Then it will break the shell with a stone held in its front paws. The sea otter cracks the shell just as you might crack nuts with a hammer or stone.

At one time, sea otters were in great danger of becoming extinct because they were hunted for their fur. The sea otter is now protected by government regulations. Only people with special licenses can hunt sea otters—and then only in limited numbers.

ALSO READ: WEASEL.

OTTOMAN EMPIRE A thousand years ago, a group of Islamic tribes called the Seljuk Turks lived in western Asia. They were very warlike people, fighting among themselves and against nearby tribes. They conquered the Persian Empire and the people who lived in the lands that are now Israel, Iraq, and Syria. One branch of the Seljuk Turks was called the Ottomans. In 1299, Osman, the leader of the Ottomans, declared war against the Turks' Christian neighbors in the Byzantine Empire. The Ottomans conquered all of the Byzantine Empire (except for the capital city of Constantinople) by the end of the 1300's. By that time, they had also conquered all of the other Seljuk tribes, as well as Macedonia and Bul-

garia. Osman's great-grandson, Muhammad II, finally captured Constantinople in 1453. The Ottomans then began to move into parts of Asia and Africa.

The empire conquered by the Ottoman Turks was strongest under Suleiman the Magnificent, who ruled from 1520 to 1566. His troops conquered all of eastern Europe as far as the outskirts of Vienna, now the capital of Austria. The Turks were never able to take Vienna, however. They were driven back from the gates of Vienna twice in famous battles with the Austrians.

After these defeats, the Ottoman Empire slowly grew weaker. Nearby countries began to conquer some of the Ottoman lands. By the time of World War I, the Ottoman Empire had lost most of its European possessions. Mustafa Kemal, a general in the Turkish army, took command of the Turks in 1922 and founded the Turkish republic in 1923. He was elected Turkey's first president in 1925. He changed his name to "Atatürk" ("father of the Turks") in 1934.

ALSO READ: BULGARIA, BYZANTINE EMPIRE, ISLAM, MACEDONIA, PERSIA, TURKEY.

▲ *Suleiman the Magnificent, greatest of all the sultans of the Ottoman Empire, besieges the city of Bucharest in what is today called Romania.*

▼ *A monument to Kemal Atatürk, who founded the Turkish republic in 1923, ending the Ottoman Empire.*

OUTLAW From about 1845 to 1885—the height of the period known as the Old West—thousands of people moved west to claim land the government was giving away. They established towns, farms, and ranches very quickly. The only law officers were sheriffs and marshals, and even they were scarce. During these years, some persons—called outlaws, gunmen, or bandits—took advantage of the unsettled conditions.

Two brothers named Frank and Jesse James organized a gang of outlaws in 1866. They roamed the West for 16 years, robbing banks and trains and murdering innocent people. Those victims and witnesses who were not murdered were usually threatened so that they were too scared to give evidence against the gang. Jesse James never was captured—he retired. He grew a beard and changed his name. He was later shot by one of his own gang members for the reward money!

One of the most notorious outlaws in the Old West had one of the shortest careers of all time. His name was William H. Bonney, but he became known as Billy the Kid. His only education was what he learned on the muddy streets in the West. He began his career of murder when a man who had befriended him was shot. Billy set out to get revenge and, it was reported, had killed three men by the time he was 17. Billy went on to add to the "notches on his gun" (kill more people). He was shot at the age of 21 by a sheriff.

Butch Cassidy and the Sundance Kid gained reputations as amiable, but determined outlaws. Butch, especially, was known as a cheerful, persuasive man. Legend says that he and his partner never killed a person except in self-defense. But they did rob banks all over the West until they had to leave the country to escape capture. A famous movie about them was released in 1969.

OWENS, JESSE (1913–1980) The greatest competitor of the 1936 Olympic Games was a black athlete, Jesse Owens. He won four gold medals in the Games. His victories were unusually dramatic because the Olympics that year were held in Nazi Germany. The Nazi dictator, Adolf Hitler, believed that Germans were superior to other peoples in everything, including athletics. Hitler had also declared that blacks were an inferior race. So it was doubly pleasing to the United States that Jesse Owens was the outstanding performer of these Games.

Owens was born in Decatur, Alabama, the son of poor sharecroppers. He had ten brothers and sisters. His family moved to Cleveland when he was a small boy. He became a member of the track team in high school and was elected president of the student council. He later worked his way through Ohio State University, where he was a track star.

As a member of the 1936 U.S. Olympic Team, Owens won gold medals in the 100-meter dash, the 200-meter dash, and the running broad jump. He set two Olympic records. He won his fourth gold medal as a member of the U.S. team in the 400-meter relay race.

ALSO READ: OLYMPIC GAMES.

OWL The owl is a bird of prey found on every continent except Antarctica. Owls have large heads, big eyes, and short, hooked beaks. Their feathers are soft and fluffy. Owls have a feathered fringe on the front of each wing. These soft feathers enable the owl to swoop silently down on its prey. The owl's strong legs are covered by feathers. Each foot has four toes, ending in long, sharp *talons*, or claws. The outer toes can be bent inward, so that the owl can grasp its prey.

Most owls are night hunters. They

▲ *Jesse James was a celebrated outlaw of the American West.*

▲ *Jesse Owens, the great U.S. athlete, performs in the running broad jump for which he won a gold medal in the 1936 Olympic Games.*

▲ *The snowy owl, as its name suggests, is colored a speckled white which helps conceal it against snow. It is fairly common in arctic regions of North America.*

▼ *The ghostlike barn owl of many folk tales has a white face. It gives an eerie shrill shriek. Rodents are its chief prey.*

feed on small mammals, birds, insects, and occasionally fish. Although the owl can locate its prey using only its sharp sense of hearing, its excellent eyesight is also helpful. Its large eyes, located at the front of its head, are fixed in their sockets. Undisturbed by any side vision, the owl can "zero in" on its prey with amazing accuracy. The pupil of the owl's eye can be greatly expanded (opened), giving it good night vision.

Owls are usually bewildered and helpless in the glare of sunlight. When surprised, an owl hisses like a cat and makes a clicking noise with its beak. Some owls have a shrieking cry, and others have a musical "hoot."

Owls build their nests in hollow trees, caves, barns, deserted buildings, and underground burrows. The *burrowing owl* of western North America often lives in the deserted burrows of prairie dogs (its favorite food) or digs its own. Owls live alone or in mated pairs. They range in size from the *elf owl*, 5½ inches (14 cm) tall, to the *great horned owl*, 25 inches (64 cm) tall and with a wingspread of 5 feet (1.5 m).

Owls have heart-shaped, humanlike faces, and their large, serious eyes

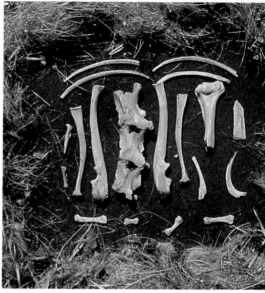

▲ *The contents of an eagle owl's pellet include bones, pieces of fur and feathers and reveal much about its hunting habits.*

and dignified appearance have given them the reputation of being wise birds. Ancient Greeks believed the owl was the companion of Athena, the goddess of wisdom.

Owls are nearly always harmless and useful birds. *Barn owls* are very common in the southern United States. They feed on harmful rodents. A barn owl may eat ten mice a day. This saves about 250 pounds (110 kg) of grain that would have been eaten by the ten mice in one year.

ALSO READ: BIRD, BIRDS OF PREY.

OX see CATTLE.

OXIDATION see OXYGEN.

OXYGEN Oxygen is the third most abundant of all the elements. Free (uncombined) oxygen is a gas that makes up about one-fifth of the volume of the air. Oxygen makes up 89 percent of the weight of pure water. Oxygen makes up half the weight of the Earth's crust, where it is com-

▲ *Welding equipment combines oxygen and acetylene to produce an oxyacetylene flame.*

bined with many other elements.

Oxygen is colorless, odorless, and tasteless. It dissolves slightly in water, enabling fish to get oxygen to breathe. If oxygen is cooled to 297° F below zero (−183° C), it becomes a liquid.

Oxygen is extremely important to all living things. No animal can exist without it. When you breathe air into your lungs, the oxygen in the air enters your bloodstream. The blood carries the oxygen to all the tissues of your body. The oxygen combines with digested food in the cells of the tissues. This produces energy. Your body uses energy for keeping warm and moving around.

Oxygen is a very active chemical element. It combines with many other chemical elements to make a very large number of compounds. These compounds are called *oxides*, and the process in which they are

▶ *Lavoisier saw that when substances burn they are reacting with oxygen. This candle will go out when the air in the jar contains no more oxygen.*

made is *oxidation*. When oxygen and another element are combined rapidly, heat and light are given off. Rapid oxidation is called *combustion*, or burning. Things burn brighter in oxygen than they do in air.

Oxygen combines slowly with some elements. For example, iron in damp air oxidizes slowly. This produces *iron oxide*, or rust. The decaying of dead plant and animal matter is caused by slow oxidation, which is aided by molds and bacteria.

Acetylene and *hydrogen* are two gases. Each can be burned in pure oxygen to produce a very hot flame used for welding (melting together) metals. In hospitals, patients with lung troubles are given pure oxygen to breathe. Mountain climbers take along tanks of oxygen that they must breathe because there is less oxygen in the air high above the ground. High-flying airplanes also carry a supply of oxygen to use when it is needed at unusually high altitudes. Fuel for space rockets usually contains liquid oxygen, called *LOX*.

Most often, oxygen is found in a form where two atoms are joined together. However, sometimes three oxygen atoms join together to form a rather different gas, *ozone*. Ozone is very bad to breathe. When people think they smell ozone by the sea, what they are really smelling is rotting seaweed!

ALSO READ: AIR, ATMOSPHERE, BACTERIA, CHEMISTRY, HYDROGEN.

There can be no fire without oxygen. La Paz, the capital of Bolivia, is about 12,000 feet (3,700 m) above sea level. At this height there is so little oxygen in the air that the city's fire engines are hardly ever used.

PACIFIC ISLAND NATIONS

Fiji

Capital: Suva
Population: 780,000
Area: 7,056 square miles
(18,274 sq. km)

Kiribati

Capital: Tarawa
Population: 70,000
Area: 359 square miles
(931 sq. km)

Nauru

Capital: Yaren
Population: 9,200
Area: 8 square miles
(21 sq. km)

Solomon Islands

Capital: Honiara
Population: 342,000
Area: 16,120 square miles
(28,446 sq. km)

Tonga

Capital: Nukualofa
Population: 101,300
Area: 270 square miles
(699 sq. km)

Tuvalu

Capital: Funafuti
Population: 8,000
Area: 9.7 square miles
(25 sq. km)

Vanuatu

Capital: Vila
Population: 170,000
Area: 5,700 square miles
(14,763 sq. km)

Western Samoa

Capital: Apia
Population: 190,000
Area: 1,097 square miles
(2,842 sq. km)

PACIFIC ISLANDS Most of the islands in the Pacific Ocean are in its southern and southwestern waters. The ocean bed in this area is deep in some places and quite shallow in others. The shallow places are formed by underwater hills or mountains. Many of these mountains are volcanoes.

Some of the Pacific islands are volcanoes that have risen high above the surface of the water. These volcanic islands are often large, with rugged mountain peaks. The Pacific island of New Guinea is the second largest island in the world. Only Greenland, in the North Atlantic Ocean, is larger. Other Pacific islands are formed from *coral*—the stony skeletons of tiny sea animals. These animals usually live on mountain peaks that lie just under the surface of the water. The coral is built up over the years until it rises above the water. Many of the coral islands are *atolls*—ring-shaped islands with a lagoon in the center.

The islands of the South Pacific are often known as *Oceania*. These islands lie in three general groups.

Melanesia ("black islands") is the group that lies scattered north and northeast of the continent of Australia. To the north of Melanesia lies *Micronesia* ("little islands"). To the east are the islands known as *Polynesia* ("many islands"). The islands of Hawaii are among the Polynesian group. (See the map with the article on PACIFIC OCEAN.)

The waters of the North Pacific Ocean are very deep. There are fewer islands in this region than in the South Pacific. One group of islands in the North Pacific is the Aleutians. These islands lie off the south coast of Alaska and are part of that state.

Some Pacific islands are independent nations. They are Fiji, Kiribati, Nauru, Tonga, Tuvalu, Vanuatu, Western Samoa, and the Solomon Islands. Such island nations as Japan, Indonesia, Taiwan, and the Philippines lie near the coast of Asia. Many Pacific islands are possessions, territories, or dependencies of other nations. The United States holds the Caroline, Marshall, and Mariana Islands (except Guam) in Micronesia as trust territories for the United Nations. New Caledonia is a French overseas territory in Melanesia.

ALSO READ: CORAL, ISLAND, MELANESIA, MICRONESIA, PACIFIC OCEAN, POLYNESIA, VOLCANO.

PACIFIC OCEAN The Pacific Ocean is the largest and deepest body of water in the world. It stretches between North and South America on the east, and Australia, the Malay Archipelago, and Asia on the west. Its northern boundary is the Bering Strait, through which it connects with the Arctic Ocean. The Pacific's southern boundary is Antarctica. Its greatest length from north to south is about 9,900 miles (15,900 km). Its greatest width is about 10,400 miles (16,700 km).

The Pacific Ocean is deepest in the

long trenches that lie parallel to some of its coastlines. The greatest depth yet found, over 36,000 feet (11,000 m), is in the Marianas Trench, off the Mariana Islands. The ocean floor also has many underwater mountains. Some, called *guyots*, have flat tops. The Pacific has several underwater *ridges*, or chains of mountains. *Continental shelves*, or plateaus, extend from the continents into the Pacific for varying distances.

Currents in the North Pacific move in a clockwise direction. Together they form one large, circular current. The California Current flows southward. When it turns westward, it is called the North Equatorial Current. It moves north along Asia's coast, where it is called the Japan Current. The eastern flow back across the Pacific is called the North Pacific Current. Currents in the South Pacific move in a counterclockwise direction.

Many small islands and island groups lie in the central, southern, and western parts of the Pacific. They are divided into three groups, according to their location and the types of peoples who live there. *Melanesia* is the southwestern group of islands. *Micronesia* consists of the islands north of Melanesia, and *Polynesia* includes the islands scattered across the central Pacific.

Asian peoples began exploring the

▲ *A typical Pacific island shoreline with abundant palm trees fringing a sandy beach. An outlining coral reef keeps the waters shallow and calm.*

▲ *On the Pacific island of Hawaii, a boy displays some of the island's flowers.*

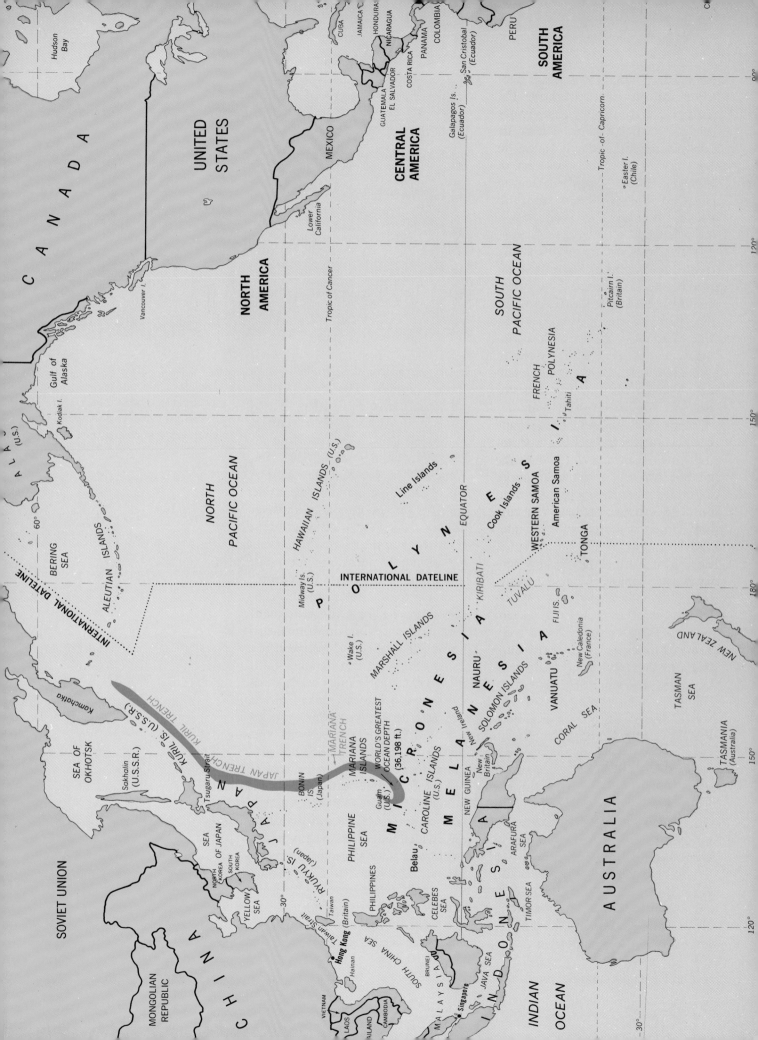

Pacific more than 2,000 years ago. Europeans began exploring the Pacific from the western side in the early 1500's. In 1513, Vasco Núñez de Balboa became the first European to sight the Pacific from its eastern shore. In 1520, Ferdinand Magellan named the ocean Pacific (peaceful) because it was so calm.

ALSO READ: BALBOA, VASCO NÚÑEZ DE; MAGELLAN, FERDINAND; MELANESIA; MICRONESIA; OCEAN; PACIFIC ISLANDS; POLYNESIA.

PAGODA A pagoda is a type of building found in many Asian countries. Pagodas are usually temples or shrines of the Buddhist religion.

Most pagodas are built in the shape of a tower, with several tiers, or stories. Each story is smaller than the one beneath it. The different stories of a pagoda represent a journey from Earth to heaven. Upward-curving roofs project outward from the building at each story. A tall mast, or spire, is on the top of most pagodas. Pagodas may be round, square, or many-sided.

Pagodas were first built in ancient India. Many Indian pagodas were shrines containing holy objects. Buddhist preachers introduced the idea of the pagoda into other Asian countries. Chinese pagodas were decorated with ivory carvings and colorful tiles. Bells were often hung from the roofs. Pagodas in Japan are usually square and built of wood. The Horyuji pagoda at Nara, Japan, is decorated with beautiful wood carvings. In Burma, devout Buddhists build pagodas as a holy task. Most Burmese villages have at least one pagoda.

Some pagodas are found in Europe. Most were built in the 1700's, when Chinese architecture was popular in Europe. They were built for ornament, not for religious use.

ALSO READ: BUDDHISM, TEMPLE.

▲ A Western Samoan in traditional dress also shows the modern side of Pacific Island life with his flashy wrist watch.

PAINE, THOMAS (1737–1809) Thomas Paine was an American Revolutionary writer on politics and religion. He was an outspoken defender of democracy and has become a hero of all lovers of liberty.

Paine was born in Thetford, England, the son of a poor Quaker corsetmaker. He came to Philadelphia in 1774. He became an editor of the *Pennsylvania Magazine* and began promoting the idea of independence from Great Britain. In January 1776, he published a pamphlet called *Common Sense*. It called for the colonies to declare independence. Paine's pamphlet sold 120,000 copies in three months. Paine then joined the Continental Army and wrote a series of 16 pamphlets called *The American Crisis*. George Washington liked the ideas in the first pamphlet so much that he ordered it to be read to his troops just before battle. The opening words are famous: "These are the times that try

▶ The ancient Indians built domed temples of Buddha. The Chinese were so impressed by one Indian temple that they based their pagoda design on the temple's spire alone!

PAINT

▲ *Thomas Paine, political writer and philosopher during the American Revolution.*

men's souls. The summer soldier and the sunshine patriot will, in this crisis, shrink from the service of their country. . . "

After the war ended, Paine went to France and England. He published *The Rights of Man* in 1791–1792. This book defended the new French and American republics. Paine became a member of the French Convention, but he was put in prison when he refused to vote for the execution of the French king. While he was in prison, he wrote most of *The Age of Reason*, which contained his views on religion. Later he returned to the United States. Paine died in poverty on his farm in New Rochelle, New York.

ALSO READ: AMERICAN HISTORY, AMERICAN REVOLUTION.

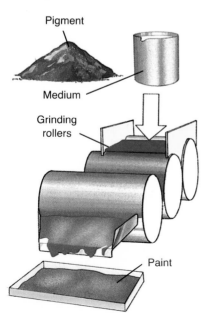

▼ *Paints are made by grinding pigments (colored powders) and a liquid medium (such as oil) between heavy rollers. More pigment or more medium may be added to change the color or thickness of the paint.*

Pigment

Medium

Grinding rollers

Paint

PAINT Paint is a colored liquid that is brushed, sprayed, or rolled onto a surface to protect or decorate it. When paint dries, it forms a thin, tough coating. Paint is made up of three parts—the *pigment*, the *body*, and the *vehicle*. The pigment gives the paint its color. It consists of a fine powder, often made of ground earth, stone, or minerals. The body of a paint forms the main protective covering when the paint dries. It is also made of a fine powder, usually white in color. Until recently, white lead was the most commonly used paint body. Now titanium dioxide is used because lead is poisonous. Many children and animals have become very sick, and some have died, from licking or eating lead paint.

The pigment and the body are mixed together in a liquid called the vehicle. In *oil paints* the vehicle is an oil, such as linseed oil, combined with a *thinner*, such as turpentine. The thinner makes the paint flow on evenly. In *alkyd paints*, the vehicle contains a high percentage of man-made alkyd resins. *Latex paints* use

water as the vehicle; these are very popular paints because of their low cost, quick drying ability, and the ease with which the paintbrush can be cleaned.

People have been using paints for about 50,000 years. Primitive people learned to make pigment from natural materials, such as chalk, charcoal, and berries. The ancient Egyptians made blue paint from sand, soda, and copper, and red paint from madder plants. They imported these red-rooted plants from India. As civilization spread, people began to use paints more and more. They learned to make longer-lasting and tougher paints from chemicals. But natural materials were often used.

There are many types of paints available today. Paints are specially made for the interior (inside) or the exterior (outside) of homes and buildings. They may be made with a *gloss* (very shiny), *semigloss* (less shiny), or *mat* (dull) finish. Gloss paints are often used by homeowners in their kitchens and bathrooms because they are washable. Mat paints are suitable for ceilings and some walls. Many other types of paints are used for specific purposes. There are *fluorescent paints* that glow at night when exposed to light. These paints are good for the sake of safety in and around the home. *Textured paints* have a thick body and are applied with special tools to give a textured effect on a ceiling or wall. Artists mix oil paints to obtain different tints and shades. And shippainters paint ship hulls with a special type of poisonous paint to keep barnacles away!

Painting can be easy and fun, too. If your bicycle is getting scratched or rusty, you may want to paint it with a bright, rust-resistant enamel. First, sand the rusted parts and clean the metal. Then follow the directions on the paint can to make your bike bright and shiny again.

ALSO READ: PAINTING.

1858

PAINTED DESERT When early Spanish explorers in the American West saw a wasteland of buttes, mesas, and canyons glowing with pastel colors, they named the place *El Desierto Pintado*, meaning "The Painted Desert."

The Painted Desert is a dry region that lies in the northeastern part of Arizona. Parts of it are in the Petrified Forest. The desert is unusual for the colors of its rocks and sand.

Iron oxides create the bright yellows and reds, and other chemical compounds make other colors in the desert. Shades of red, yellow, and purple mixed with white, gray, blue, and brown are seen. Colors seem to change with differences in heat and sunlight. Wind and rain have eroded the soft rocks into many strange shapes. Few plants grow here. An occasional scorpion or snake crawls across the hot ground. Sunset Crater, a volcano, stands in the Painted Desert near Flagstaff, Arizona.

If you were to stand in the Painted Desert in late afternoon, you would see a kind of color movie show. As the sun sinks, the desert casts its reddish glow. Rocks change color before your eyes.

Look around in your own neighborhood and in fields and woods nearby. See if you can find any unusual color patterns that nature has provided. Make a list of them and try to discover what causes the different colors.

ALSO READ: ARIZONA, DESERT, PETRIFIED FOREST.

PAINTING Can you remember some of the paintings you have created? Perhaps you used fingerpaints, watercolors, or poster paints. You might have painted something real, such as a person you know or the street you live on. Maybe you painted an imaginary person or scene, or per-

▲ *The late afternoon sun casts a pattern of light and shadow over the hills of the Painted Desert in Arizona.*

haps you just made a colorful design.

Painting means creating a picture, or *image*, by putting colors (called *pigments*) on a surface. There are two basic ways of doing this—*mural painting* and *easel painting*.

In mural painting, the artist applies pigments to a whole wall. The most lasting type of mural painting is the *fresco*. The artist uses a brush to paint with pigments on wet plaster. The plaster absorbs the colors. When dry, the fresco actually is part of the wall. The fresco artist must work with great speed, doing only one small section of the painting at a time before the plaster dries. Once completed, a fresco will last as long as the wall. The *Delphic Sibyl* (shown on the next page) is one of the great frescoes created by Michelangelo for the Sistine Chapel. *Fresco secco* (dry fresco) is painted on dry plaster. The pigments do not get absorbed by the plaster, and the colors can chip off easily if not carefully protected.

Easel painting is done on canvas, paper, wood, or any other movable surface—unlike a mural painting that cannot be moved because it is part of a building. An easel is a stand that holds a painting while the artist works on it. Easel paintings are usually framed and can be hung anywhere, whereas mural paintings must be created to fit the room in which they are painted. There are several techniques of easel painting.

▼ Fiord *by Emil Nolde.*

▲ *The* Delphic Sibyl *by Michelangelo, from the ceiling in the Sistine Chapel.*

▼ *A detail from* View of Venice from the Lagoon *by J.M.W. Turner, a British painter of the early 19th century.*

FINGER PAINTING. The pigments used in finger painting are pasty substances that are mixed with water and smeared on slick paper with the fingers. Many designs can be made by using different parts of your hands to smear the paint.

WATERCOLOR. Watercolor pigments are mixed with water and applied to paper with a brush. The colors are transparent, which means that if you paint over a color with another color, the color underneath will show through. Mistakes are not easily correctable with watercolors. The painting by Joseph Turner (below) and Emil Nolde (page 1859) are good examples of different effects you can get from watercolors. Turner used very pale colors. The white from the paper gives a glowing atmosphere to the scene. The city, water, and sky all blend together. Nolde uses bright colors—blue, purple, orange, red, and yellow outlined in black. He has not blended the water and land together as Turner did.

Gouache, or poster paint, is a type of opaque watercolor. Colors can be painted over one another, and those underneath do not show through. *Casein* paint is similar to gouache, but when it dries it is very brittle. Casein should be used on a stiff surface, such as wood, rather than on paper or canvas.

TEMPERA. The word "tempera" usually refers to pigments that have been mixed with egg and with water or oil. Egg tempera is painted on wooden boards that have been covered with a hard plaster called *gesso*. Tempera paints produce deep, rich colors and clear, sharp lines. The Chinese tempera painting (page 1861) was painted during the 1400's.

OIL PAINTING. Oil paints are made by mixing pigments with oil to form a thick substance feeling a little like toothpaste. Oil paints are usually applied to canvas material which has been stretched tight over a wooden frame or board and coated with a special white paint. Oil paints and the newly developed *plastic paints* (made from artificial materials, such as acrylics) are very popular with artists. Plastic paints are like oil paints to use, but they dry more quickly. They are also cheaper and do not discolor over the years, as oil paints do.

Oil paint can be thinned with turpentine so that it is transparent like watercolor. Or it can be applied in thick layers straight from the tube. The artist can apply the paints with a brush or, in the case of thick paint, with a flexible instrument called a *palette knife*. He or she can get effects by using an *impasto* technique—building up layers of paint to make it thicker in some spots. The artist can use a very dry pigment or leave brushmarks in the paint to achieve other effects. Oil paint dries very slowly, especially if it is thick. But once it dries, colors can be painted over and corrections made.

Still Life: Apples and Pomegranate, by Gustave Courbet (shown on page 1861), is very realistic. Compare it with the painting beneath it by Paul Klee, who has used paint to bring out the colors and shapes of his imaginary scene.

PASTELS. Pastel paints are pigments molded into sticks similar to chalk. The paints are drawn on paper or canvas in the same way you would use crayons. Once applied, pastel paints smudge easily and must be protected by being sprayed with a *fixative*, a preparation that keeps the pigments in place.

ENCAUSTIC. This painting technique was widely used in ancient Greece, Egypt, and Rome. The pigments are mixed with melted beeswax and then painted on a warm wooden surface. When the painting is complete, the surface is heated a final time to fuse the colors to each other and to the wood. The process takes a long time, and the artist must work in constant heat. Encaustic was finally replaced by tempera paints.

ILLUMINATION. Illumination is the application of pigments, often gold leaf and tempera, to book pages, certificates, and other items to make illustrations and decorative lettering. It was most popular before the beginning of book printing around 1450, but it is still sometimes done today.

Elements of a Painting When an artist paints, he or she organizes lines, shapes, colors, and textures to form a pleasing picture. By comparing four pictures of a similar subject, you will be able to see how different artists have used these elements. Four paintings shown on pages 1862 and 1863

▼ *An old Chinese tempera painting of three ladies.*

are all portraits of people, by Giovanni Bellini, Pierre Auguste Renoir, Henri Matisse, and Rufino Tamayo. Each artist has used the element of line in a different way. Bellini used soft lines at the edges of the face and hands to show the feel of skin. But the lines about the jewelry are sharp, indicating something hard. Renoir, however, has used very soft and fuzzy lines for both the skin and the jewelry. Matisse has used dark lines to outline the girl. He put thicker lines about the face, and thinner ones on the blouse and hands. The lines in Tamayo's painting are very angular—more like a design than a portrait. The lines in each painting are different, but they all mark edges

▲ Still Life: Apples and Pomegranate (top) *by French painter Gustave Courbet.* Around the Fish (above) *by Paul Klee.*

PAINTING

▲ *A detail from* The Nooning *by the American painter Winslow Homer in the 1870's. Homer painted unmistakably American scenes.*

▲ The Singer *by Rufino Tamayo, one of Mexico's leading modern painters.*

or give a pattern or feeling.

The shapes in a painting may be areas bordered by lines, or they might be just patches of color. In the Matisse painting, the girl's blouse is really one large white shape. The red background forms another shape, and the blue skirt yet another. In the Renoir, the lady's head and neck form a definite shape, but so do the two dark areas extending down from either shoulder. The dusky violet patch on the upper side forms another shape, as does the rose in her hair. Bellini emphasized three important shapes—the woman's face, neck, and her hands. Notice how they stand out in comparison to the rest of the painting. The shapes in Tamayo's painting are set off both by lines and by colors. How many different shapes can you find in Tamayo's picture?

An artist can arrange colors to emphasize areas of a painting, to give a feeling of roundness to objects, or to give a special mood to a painting. Bellini used colors not only to record accurately the woman he painted, but also to set a mood. Notice that two or three areas of the portrait are quite light, but the rest is dark. What sort of feeling does this give you? Notice, too, that Bellini has used shadings of color to show the shapes of objects. The tip of the woman's nose is a bright color, but the side of her nose

is darker. Down at the bottom of the picture, Bellini has even shaded dark areas to show the wrinkles of the woman's sleeve. This kind of shading is called *chiaroscuro*.

Renoir did not use a lot of different colors in this painting. Most of the painting uses only two—violet and brown-black. By adding white to the violet color, Renoir was able to make the pink in the rose and the even paler pink of the woman's skin. Notice how the whole composition is tied together by skillful use of violet and brown shades.

Matisse used what is called *flat color*. There is very little shading at all, and the colors do not vary. Matisse has depended almost entirely on lines to show the girl's shape. Both Matisse and Tamayo have used colors that are very similar together. Notice the orange and red in the Matisse, and the red and violet in the Tamayo. Notice the patchlike use of color in the background of Tamayo's painting.

▼ *A detail from* The Balcony *by Pierre Auguste Renoir.*

▲ Mary Magdalene *by Giovanni Bellini.*

The *texture* in a painting is either the feel of the paint itself or the way the artist has represented objects in the painting. Bellini has tried to paint so exactly that you almost seem to feel the texture of the woman's hair, skin, and jewelry. Renoir has not painted the girl *exactly* as she would be in real life. He has blended and fused colors and lines so that the whole painting seems to have a soft, filmy feeling. Matisse does not use texture at all in his painting. The surface is very flat, and the colors and shapes do not suggest any special texture. Neither was Tamayo so concerned about texture. There seems to be no difference in feeling between the guitar, the hand, and the shirt.

All of these paintings have as their subject the same thing: a beautiful young woman. Yet all of the paintings are very different from each other. Why do you think this is? Every artist has a different way of *seeing* things. The greatest artists are those whose pictures make other people see things the way the artist saw them. Thus, Tamayo and Bellini are really trying to make you see the same sort of young woman, yet the visual images they have produced are very different. If you go to an art gallery or museum, you will see paintings of young women by other painters. All will have the same subject, but all will be very different.

Perspective Perspective is a way of creating the illusion of space and depth on a flat surface. You can do this by painting faraway objects much smaller. Lines that move off into the distance in your painting should be made to come closer together the farther away they get. Also, you cannot see a faraway object as clearly as you can one that is closer. By slightly blurring distant objects in your painting, they will seem farther away. Notice the woman's left hand in the Bellini painting. The edges of the fingers are fuzzier than those on the right hand, which is closer to you. Also notice that the left-hand fingers are short little stumps. Because the hand is pointed away from you, the fingers are *foreshortened* (made to look shorter because they are headed into the distance). In the Tamayo painting, the lines marking the corners of the ceiling and walls are arranged in perspective so that the walls look as if they extend way back behind the guitar player.

Each of these paintings has a style, a mood, and a personality all its own because each of the artists was different. Therefore, each artist's work is unique.

The next time you decide to paint a picture, try experimenting with new ways of using lines, colors, textures, and shapes. You'll be surprised at the fascinating results.

ALSO READ: ART, ART HISTORY, CARTOONING, COLOR, DESIGN, DIMENSION, DRAWING, GRAPHIC ARTS, MINIATURE, PAINT.
For individual artists see Index at name.

▲ The Rumanian Blouse *by Henri Matisse.*

SOME FAMOUS PAINTERS

Giotto di Bondone, Italian (*c.* 1266–1337)
Jan van Eyck, Flemish (*c.* 1387–1440)
Sandro Botticelli, Italian (*c.* 1444–1510)
Leonardo da Vinci, Italian (1452–1519)
Albrecht Dürer, German (1471–1528)
Michelangelo, Italian (1475–1564)
Titian, Italian (1477–1576)
Raphael, Italian (1483–1520)
El Greco, Spanish (*c.* 1541–1614)
Rubens, Flemish (1577–1640)
Velasquez, Spanish (*c.* 1599–1666)
Rembrandt van Rijn, Dutch (1606–1669)
Goya, Spanish (1746–1828)
J. M. W. Turner, English (1775–1851)
Edouard Manet, French (1832–1883)
Paul Cézanne, French (1839–1906)
Henri Rousseau, French (1844–1910)
Vincent van Gogh, Dutch (1853–1890)
Vassily Kandinsky, Russian (1866–1944)
Henri Matisse, French (1869–1954)
Edward Hopper, U.S. (1882–1967)
Pablo Picasso, Spanish (1881–1973)
Jackson Pollock, U.S. (1912–1956)

▲ *Farmland irrigated by ditches in Pakistan.*

PAKISTAN A country whose two sections were separated from each other by 1,000 miles (1,600 km) has now been made into two independent countries. Pakistan, formerly made up of West and East Pakistan, is now the name for the western part. Bangladesh has been the new name for East Pakistan since it became independent late in 1971.

Pakistan covers an area about twice the size of California and has more than three and a half times as many people as that state does. It is bordered by India on the east, Iran on the southwest, Afghanistan on the northwest, and the Arabian Sea on the south. (See the map with the article on INDIA.) Highlands and towering mountains cover most of western and northern Pakistan. Passes cut through the high mountains in several places. The famous Khyber Pass connects Pakistan with Afghanistan. Islamabad, the country's beautiful capital city, is located in the northern highlands. People called *Pathans* live in the mountains of Pakistan, and wandering nomads tend flocks of sheep and goats in the highlands and on the plains.

Pakistan's chief river is the Indus, which flows through the eastern half of the country. Wheat, rice, cotton, and other crops are grown on the fertile Punjab and Sind plains along the Indus. Most of Pakistan's people live in these areas. Karachi, the largest city, is on the Sind plain near the Indus River delta. Large deposits of natural gas have been discovered in central Pakistan. Copper and iron ore are in the highlands.

Pakistan, part of India until 1947, was invaded by many Asian peoples through the centuries. The Muslims came in several waves from the early 1000's to the 1500's. The Muslims kept their own religion and did not become Hindus (the religion of most Indians) during their rule of India. The British took control of the whole subcontinent of India in the 1700's.

In 1947, the mostly Muslim areas of India gained independence as Pakistan, which was divided into two widely separated sections. Muhammad Jinnah became Pakistan's first president. Fighting broke out between Muslims and Hindus. About 7 million Muslims fled from India to Pakistan, and about 6 million Hindus left Pakistan for India.

Later, the Bengali Muslims of East Pakistan wanted more self-government. West Pakistan refused their demands and sent troops to East Pakistan in 1971. The Indian army helped the Bengalis defeat the West Pakistan army. Bangladesh, meaning "Bengal nation," was born.

Pakistan is an Islamic republic. The civilian government was ousted in 1977, when a military group took control. The country's state and national assemblies were dissolved.

ALSO READ: BANGLADESH, INDIA.

PAKISTAN

Capital City: Islamabad (250,000 people).
Area: 310,404 square miles (803,943 sq. km).
Population: 113,500,000.
Government: Islamic republic.
Natural Resources: Natural gas, coal, copper, iron ore, oil.
Export Products: Cotton and cotton goods, rice, wool carpets, leather.
Unit of Money: Rupee.
Official Languages: Urdu, English.

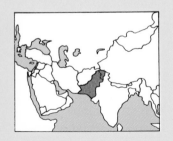

PALEONTOLOGY Living things have been on Earth for more than three billion years. Remains of some plants and animals that lived in the past have been preserved as fossils. Generally fossils are rocky—the original animal or plant tissues have been replaced by substances that form stone. Sometimes fossils are found in tar, in a mineral called amber, and in ice—these fossils are the preserved remains of the animal or plant.

Animal fossils most commonly include hard body parts, such as bones, teeth, and claws. Some animal fossils are just traces, such as footprints, claw marks, and burrows. Plant fossils are generally found in the form of leaf and stem imprints in rock and coal. But whole petrified plant stems and fruits have also been found.

Paleontology uses fossils to study the living things of the ancient past. It is usually thought of as a branch of geology, the study of the Earth, including its rocks, because most fossils are found in rocks. Paleontology is divided into two main parts: *paleobotany*, the study of plant fossils, and *paleozoology*, the study of animal fossils.

Millions of fossils have been found, but many, many more must still be buried in the rocks. The oldest fossils are usually buried the deepest. The very old rocks containing these fossils are exposed to view in only a few places. For this reason, there are gaps in the record of past life. *Paleontologists* (people who work in paleontology) spend much time and effort searching for fossils. They are always hoping that some of the fossils they find will fill in some of the gaps in the record of past life. By studying fossils, they can find out about *evolution*—the way that living things change over millions of years.

Paleontology is useful to the oil industry. Paleontologists have found that certain kinds of very tiny fossils are found in and near rocks that contain oil, so finding the fossils helps find the oil.

ALSO READ: DINOSAUR, EARTH HISTORY, EVOLUTION, FOSSIL, GEOLOGY, MAMMALS OF THE PAST, PLANTS OF THE PAST.

PALESTINE Palestine is the "Holy Land" of the Bible. It is a region on the eastern coast of the Mediterranean Sea that is sacred to three religions—Christianity, Judaism, and Islam. Judaism and Christianity began here. Israel now covers most of this historic land.

The Phoenicians and Canaanites first lived in Palestine, then called Canaan. Between 1300 and 1100 B.C., tribes of Philistines and Israelites moved in. Palestine is the Hebrew word for *Philistine*. The Israelites slowly conquered the other tribes. Around 1030 B.C., the 12 tribes of the Israelites formed a kingdom.

The kingdom split in half around 933 B.C., becoming Judah (Judea) in the south and Israel in the north. Assyrians and Babylonians invaded. Next Persians conquered the land. Then Alexander the Great added Palestine to his list of conquests. Egypt claimed it, and then Syria. In 63 B.C., Palestine became part of the Roman Empire, and later the Byzantine Empire. And in A.D. 1516, Palestine became a Turkish province. During World War I, Great Britain took it over.

In 1917, the British government issued the Balfour Declaration, which favored the establishment of Palestine as the Jewish homeland. The League of Nations in 1922 appointed Great Britain to rule Palestine as a *mandate*. Part of Palestine had been made into the state of Trans-Jordan by the British in 1920. Jews came from many countries to settle in Palestine in the 1930's. The Arabs of Palestine wanted Palestine to be an Arab state and began fighting the Jews. In 1947,

▲ *Map of the Middle East showing the historic land that was called Palestine.*

▲ *Digging up the fossil skeleton of a plesiosaur (a type of extinct reptile). Paleontologists do this with great care so that the fossilized bones are damaged as little as possible.*

Chusan
Palm

▲ *The Chusan Palm is a native tree of China and Japan but can be grown in other warm regions. It reaches about 36 feet (11 m).*

the U.N. divided Palestine into two states: one Jewish, one Arab. Jerusalem was made an international city and the British ended their mandate. Five Arab countries attacked the new state of Israel but were turned back. Israel won Jerusalem and other land in the Arab-Israeli War of 1967. But the Palestine Liberation Organization (PLO) had been founded in 1964 to try and create a Palestinian state.

The PLO has continued to have bitter border disputes with Israel and to withhold information about Israeli soldiers killed in action. In 1991, this information was released. This helped to speed up the freeing of many Western hostages, such as the American Terry Anderson, held in the Middle East. The disputes between the PLO and Israel were one of the key issues of the 1991 Madrid Conference which began the long process of seeking peace in the Middle East.

ALSO READ: DEAD SEA, ISRAEL, JERUSALEM, JORDAN, MIDDLE EAST.

▼ *Each of the leaves of the dwarf fan palm is made up of a "fan" of between 12 and 15 stiff, pointed leaflets. Its small, yellow flowers are in dense clusters that are at first sheathed in a red covering.*

PALM Palms are among the most valuable of all plants. They grow in the warmer parts of the world. Palms provide people who live in tropical lands with a large number of things they need for daily living.

There are more than 2,600 kinds of palms. Most of them are trees, some of which grow more than 100 feet (30 m) tall. But some are shrubs that grow only 3 or 4 feet (90–120 cm) tall, and others have vinelike stems several hundred feet long. Most palms are evergreen. They produce leaves, flowers, and fruit all year long. Palms can be divided into two big groups according to the shape of their leaves—those with broad, flat leaves, and those with feathery leaves. Most types of palm trees have no branches. The leaves usually form a tuft at the top of the trunk.

Palm leaves are often used to thatch the roofs of tropical houses. The tree trunks are used for timber. Strips of fresh leaves are woven into mats, baskets, and wall screens. Fibers from palm leaves are made into cloth for clothing and hats. Many kinds of palm fruits—including dates and coconuts—are nourishing foods.

Coconut palms are grown commercially for the many useful things they produce. They are feather-leaved palms that grow 60 to 100 feet (18–30 m) tall. Coconut palms thrive near water and grow naturally on almost all the islands in the South Pacific. Coconut palms produce large clusters of coconuts. Each coconut is a large one-seeded fruit with an outer tough fiber husk. Within this husk is the coconut you see in grocery stores—the "shell" is actually the hard inner layer of the fruit. Inside the shell is a thick layer of nourishing "meat," which surrounds a hollow filled with coconut "milk." The milk may be fermented to make a beverage. The meat is made into soap, wax, food, and oil.

ALSO READ: PLANT, PLANT DISTRIBUTION, PLANT PRODUCTS, TREE.